The Cinema of Manoel de Oliveira

The Cinema of Manoel de Oliveira

Modernity, Intermediality and the Uncanny

Hajnal Király

BLOOMSBURY ACADEMIC
NEW YORK · LONDON · OXFORD · NEW DELHI · SYDNEY

BLOOMSBURY ACADEMIC
Bloomsbury Publishing Inc
1385 Broadway, New York, NY 10018, USA
50 Bedford Square, London, WC1B 3DP, UK
29 Earlsfort Terrace, Dublin 2, Ireland

BLOOMSBURY, BLOOMSBURY ACADEMIC and the Diana logo are trademarks of
Bloomsbury Publishing Plc

First published in the United States of America 2022

Copyright © Hajnal Király, 2022

For legal purposes the Acknowledgements on p. x constitute an extension of this
copyright page.

Cover design: Eleanor Rose
Cover image: Leonor Silveira in *Abraham's Valley* (*Vale Abraão*), 1993,
Dir. Manoel de Oliveira © Madragoa Filmes / Collection Christophel /
ArenaPAL www.arenapal.com

All rights reserved. No part of this publication may be reproduced or transmitted
in any form or by any means, electronic or mechanical, including photocopying,
recording, or any information storage or retrieval system, without prior permission
in writing from the publishers.

Bloomsbury Publishing Inc does not have any control over, or responsibility for, any
third-party websites referred to or in this book. All internet addresses given
in this book were correct at the time of going to press. The author and publisher
regret any inconvenience caused if addresses have changed or sites have ceased
to exist, but can accept no responsibility for any such changes.

Library of Congress Cataloging-in-Publication Data

Names: Király, Hajnal, 1974– author.
Title: The cinema of Manoel De Oliveira : modernity, intermediality and the uncanny / by
Hajnal Király. Description: New York : Bloomsbury Academic, 2022. | Includes bibliographical
references and index. | Summary: "Organized by tropes and topics, rather than
chronological order, this volume creates a unique lens with which to focus on the links
between cinema, literature, painting, and other art forms in Manoel de Oliveira's work.
Hajnal Király reads the films in relation to 20th-century Portuguese, European and global
history. Many of Oliveira's over 50 films are discussed, including Rite of Spring (1963) and
Eccentricities of a Blonde-haired Girl (2009). The only book to cover his later films, this book
uncovers the persistent topics that permeates his oeuvre"– Provided by publisher.
Identifiers: LCCN 2021052325 (print) | LCCN 2021052326 (ebook) |
ISBN 9781501378652 (hardback) | ISBN 9781501378621 (paperback) |
ISBN 9781501378645 (epub) | ISBN 9781501378638 (pdf) |
ISBN 9781501378614
Subjects: LCSH: Oliveira, Manoel de, 1908-2015–Criticism and interpretation. |
Motion pictures–Portugal–History. | Motion picture producers and directors–Portugal–
Biography. Classification: LCC PN1998.3.O44 K57 2022 (print) |
LCC PN1998.3.O44 (ebook) | DDC 791.4302/33092 [B]—dc23/eng/20220204
LC record available at https://lccn.loc.gov/2021052325
LC ebook record available at https://lccn.loc.gov/2021052326

ISBN:	HB:	978-1-5013-7865-2
	ePDF:	978-1-5013-7863-8
	eBook:	978-1-5013-7864-5

Typeset by RefineCatch Limited, Bungay, Suffolk

To find out more about our authors and books visit www.bloomsbury.com
and sign up for our newsletters.

I think that in Manoel de Oliveira there is a closed door he never enters, he does not want to enter, he lost the key of this door and doesn't want to pass through it.
—Agustina Bessa-Luís

Contents

List of figures	viii
Acknowledgements	x
Introduction	1

Part One The beautiful automaton

1 Cinema and/as the myth of modernity	17
2 Towards an Oliveirian aesthetics of stillness	27
3 The trope of the doll	39

Part Two Camões and Don Quixote

4 The cultural philosophy of Oliveira	59
5 Profanations	83
6 Cultural mimicry	95

Part Three Doomed loves

7 Disturbing adaptations	113
8 Letters on the screen	131
9 Sounding letters	145
Coda: A melancholic cinema?	159
Index	169

Figures

1.1–1.4	An analogy between the family altar and the mirror in *Abraham's Valley*.	25
2.1–2.4	Frames and grids as metaphors of entrapment and stillness in *Doomed Love*.	31
2.5–2.6	Ema 'framed' as a picture in *Abraham's Valley*.	32
2.7–2.10	Leg and foot fetishism in *Abraham's Valley*.	36
3.1–3.2	The doll in the window and the unidentifiable gaze in *Aniki Bobó*.	42
3.3–3.4	The trope of the doll in *A Talking Picture* and *The Letter*.	43
3.5–3.6	The torso and artificial limbs as tropes of the stillness–movement dichotomy in *The Cannibals*.	45
3.7–3.8	Variations on 'dollness' in *Eccentricities of a Blonde-Haired Girl*.	46
3.9	An aesthetics of death in *Magic Mirror* and *Francisca*.	48
3.10–3.11	The painterly image of the dead woman in *The Strange Case of Angelica* (2010), echoing Renoir's *Madame Monet Reading* (1872).	49
3.12–3.13	The uncanny effect of the 'living photograph' in *Benilde or the Virgin Mother* (1975).	50
4.1	The recurring etching of Don Quixote, an illustration of the uselessness of human efforts.	62
4.2–4.3	The external gaze on 'Portugueseness' attracted into Faust-like contracts in *The Convent*	72
4.4–4.5	Allegorical personification of Portugal in *Cristopher Columbus – The Enigma*.	74
4.6–4.7	The statue of Pedro Macau, illustrating the burdens of masculine identity in *Voyage to the Beginning of the World*.	78
5.1–5.2	Painterly references to a religious family ideal and values in *The Uncertainty Principle*.	90
5.3–5.4	Multiple mirrors as figure of delusion and the forgery serving it in *Magic Mirror*.	94

6.1	Presentation of the act of reading as revelation of the French influence in *Abraham's Valley*.	100
6.2–6.3	The group of statues in the Parisian park as representation of the melodramatic situation of the novel.	103
6.4–6.5	Pop star Pedro Abrunhosa framed by a statue representing the core dramatic situation in *The Letter*.	103
6.6–6.7	Statues emphasizing the animate–inanimate, eternal–contingent (values) opposition in *The Uncertainty Principle*.	104
6.8–6.9	Adopting, through a painterly reference, a subversive artistic attitude in *Anxiety*.	105
6.10–6.11	The chiaroscuro effect as figure of 'the moment of truth' in *Voyage to the Beginning of the World*.	106
6.12	The chiaroscuro effect as figure of the quest for the truth in *Gebo and the Shadow*.	107
7.1	Édouard Manet, *Jeanne Duval, Baudelaire's Mistress, Reclining* (*Lady with a Fan*), 1862, a painting echoed by the character of Ema.	127
8.1–8.2	The representation of the 'late letter' in Ribeiro's and Oliveira's version of *Doomed Love*.	134
8.3–8.4	The letter-writing and reading scenes in Oliveira's *Doomed Love*.	139
8.5–8.6	Gabriel Metsu, *Man Writing a Letter* and *Woman Reading a Letter* (1662–5).	140
8.7	The main character reading the book, *Doomed Love*, that becomes a moral code in the film of Mário Barroso.	144
9.1–9.2	Letter-reading and intercepting scenes as key dramatic moments in *Francisca*.	147
9.3	Musical scenes as emotional/romantic scenes in seventeenth-century Dutch painting, Gerard ter Borch, *A Music Lesson* (1668).	152
C.1–C.2	The interchangeable photographic and cinematographic as figures of death and life in *Angelica*.	162

Acknowledgements

The chapters of this book were written with the support of two different funds, the Portuguese FCT (Fundação para a Ciência e a Tecnologia) and the Romanian UEFISCDI (Executive Unit for Financing Higher Education, Research, Development and Innovation), within the framework of two different research projects and theoretical backgrounds. However, there was continuity and overlapping in the topic of the two projects: the FCT project focused on film adaptations of the iconic nineteenth-century Portuguese novel *Doomed Love*, with emphasis on Oliveira's controversial adaptation placed in the larger stylistical and thematic context of the director's oeuvre, while the Romanian one, part of a group research, provided its intermedial conceptual and discursive apparatus. This latter project has also considered the cinema of Oliveira as exemplary of an intermediality conceived as 'in-betweenness' between expressive forms of different arts and media. The cultural and psychoanalytical approach that I chose, with the Freudian concept of uncanny at its centre, helped me to illuminate the Oliveirian artistic and private persona behind the films that I initially sometimes found intriguing, even unnerving. In this respect, I hope that this book complements the existing scholarship on Oliveira with insights on the 'disturbing' aspects of his cinema, greatly related to its intermediality – theatricality, pictoriality, musicality and literariness. I was in the fortunate position to be led and accompanied on this intercultural and intermedial journey by prominent Portuguese and Romanian scholars, to whom I am very grateful. I would like to thank Ágnes Pethő, the leader of the Romanian project and former head of the Film, Photography and Media Department at the Sapientia Hungarian University of Transylvania, who has been a mentor to me in all my intermedial projects. I am grateful to my fellow project members for reading my articles many times and advising me on them. My cooperation with my Portuguese project coordinator, Clara Rowland, at the University of Lisbon, was also very effective. I would like to thank her for encouraging me to apply for postdoctoral research funding with this topic, and for supporting me all along the process of completion of the research at the Centre for Comparative Studies of the University of Lisbon. I would also like to express my gratitude to all those who

Acknowledgements

have read the chapters and advised me at different stages of the project: Tiago Baptista, Filipa Rosário, Adriana Martins, Paulo Cunha and last, but not least, Professor Helena Buescu at the University of Lisbon, who put me in contact with the Portuguese intermediality research and ultimately launched the process resulting in this book.

Introduction

Manoel de Oliveira is not only the longest-lived film director of all time, active until his death, which occurred at the very advanced age of 106, but also one of the most curious personalities of film history. Despite a scholarly interest in his films, which used to be regularly presented at prestigious European festivals, they were very little shown in film theatres, therefore his work remains an 'exquisite delicacy' for cinephiles. While praised by Serge Daney (2001), Jonathan Rosenbaum (1995) and David Bordwell (2013), to name a few *connaisseurs*, most critics are puzzled when trying to discover a clue to his cinema, a task as difficult as finding out the secret of his long life. These preoccupations are at the origin of numerous interviews, portrait films and television reports (see, for example, Costa 1981; de Baecque and Parsi 1999; Araújo 2014; and Costa Andrade 2008), all keen to set up new categories, periods, concepts and comparisons for his somehow familiar, but still uncanny, approach to cinema. The divide of the Salazar dictatorship, the tetralogy of 'frustrated loves' (see Parsi 1981) – as Oliveira himself used to call the films with the same topic: *Past and Present* (*O Passado e o Presente*, 1972), *Benilde or the Virgin Mother* (*Benilde ou a Virgem Mãe*, 1975), *Doomed Love* (*Amor de Perdição*, 1979) and *Francisca* (1981) – the collaboration with Paulo Branco and Agustina Bessa-Luís, the preference for literary adaptations, cultural-historical topics and painterly allusions (especially to the French Impressionism), are only but a few persistent points of reference that help illuminate some aspects of his work, without providing, however, a coherent clue to the interpretation. Similarly, after a comparison of his style to different moments of film history, such as the German avant-garde (*Labor on the Douro River* [*Douro, Faina Fluvial*, 1931] to Walter Ruttmann's, *Berlin: A Symphony of a Great City*, 1927), the Italian neorealism (*Aniki Bobó*, 1942), the films of Robert Bresson and his model-theory, some films of Eric Rohmer (his *The Marquise of O / La Marquise d'O*, 1976, and his moral tales), and Buñuel (his predilection to parody, the critique of the bourgeoisie and the Catholic Church, as well as the thematization of fetishism), it can be stated that none of these similarities became constant in his work. Moreover, these do not even provide a sufficient basis to call him a 'modernist' filmmaker.

There are, however, persistent topics and features in this huge work overarching almost a century of cinema that instigate a person to find a perspective that would bring closer both the films and the man behind them. His obsession with death, feminine mystery, the ambivalence of human behaviour, the impossibility of an ideal love, the stakes of sacrifice and redemption (both personal and national), attract narrative and visual patterns that constantly destabilize the spectator. Although many of these aspects have been repeatedly analysed, little has been said about the *effect* – surprising, irritating, unsettling, unnerving or even boring – that these verbally and visually loaded films exercise over spectators. Coming from a different culture, I found it difficult to penetrate the 'familiar unfamiliarity' of these films, just to realize that the existing critical material gives little insight to the personal and cultural mechanisms underlying the peculiar Oliveirian universe. Many critical writings, both Portuguese and non-Portuguese, remain case studies, comparisons and analyses of some particular features of these films, or more comprehensive studies about distinct segments (such as the journey films and transnationalism, geopolitics, postcolonial approaches, adaptations, genres, etc.). These approaches are represented by essay collections, such as *Olhares: Manoel de Oliveira* (2010, edited by Michelle Sales and Paulo Cunha and published in Brazil), *Manoel de Oliveira – Novas perspectivas sobre a sua obra* (2013), *Dekalog 02: On Manoel de Oliveira* (2009), both edited by Carolin Overhoff Ferreira, and *Manoel de Oliveira: Uma Presença* (2010), edited by Renata Junqueira.

The most complete non-Portuguese presentations so far have been realized by Randal Johnson's book in English, *Manoel de Oliveira* (2007), and Mathias Lavin's monograph in French, *La Parole et le lieu* (2008). The two books represent two completely different critical and methodological approaches: that of Johnson excels in the 'close reading' of these films, revealing a remarkable sense of the details and a good knowledge of the existing writing on Oliveira, the cultural background, but he rarely enters into theoretical discussions of the coined phenomenon in order to defuse the private and artistic personae of Oliveira. Moreover, his chronological overview, organized in more or less loose thematic clusters, ends in 2005, and thus misses almost ten active years of the director's work. Lavin's book (2008), on the other hand, is more preoccupied with the 'Oliveira phenomenon', the 'auteur in question', focusing on fundamental aspects of the Oliveirian cinema: the problematic relationship between word and image (of places and scenes), the gaps, delays and excesses that are responsible for the often disturbing effect it has on spectators. This latter book sets up a coherent

Introduction 3

method for the analysis, relying extensively on French theoretical literature and Portuguese critical works and interviews about Oliveira.

Admitting that the image–word discrepancy is a major characteristic of this cinema, rich in exuberant visual and oral details, I contend that there is a relevant aspect of Oliveira's cinema that has not been addressed by critics: the figurative potential of its intermediality, in both personal and cultural terms. I refer here to the importance of the stillness–movement dynamics, the relevance of the single, still(ed) image (pictorial or photographic) as a surface of projection of artistic and philosophical ideas and emotions, or as a link between theatricality and film (the case of *tableaux vivants*), also responsible for the 'literariness' of Oliveira's literary adaptations. Accordingly, in the light of already existing Portuguese and non-Portuguese critical material, as well as theoretical writings of the new disciplines of intermediality and cultural studies, I conceived my monograph in a format balancing between the two types of approaches, incorporating both close analyses and theoretical insights into what I consider to be the all-pervasive features of Oliveira's cinema: its strong affinity with the myth of modernity, conceived as the coexistence of tradition (stability) and the contingency brought about by the technological innovation; its intermediality as manifestation of a constant dialogue between the classic arts (painting, sculpture, theatre, literature and music) and the moving image; and, finally, *the uncanny* deriving from the previous two aspects, that is, the experience of the unfamiliar in the familiar (movement in stability, the modern in the classical, tradition in innovation and the other way around). I also understand the concept of the uncanny in the case of the cinema of Oliveira as a spectatorial experience (familiar in evoking well-known styles, but somehow strange in pairing these styles with bizarre topics, apparently without actuality), as an effect generated by a peculiar (slow, repetitive, allegoric) narrative technique and alienating style (long shots, painterly compositions, expressionless acting), as well as a personal and artistic attitude, characterized by an obsessive return to the same topics, characters and actors.

As Freud points out in his short article, *The Uncanny (Das Unheimliche)*, 'animism, magic and witchcraft, the omnipotence of thoughts, man's attitude to death, involuntary repetition and the castration-complex comprise practically all the factors which turn something fearful into an uncanny thing' (Freud [1919] 2003, 14). I argue that this definition of the uncanny (also viewed as the emergence of the unfamiliar in the familiar and the uncertainty of whether something is what it seems to be) does not only apply to most of the topics of Oliveira's films, but is equally true for Oliveira's vision of cinema, including his attitude to the magic of still and moving images, resulting in intermedial connections, the stubborn repetition of certain topoi, the obsession with the image of the (dead and dying) woman, his relationship with cinematic and wider cultural heritage, the link between recurring actors and their roles, as well as the effect that all of this has on the spectator. Thus, I contend that the applicability of the concept of *uncanny* to the cinema of Oliveira as a whole, instead of generating contradictions, rather reveals a close interconnectedness between the different layers of his work, that constantly reflect and figurate each other. I do not aim, however, to see the uncanny elements of these films solely as symptomatic of psychological phenomena (of characters, of the author or of historical eras). Freud's text is not strictly psychoanalytical either and it has been referred to in most varied contexts. It is also relevant in terms of representation of the uncanny in artistic works, armed, as Freud puts it, with a far greater range of means than real life. I do think that all films of Oliveira epitomize the workings of the uncanny, many of them in an evident manner, on the level of the story or topoi, others on a metanarrative level, by creating a tension between past and present, words and images (the case of numerous adaptations) or other media (film and painting, film and theatre, film and music), or by the uncertainty principle that affects the image: Is it moving or not? Is the character dead or alive? Is the idealized woman a doll/machine or human? Is the image revealing or hiding the truth/reality?

Beyond the above mentioned ambivalent relationship to the cinematic tradition, the concept of uncanny also applies to Oliveira's interpretation of modernity, after Charles Baudelaire, as a unity of stability and contingency, tradition and technology, old and new, stasis and movement, all perfectly represented by cinema and the cinematic apparatus itself. The uncanny can be also discovered in his sometimes 'too faithful' adaptations of literary texts and plays: the intermedial exchange is never smooth in these films, as, in them, re-mediation means a tensioned coexistence between the old and the new medium, the familiar and the unfamiliar. Repetition is an all-pervasive feature of this cinema, it appears in its urge to adapt literary works, its many art references, its recurrent topics, characters and actors, repetitions even inside the same narrative. I argue that the visual mannerism and tendency of aestheticization epitomized by intermedial, painterly references and the preference for *tableaux vivants* in Oliveira's films, is nothing else than a figuration of his constant preoccupation with the mystery of life and death, history (of Portugal, in a global context) and ultimately, time. His attraction to sinister, unusual, uncanny topics, reflected in many of his titles containing words like 'doomed', 'strange', 'magic', 'eccentric', 'uncertainty', 'anxiety', is paired with a style that often seems familiar, just to be subverted, parodied, interrupted most unexpectedly, triggering an uncanny effect.

What is also striking about these films and responsible for the uncanny effect is the anachronism of their narratives, missing all connections to the present: young women dying of tuberculosis (TB), people dying of grief and longing, moral stories about a decadent bourgeoisie, the self-destructive life of a nineteenth-century author, lives of historical and cultural personalities from the nineteenth and earlier centuries, meditations over Portugal's historical past and greatness, to name but a few topics. These are not heritage films in the sense that they are not meant to bring the past to the present: instead, in them the past remains a distant load, to which one needs to return regularly in order to achieve the desired understanding of the present. Accordingly, settings and décors are not revelatory of any specific moment of the twentieth century: costumes, fashion items, cars and interiors represent a great heterogeneity of styles and periods that undermine the actuality of the narrative and become another source of the uncanny. At the same time, the mannerism and aestheticization, the all-pervasive preference for the still(ed) image, painterly compositions and *tableaux vivants* reflect on the constant intention of the Western man to hold back time and grab the instant, in accordance with Giorgio Agamben's view on aesthetics as the destiny of contemporary art. As he points out, 'aesthetics is not simply the privileged dimension that progress in the sensibility of Western man has reserved for the work of art as his most proper place; it is, rather, the very destiny of art in the era in which, with tradition now severed, man is no longer able to find, between past and future, the space of the present, and gets lost in the linear time of history' (1999, 69).

All of Oliveira's work after his return to very prolific filmmaking at the beginning of the 1970s, after a long silence, can be seen as an intention to save tradition, retrieve memories and fulfil unfinished projects from the Salazar era, when he was politically marginalized. Unwilling (or unable) to recognize himself in the present (he is already in his sixties at the time of his return, an age at which many other filmmakers retired), he chose reconcile the past to the present, arguably with the aim of making the present more familiar. This is the role of his many literary adaptations (most of them from Portuguese works) and a few films of Portuguese historico-cultural interest. Under the circumstances of relativized temporal relationships, only one reality persists: that of the single image that becomes the sole present, or rather, *a presence.*

This book relies also on the assumption that the concept of the uncanny is also descriptive of the spectatorial experience whenever coming across the major, intertwining themes of the Oliveirian cinema: the safeguarding of universal or local, civilizational and cultural values, Portugal's role in their consolidation and Oliveira's life as a private person and his work as testimony of all this. These topics are structured by oppositions echoing the familiar-unfamiliar duality of the uncanny concept (stillness–movement, old–new, traditional–modern, visible–invisible, presence–absence, life–death), paired with a style (repetition, interruption, doubling, mirror-effect, intermedial exchanges) meant to figurate it. Oliveira's approach to cultural artefacts and most prominently to cinema shows striking similarities with that of cultural philosophers from the first part of the twentieth century (Ernst Bloch, Walter Benjamin, Siegfried Kracauer), and, more recently, Giorgio Agamben, for example – who had positioned themselves as experiencing subjects of arts and cultural practices. All films of Oliveira emanate a belief in the utopian function of art formulated by Bloch, the only source of hope and bearer of the illuminating anticipation that only art is capable to complete the world without destroying it (Bloch [1988] 1996: 72). In my view, Oliveira conceives of cinema as the technical medium that might counter humanity's miscarried reception of technology and be the perfect reflection of a fallen world and a life without substance of a decadent bourgeoisie, a recurrent topic of his films. However, I do not see the work of Oliveira as a simple illustration of these theses and theoretical views, but rather as a coherent discourse on its own on the responsibility of art and the artist in the century of cinema, witness of great societal crises and transformations, of the relativization of values and radical changes in the ways of looking.

Although I aim to provide an overall picture of the manifold occurrences of the myth of modernity, closely connected to the intermedial dialogues and the uncanny effect in Oliveira's work, the monograph does not have the ambition to cover the full list of his films (over 50 titles). Instead, it will refer to most of his feature films that will be included in more or less detailed analyses as follows: *Aniki-Bobó* (1942), *Rite of Spring* (1963), *Past and Present* (1972), *Benilde or the Virgin Mother* (1975), *Doomed Love* (1978), *Francisca* (1981), *The Cannibals* (1988), *No, or the Vain Glory of Command* (1990), *Abraham's Valley* (1993), *The Divine Comedy* (1991), *Voyage to the Beginning of the World* (1997), *Anxiety* (1998), *The Letter* (1999), *The Uncertainty Principle* (2002), *A Talking Picture*

(2003), Magic Mirror (2005), Cristopher Columbus – The Enigma (2007), Eccentricities of a Blonde-Haired Girl (2009) and *The Strange Case of Angelica (2010),* as well as *Gebo and the Shadow (2012).*

In the light of the above described aspects of the Oliveirian cinema, apart from an introductory and closing chapter, I structure the book in three parts, each comprising three chapters, with titles alluding to tropes and films representative of certain uncanny aspects. This involves having some films addressed more than once, due to their relevance for the theoretical issue raised in the particular chapter. These repeated occurrences are not, however, simple repetitions, as they are illuminated from different theoretical and conceptual perspectives.

Part One, 'The beautiful automaton', is built around the trope of the *beautiful automaton*, one of the central examples of Freud's essay that epitomizes the uncanny as an effect triggering (just like in its paradigmatic example, Hoffmann's, *The Sandman*) the uncertainty whether a character, a woman is living (human) or not (a machine), is still or moving. I find this trope descriptive of cinema in general (contemporary with Freud's essay) and three aspects of Oliveira's cinema, in particular, each to be tackled in separate chapters. The first chapter, 'Cinema and/as the myth of modernity', considers the beautiful automaton as a metaphor of cinema seen in its historical evolution from the classic visual arts to the technologically manipulated, moving image. I argue that the concept of cinema, seen as an accomplishment of the myth of modernity, defined by Baudelaire as a dichotomy between the eternal and ephemeral, art and fashion, stillness and movement (Baudelaire [1863] 1964), cannot be ignored in the case of a film director who started his career in the silent era. His return to this myth of origin, revealing a coherent personal philosophy of cinema, can be detected in a constant preoccupation with the human–machine duality, equally present in his early *Labor on the Douro River (Douro, Faina Fluvial,* 1931), and one of his latest features, *The Strange Case of Angelica* (2010), where a dead woman is seen as alive through the lens of the camera. The trope of missing and mechanical limbs (in *The Hunt,* 1963, and *The Cannibals,* 1988), as well as the fetishism of legs (most prominently in *Abraham's Valley*) are invoking modernity through the uncanny effect that presents cinematic movement as an illusion, a technologically adjusted ability of the still image. Similarly, a number of films that thematize blindness, voyeurism, the act of looking or visual creation (*The Box/A caixa, Abraham's Valley, Eccentricities of a Blonde-Haired Girl, Angelica, Belle Toujours, No, or the Vain Glory of Command, Voyage to the Beginning of the World, A*

8   *The Cinema of Manoel de Oliveira*

Talking Picture) participate in the discourse on cinema seen as technical (optical) prosthesis of the human body meant to overcome the uncanny fear of losing one's eye/sight, as well as the ultimate fear of dying before having seen everything.

Besides Charles Baudelaire, the art of Édouard Manet is another link connecting Oliveira to the myth of modernity, not only by representing the act of looking or by direct painterly references (in *Anxiety* or in *Angélica*), but first of all by introducing a disturbing element in his images of women, who often act as posing models, aware of being watched. The 'pose and pause' correlation resonates with Baudelaire's vision of modernity as the paradoxical relationship between an attraction towards the ephemeral, the contingent, like fashion, and the urge to grab the moment. This duality also permeates the cinema of Oliveira.

The second chapter in Part One, 'Towards an Oliveirian aesthetics of stillness', aims to explore further the beautiful automaton trope in the context of Oliveira's obsession with the still(ed) image. Relying on the discourses of slowness and stillness in cinema, by Roland Barthes, Pascal Bonitzer, Raymond Bellour and Laura Mulvey, for example, I argue that, while carrier of an unspeakable meaning (death drive, the sacred, a miracle or a taboo), the still, isolated image in the films under analysis becomes a fetish, just like the (female) body it represents. In many cases (for example in *Doomed Love, Francisca, Benilde, Past and Present*), the images of the film imitate the composition, colouring, texture, lighting and attention for the detail of paintings, photographs that the characters contemplate, creating an intermedial 'surface' where concealed meanings are projected, as an analogue to the literary style (in the case of adaptations). In the light of writings by Angela Dalle Vacche, Susan Felleman, Brigitte Peucker and Steven Jacobs, the intrusion of the painterly in film, beyond an atavistic animism that is part of the magic relationship between representation and death, functions as the memory of cinema, its 'subconscious', emphasizing Oliveira's historical view of the medium. I aim to show how the intermedial genre of *tableau vivant*, characteristic of his films that have been coined 'filmed theatre' (*Benilde, The Divine Comedy, Gebo and the Shadow*, for example), mediate between theatre and film, marking the culmination of the drama, the collapse between the signifier and the signified, as well as a still assumed modernist self-referentiality, a media-historical vision of cinema.

The last chapter in Part One, 'The trope of the doll', deals with a specific case of the beautiful automaton, that of the 'doll in the window' and its various occurrences in the films of Oliveira, starting from *Aniki Bobó*. But while animism is a natural ingredient in the play of the child protagonists of this film, the same

Introduction

attitude appears as an uncanny experience in the films of the so-called Tetralogy of Frustrated Loves (*Past and Present, Doomed Love, Benilde* and *Francisca*) and in *The Strange Case of Angelica, Eccentricities of a Blonde-Haired Girl, Abraham's Valley* and *The Letter*. All these films are built around the voyeuristic scene of a man contemplating a woman who seems unattainable, questionably animate/not animate, living/not living, like a picture or a statue. In this chapter, relying on the theoretical considerations of the previous two, my aim is to track the line of transformations of an emblematic object into an 'image', an aesthetic object based on the principle of stillness, a 'to-be-look-at-ness' demanding a contemplating spectator.

Part Two, titled, 'Camões and Don Quixote', focuses on another aspect of the uncanny experience, repetition and doubling. Invoked in the last short film of Oliveira, *The Old Man of Belém* (*O Velho de Restelo*, 2014), together with other key characters of the director's oeuvre, the recurring literary personalities embody central cultural concepts raised in a series of films tackling artistic responsibility for what he considers as national destiny. The emblematic figure of Camões stands for a heroic past and topics related to the preservation of national and cultural identity, while that of Don Quixote, invoked in the recurring quotation of the fight with the windmills scene from Grigor Kozintsef's homonymous 1952 film, remains a constant emblem of struggles with illusions, both individual and national. The artistic strategies of allegorization, profanation and parody, as well as cultural mimicry, as forms of repetition and imitation, serve Oliveira's cinematic reflections on Portugal's cultural heritage, conceived as a tensioned relationship between the global and the local, Western and Southern, European and non-European, as well as official and unofficial/personal discourses. The stubborn return to these familiar topics tackled from unfamiliar perspectives, mostly in films made after 2000, also generates an uncanny effect, revealing, at the same time, the vision of an artist who feels that a critical reframing of national identity discourses is his major responsibility. The sub-chapters of this section will illuminate different aspects of the complex discourse of Portuguese national and personal identity, as represented in the films of Oliveira. The one entitled *Historical Allegories and Identity Quests* tackles the phenomenon of historical/cultural allegory described by Ismail Xavier as a figuration open to moralization and educational purposes, typical of periods of transition and crisis – in this case, from the isolation during dictatorship to a membership of the European Community ([1999] 2004). In Oliveira's approach, this crisis appears as an intense search for identity, detectable in a preoccupation with the national character and stereotypes, the reflection of big historical movements in individual destinies, as well as a wish to find the place of Portugal among the other nations of Europe.

Chapter 4, 'The cultural philosophy of Oliveira', explores the manifold aspects of Oliveira's cultural philosophy: the sub-section headed, 'The Spirit of Negation', is a detailed analysis of *No, or the Vain Glory of Command* and *The Fifth Empire*, both revealing an ambivalent attitude towards Portugal's colonial past; the section subheaded, 'Spectres of Nostalgia', focuses on the films *Cristopher Columbus – The Enigma*, where national and personal identity quest intertwine in a strictly Portuguese definition of nostalgia: *saudade*; and finally, the section subheaded, 'The Road to a Transnational Identity', is a detailed analysis of *Voyage to the Beginning of the World. A Talking Picture* is presented as an allegory of Portugal's position among European nations, permeated with the urge 'to see it all' stemming from the (uncanny) fear of darkness, of losing one's eye(sight) and of (both individual and national) death.

The second chapter of Part Two, Chapter 5, 'Profanations', is built around the concept of repetition as 'profanation' of religious mysteries and miracles, seen by Giorgio Agamben as a loss of aura of the original event (2007). Profanation, as well as parody, considered by Agamben as the unique way to approach mysteries, a confrontation of the own with a universal grammar (in this case, with the sacred texts of the Bible) will be interpreted in three detailed analyses: that of *Rite of Spring* (where the filming process itself becomes part of the re-enactment), *The Divine Comedy* (a series of re-enactments of resurrection scenes, accompanied by dialogues and monologues corresponding to contradictory voices in a personal discourse of Oliveira, seeking answers after the death of his grandson) and, finally, *The Uncertainty Principle* and *Magic Mirror*, both structured along a profane aspiration towards the sacred seen as ideal (the holy family, the Virgin Mary, Saint Joan) of an upper-middle-class frozen in pure formalities and appearances. The third chapter, Chapter 6, 'Cultural mimicry', turns towards the topic of cultural identity, Portugal's position in contemporary Europe, its geopolitical liminality that triggers an urge of 'mimicry' of the Western cultural, especially French, colonizers that also goes hand in hand with an ironical distanciation. This topic will involve the discussion of the 'French connection' of a number of films by Oliveira (actors, locations, co-production, financing, painterly style), the so-called Paulo Branco (the producer of many of his films) factor, as well as the many other references connecting them to the wider European (visual) culture. The films referred to – *The Satin Slipper, Anxiety, The*

Letter, Belle Toujours, Gebo and the Shadow, as well as *Voyage to the Beginning of the World* – are all representative of a Portuguese cultural identity seen by Oliveira as 'the other' of Western European values and identities.

In Part Three, the last set of chapters targets a special group of films in the Oliveirian oeuvre, the literary adaptations as special examples of intermediality reuniting his views on the visual representability of words and poetic ideas. Although this is one of the most interpreted sections of the director's work, involving more than half of his films, I argue that they raise dilemmas that cannot be grasped solely in the word–image discrepancy. I aim to reiterate the assumptions regarding the figurative role of intermediality, already discussed in the previous chapters to some extent – most prominently the 'intrusion' of the painterly into the filmic text – both in terms of narrative signification and intercultural dialogue. Oliveira's paradigmatic *Doomed Love*, an adaptation of a novel by Camilo Castelo Branco, epitomizes his view that the fatal attraction between literature and film can be only problematized, but never solved. This assumption is reflected in a set of uncanny effects (such as repetition, interruption, stillness) that make the intermedial exchange visible and result in 'disturbing adaptations' that will be analysed in Chapter 7, also titled, 'Disturbing adaptations' (*Past and Present, Francisca, Benilde, Abraham's Valley, Eccentricities of a Blonde-Haired Girl*). *Doomed Love* will be interpreted in detail in a subsequent chapter, Chapter 8, 'Letters on the screen', comparing Oliveira's version to three other Portuguese adaptations of the novel, in order to explore, through the differences detected, the underlying Oliveirian discourse on authorship, cinema as writing, fidelity, the word–image relationship, the visible and the invisible, as well as the absence–presence dichotomy. The signifying potential of the interaction between the visible and audible, the letter and the voice, or music, is explored in the last chapter of this part, Chapter 9, 'Sounding letters', in connection with two other films that have as their central narrative trope the letter, its writing and reading process (*Francisca* and *The Letter*). The analyses will be placed in a wider cultural context of visual representations of writing and music making in paintings (especially the seventeenth-century Dutch tradition).

The concluding chapter, 'Coda: A melancholic cinema?', aims to reframe the obstinately repeating topics and experiences tackled in the previous parts (and responsible for the uncanny effect of films) from the perspective of a real or imagined, even anticipated, individual and national loss: mourning, longing, loss of identity, Portugal's loss of global prestige, loss of youth and health, as well as own death. I argue that melancholia is a common denominator in Oliveira's films, that, together with the nostalgia for a glorious past (of Portugal, of the Oliveira family and their social class), is the ingredient of *saudade*, a specifically Portuguese (and Brazilian) form of yearning. The desperate longing for the lost object (the Mother-Thing being its archaic image) surfaces in stubborn repetitions of the same 'unfinished business', of the topic of frustrated love affairs, fetishism, a preference for melodramas and stillness, as well as the death drive of his narratives. I contend that the work of Oliveira can be interpreted as a continuous attempt to sublimate an unspeakable sense of loss, a powerful drive that fuelled his active and creative cinematic work. In this respect, cinema as filmmaking can be seen as an *object of transition* for him that made his passage to death smooth, from the familiar facts and acts of life to the unfamiliar and unrepresentable Big Unknown.

References

Agamben, Giorgio. 2007. *Profanations*. New York: Zone Books.

Araújo, Nelson (ed.). 2014. *Manoel de Oliveira. Análise Estética de uma Matriz Cinematográfica*. Lisboa: Edições 70.

Baecque, Antoine de and Jacques Parsi. 1996. *Conversations avec Manoel de Oliveira*. Paris: Cahiers du Cinéma.

Baudelaire, Charles. [1863] 1964. 'The Painter of Modern Life'. In *Baudelaire: The Painter of Modern Life and Other Essays*, ed. and trans. Jonathan Mayne, 1–41. London: Phaidon Press.

Bloch, Ernst. [1988] 1996. *The Utopian Function of Art and Literature*. Cambridge, MA: MIT Press.

Bordwell, David. 2013. *Observations on Film Art: David Bordwell's Website on Cinema*, blog entry on Il Cinema Ritrovato Festival. Available at: http://www.davidbordwell. net/blog/category/directors-oliveira/ (accessed 2 July 2019).

Costa, João Bénard. 1981. 'Diálogo com Manoel de Oliveira'. In *Manoel de Oliveira*, 31–46. Lisboa: Cinemateca Portuguesa.

Costa Andrade, Sérgio. 2008. *Ao correr do tempo. Duas decadas com Manoel de Oliveira* [*Over Time: Two Decades with Manoel de Oliveira*]. Lisboa: Portugália Editora.

Daney, Serge. 2001. 'Notes sur les films de Manoel de Oliveira'. In *La Maison Cinéma et le monde, 1: Le Temps des Cahiers* [*The Cinema House and the World, 1: The Time of the Cahiers*], 225–7. Paris: P.O.L.

Freud, Sigmund. [1919] 2003. *The Uncanny*. London: Penguin Classics.

Hoffmann, E. T. A. [1815] 1992. 'The Sandman'. In *The Golden Pot and Other Tales*, 85–118. Oxford: Oxford University Press.

Johnson, Randal. 2007. *Manoel de Oliveira*. Champaign, IL: University of Illinois Press.

Junqueira, Renata (ed.). *Manoel de Oliveira: Uma Presença* [*Manoel de Oliveira: A Presence*]. São Paolo: Perspectiva.

Lavin, Mathias. 2008. *La Parole le lieu: Le Cinema selon Manoel de Oliveira* [*The Word and the Place: The Cinema According to Manoel de Oliveira*]. Rennes: Presses Universitaires de Rennes.

Overhoff Ferreira, Carolin (ed.). 2009. *Dekalog 02: On Manoel de Oliveira*. London: Wallflower Press.

Overhoff Ferreira, Carolin (ed.). 2013. *Manoel de Oliveira – Novas perspectivas sobre a sua obra* [*Manoel de Oliveira: New Perspectives on His Oevre*]. São Paulo: Fap-Unifesp.

Parsi, Jacques. 1981. 'A *trilogia dos amores frustrados*' ['The Trilogy of Frustrated Loves']. In *Manoel de Oliveira*, 71–8. Lisbon: Cinemateca Portuguesa.

Rosenbaum, Jonathan. [1981] 1995. '*Doomed Love*: A Masterpiece You Missed'. In *Placing Movies: The Practice of Film Criticism*, 213–17. Berkeley, CA: University of California Press.

Sales, Michelle and Paulo Cunha (eds). 2010. *Olhares. Manoel de Oliveira*. Rio de Janeiro: Edições LCV/SR3/UERJ.

Xavier, Ismail. [1999] 2004. 'Historical Allegory'. In *A Companion to Film Theory*, eds Robert Stam and Toby Miller, 333–62. Malden, MA, and London: Blackwell Publishing.

Part One

The beautiful automaton

1

Cinema and/as the myth of modernity

In a memorable scene of *The Strange Case of Angelica*, Isac, the Jewish photographer (played by Oliveira's grandson, Ricardo Trêpa), hired to take photographs of a dead young woman, Angelica, asks for another electric bulb in order to improve the lighting of the scene. He hangs up the old one on the spot, surrounded by the grieving circle of relatives. This odd scene can be attributed multiple significations: it creates an uncanny effect by opposing everyday gestures (the familiar) to death (the unfamiliar); it also models the directorial planning and aesthetic distanciation, but beyond that, it is a historical memento of the Oliveira family, owners, at the beginning of the twentieth century, of a factory manufacturing electric devices. The scene places the film in a family lineage of pioneers of technology and in the universal heritage of modernity at the same time. The concept of cinema seen as an accomplishment of the myth of modernity, defined by Baudelaire as a dichotomy between the eternal and ephemeral, art and fashion, art and technology, as well as stillness and movement (Baudelaire [1863] 1964), is central in the cinema of Oliveira, overarching the whole of the twentieth century.

In his essay, *Acte de filmer et conscience filmique dans mon cas particulier* (*The Act of Filmmaking and Cinematic Consciousness in My Particular Case*, 2009, 38), Oliveira specifies his *ars poetica* as an intention 'to restart everything, but armed with the whole inherited baggage'.[1] No definition of cinematic modernity or modernity in general could be more to the point: it touches upon the constant affinity of modernity with a classic heritage while relentlessly trying to move on, relying on new technologies and fashions. In the case of film, an ambiguous relationship to both the filmic and literary tradition, first of all the romantic heritage has been repeatedly pointed out by theorists of cinematic modernity. This is what John Orr calls the paradox of modern cinema: 'recurrence as

---

[1] 'tout recommencer, mais muni de tout bagage hérité'; author's own translation.

completion of form through technology' (1993, 3). But, as the work of Oliveira testifies, cinema itself can be seen as a metaphor of modernity, a technology that incorporates the heritage of classic arts. Baudelaire, in his famous essay, *The Painter of Modern Life*, defines modernity as if describing cinema, as 'the ephemeral, the fugitive, the contingent, the half of art whose other half is the eternal and the immutable' ([1863] 1964, 13). After 150 years, this puzzling essay is still referred to by theorists of cinematic modernity, visual culture, phenomenology, feminist film theory, related to concepts like 'the body', 'spectacle', 'mise-en-scène', 'glamour', 'search for perfection', the 'issues of the self', 'performance' or the 'look/gaze'. With titles like *The Man of the World*, *The Dandy*, *Pomps and Ceremonies*, *Cosmetics*, *Women* and *Prostitutes*, *Carriages*, Baudelaire's essay is seen by many as an anticipation of the visual mass culture and film. I contend that this is also a list of the main topics and preoccupations in the films of Oliveira, himself a dandy and a man of the world as a young man, an apt critic of middle-class ceremonies and formalities and a relentless researcher of the secret of the feminine spell as a filmmaker.

Philosopher Stanley Cavell identifies in Baudelaire's compelling presentation of aspects of modernity the myths of film, the modern medium being the only one capable of satisfying 'the specific simultaneity of presence and absence', of stability and futility, stillness and movement (1979, 42). Moreover, according to Cavell, Baudelaire is having a prophetic hallucination when describing the 'mysterious and complex grace' of movement of carriages, difficult to note down in shorthand (if not impossible), but which is the essence of cinema and the 'pleasure that the artistic eye obtains [. . .] from the series of geometrical figures that the object in question [. . .] successively and rapidly creates in space' (1979, 43–4). Carriages, cars and machines in movement have become metaphors of the moving image throughout Oliveira's career, a former race-car driver himself. Featured in a contrasting montage of human force and machines in *Douro, faina fluvial*, in a very long shot of the moving carriage wheels in *O dia do desespero* (*The Day of Despair*) alluding both to the passing time and the film reel, and as the sports car of Ema in *Abraham's Valley* (*Vale Abraão*), compensating for the heroine's limp (to name some prominent examples), cars are fetishistic objects in his films, paradoxically connected to both the desire to live and the death drive.

In film history, the modern, individual and fashionable woman also became the driving force of both the film narration (as the recognition of her sexuality grants her independence and the freedom of movement and action) and filmmaking/production. As Cavell puts it:

Cinema and/as the Myth of Modernity 19

Remarkable directors have existed solely to examine the same woman over and over through film. A woman has become the whole excuse and sole justification for the making and preserving of countless films: in many of Garbo's films, or Dietrich's, next to nothing may be memorable, or even tolerable, but these women themselves. The miracle is that they are enough.

1979, 48

For Oliveira, this fetish-actress is Leonor Silveira, often playing an apparently naive, girly, but mysterious and ever-changing woman over and over in his films, and contrasting the more two-dimensional male characters. John Orr, when discussing the paradox of the modern in film, comes to a similar conclusion: 'While male roles often continue to display older forms of patriarchy and authority, the modern female persona challenges these conventions dramatically. Thus both modern cinema and its modern women spring from changing forms of modernity, but both subsequently challenge existing forms of modernity' (1979, 49).

The movement–stillness opposition, closely related to a strong belief in the poetical possibilities of the single image (often that of a woman) and the unchanged (man) – changeable (woman) binary are at the very core of the whole work of Oliveira. *Doomed Love* (*Amor de Perdição*, 1978), from the *Tetralogy of Frustrated Loves* (also including *Past and Present Benilde or the Virgin Mother / Benilde ou a Virgem Mãe*, 1975, and *Francisca*, 1981) and *Abraham's Valley*, seem to recycle the main titles of the Baudelaire-ian essay and modernity by focusing on the concept of movement and stilled movement, as well as fashion and glamour, that more on visual attractions (mostly provided by the changing image of a woman) than on narration and story. Both films are re-mediations of nineteenth and twentieth-century novels and represent an original approach of the modern film to the romantic myth of love. They were made after Oliveira's return to filmmaking after some twenty-five years of almost complete silence, and belong to a long series of films on frustrated loves and aborted marriages, a topic characteristic to the modern film. According to Orr, in films, 'The loss of romantic love often portrayed as irreversible has drawn responses … ranging from stoicism and acceptance to irony and despair' (1993, 9). In *Doomed Love*, the still image or rather the images of stilled movement – *tableaux vivants* – are metaphorically doubling the story of a fatal love, causing the illness and ultimately the death of the protagonists. I argue that *Doomed Love* and *Abraham's Valley*, as well as the whole *Tetralogy* and many other films by Oliveira are also about the *fatal attraction and frustrating* relationship between image and movement, a recurrent topic in film theory, most prominently in phenomenological approaches and the theories of the spectator.[2] For Oliveira, 'restarting' filmmaking does not mean technological updating, but rather a conceptual approach to cinema: all his films made after his return can be conceived of as a series of allegories of cinema as a par excellence modern medium, as a private philosophy of the tensioned 'marriage' between image, movement and narration.

Doomed Love: Melodrama as a stillness–movement dynamics

Oliveira missed most of the period of European cinematic modernism, as he stopped making films in the 1940s, except for some short movies and *Rite of Spring* in the 1950s and 1960s, returning to active filmmaking at the beginning of the 1970s. He could have caught up with the late modernism by simply adopting a modernist style. But he rather went back to the original modernity definition of Baudelaire and was re-enacting the myth of modernity *on film and by film*, staging its paradoxical position between the stability and stillness of plastic artworks – paintings and statues – and the futility represented by the moving image. The ninneteenth-century literary works he adapted also stood for the romantic tradition with which modernity had always been in a love and hate relationship. This tendency is evident in the modernist melodrama where the story is always reflected upon or deconstructed by a peculiar style of the camera movement, acting, lights and editing. Oliveira is staging the relationship of film to this tradition neither by using a style reflecting on the story (either ironically or parodically) nor by alternating the story by representing alienation as a modernist version of melodrama. *Doomed Love*, an adaptation of Camilo Castelo Branco's homonymous novel from 1862, is a Portuguese *Romeo and Juliet*, the tragic love story of Simão and Teresa, who become victims of the enmities between their families: Teresa dies of tuberculosis and, heartbroken, Simão dies from despair on the boat taking him to the colonies. This film, just like all melodramas of Oliveira, does not fit entirely in either of the film genre of classic or modernist melodrama as presented by András Bálint Kovács (2007): its style is vaguely minimalist-modernist, reminding one of Bresson's model theory, Rohmer's *The Marquise of O* (1976) or Alain Resnais' *Last Year in*

---

[2] See, for example, Mulvey (2006a, 2006b), Sobchack (1992, 2004) and an overview by Remes (2012).

Marienbad (1961), but apparently without a drama of the modern subjectivity or social alienation at the level of the story. Instead, the alienation happens between image and narration, style and story: Oliveira creates a film language completely alienated from the narrative, as if representing the incapacity of the modernist film to get hold of the romantic tradition of the genre, too distant thus inaccessible.

As one of his critics has pointed out about *Doomed Love*, in most films of Oliveira, there is a 'gap between the character and the actor, the actor and the model, the frame and the scene and the world, the image and the text' (Lévy 1998, 51–3).[3] This is also evident in the much emphasized discrepancy between the *voix-off* narration and images in *Doomed Love*: the former is not interpreting images and images are not illustrations of the *voix-off* narration. We can rather talk about a complementary relationship between two independent entities. There is also a gap between the literary tradition of romantic melodrama and the actuality of film: as Francis Ramasse (1979) points out, the tuberculosis as vector of melodrama is not plausible any more in 1978. We can say, by referring to Susan Sontag's essay, *Illness as Metaphor* (1978), that sickness appears here rather as a metaphor of the depicted society. While assuming that illness is not a metaphor, Sontag provides a cultural history of artistic and political discourses using tuberculosis as metaphor of a certain type of personality in nineteenth-century Romanticism. Sontag compares systematically the literary imagery of tuberculosis with that of the cancer metaphor, characteristic of the depiction of the individual and societal crises of the twentieth century. She brings both literary and cinematic examples to demonstrate the aestheticizing tendency in the representation of tuberculosis. Through the literary works adapted in *Doomed Love* and *Francisca*, both invoking the romantic persona of the Portuguese nineteenth-century writer Camilo Castelo Branco, Oliveira also adopts this aesthetic tradition: he uses the image of a young woman with tuberculosis as a metaphor of both the activity–passivity dynamics of the relationships between the characters and of a society consumed by inner tensions and unfulfilled ideals. As Sontag argues, TB makes the body transparent, but at the same time rich in visible symptoms (1978, 12), susceptible for visual aestheticization: Oliveira depicts both Teresa, the female protagonist of *Doomed Love* and *Francisca* from the eponymous film, as very pale, fragile, transparent, slowly fading away. Sontag also calls TB 'a disease of time' that 'speeds up life,

---

[3] 'L'écart entre le personnage et l'acteur, l'acteur et le modèle, entre le cadre et la scène et le monde, entre l'image et le texte' (author's own translation).

highlights it, spiritualizes it' while being, at the same time, represented in literature as the prototypical passive death, 'a kind of suicide' (ibid., 24).

In terms of cinematic representation, and in particular in the case of the two above mentioned films, this decline into passivity following intense emotional scenes resonates with the death drive that Laura Mulvey identifies in melodramas. According to Mulvey, the death drive manifests in the tendency of filmic action and movement to slide into non-action, stillness and ultimately death. Stillness also resonates with the tendency of film to return to the photographic stage: 'Stillness may evoke a "before" for the moving image as filmstrip, as a reference back to photography or to its own original moment of registration.' The death drive negotiates between the narrative and cinema, including, as it does, movement towards an end as the desire to return to an 'earlier' state. So, there is an analogy – if not a metaphoric relationship – between death drive, narration's movement towards a final halt and the inclination of the moving image towards stillness (Mulvey 2006a, 67–81).

The same active–passive dynamics and a gradual turn into stillness characterizes the male character of *Doomed Love*, Simão. Clara Rowland and Abel Barros Baptista, following Lawton's analyses of the novel *Doomed Love*, have pointed out in a revision of Castelo Branco's novel that in contrast to the second part, its first part is very dynamic. We are acquainted with an action-hero Simão, who is impulsive, destructive, has revolutionary ideas and, finally, kills his rival in revenge (Rowland 2009, 59–80 and Baptista 2009, 81–112). After being injured and jailed following the murder, we witness a gradual sliding into stilled-ness, an almost catatonic state, lack of any bodily expression. In the second part, characters are represented mostly frontally, as a reminiscence of the Bressonian model-theory. Oliveira's film is masterly in reproducing the turning point from movement and action into non-action and meditation that occurs when Simão sees Teresa through the window and falls desperately in love with her. This structure also corresponds to Simão's personality, impulsive and melancholic at the same time, which also gives way to such critical assumptions that Simão doesn't fall due to his love and social circumstances, but his personality.[4] Assuming this revised approach of the novel, Oliveira turns the bipolarity of the hero into a play between action and stilled movement. This corresponds to a Deleuzeian distribution of movement and time images, that creates 'a cinema of the seer and no longer of the agent' (Deleuze [1985] 1989,

---

[4] See, for example, Baptista (2009, 81–112).

Cinema and/as the Myth of Modernity   23

126–9). As Ramasse pointed out, in the second part of the film, 'participation gives place to contemplation, emotion to intelligence and what has been proper melodramatic pleasure becomes intellectual pleasure' (1979, 65–6).[5] By repeatedly transforming the moving image into *tableau vivant*, Oliveira does not only invoke film's indebtedness to plastic arts and photography, but also models the double face of modernity, oscillating between 'the eternal and immutable' and 'ephemeral and fugitive'. Beauty and emotional power, linked by Lord Byron with 'an element of the sinister or at least the doomed and the damned',[6] is transformed into visual power, manifested in a systematic and excessive use of frames (windows, doors, mirrors and jail bars) and symbolic compositions meant to be deciphered by a cinephile spectator.

Fashion, pose and cultural symbolism in *Abraham's Valley*

Baudelaire defines modernity as a correlation between beauty, happiness and fashion, and this latter as responsible for its ephemeral aspect:

> By modernity I mean Fashion itself that appears as a symptom of the taste for the ideal which floats on the surface of all the crude, terrestrial and loathsome bric-a-brac that the natural life accumulates in the human brain: as a sublime deformation of Nature, or rather a permanent and repeated attempt at her reformation.
>
> [1863] 1964, 31

In *Abraham's Valley*, an adaptation of the homonymous novel by Agustina Bessa-Luís from 1991, with strong references to Gustave Flaubert's *Madame Bovary* (1857), Oliveira finds another way to celebrate the aesthetical potentials of the still image: fashion and subsequently *posing* become, once again, allegorical representations of the oscillation between stillness/stability and movement or contingency. Ema, the bored middle-class housewife, constantly poses and looks into mirrors: she is 'half-doll, half-idol',[7] a female dandy. Dandyism, as described by Baudelaire and fashion theorists as a 'performance', a 'mise-en-scène', is presenting 'one's self as a work of art': a dandy's

---

[5]   'La participation cède la place à la contemplation, l'émotion á l'intelligence, ce qui était proprement le plaisir mélodramatique devient plaisir intellectuel' (author's own translation).

[6]   Quoted by Wilson (2007, 96).

[7]   See more about the 'fin-de-siècle' visual culture and fashion in Steele's essay (2004).

24   *The Cinema of Manoel de Oliveira*

solitary profession is elegance, 'the eternal pursuit of happiness' (Baudelaire [1863] 1964, 26). Ema sets off for a search for perfection, love and happiness by creating herself a glamorous image, mesmerizing all her entourage. The meaning of the very term *glamour*, of Celtic origin, is closely related to 'occult learning and magic' (grammar, grammarye): 'when devils, wizards or jufflers deceive the sight, they are said to cast a glamour over the eye of the spectator (early eighteenth century)'.[8] Ema is looked at, admired and talked about, and these are, according to John Berger, the ingredients of glamour: 'the state of being envied is what constitutes glamour. And publicity is the process of manufacturing glamour' (Berger 1972, 131). Her posing, at parties or during her long discussions with one of her admirers evokes the femme fatale image of the Hollywood star system: she *is turning herself into an image*. A pose evokes the nature of photography and 'allows time for the cinema to denaturalize the human body', 'is a tool of delaying cinema, resisting narrative linearity, addressing a fetishistic spectator more fascinated by image than plot' (Mulvey 2006b, 164). In this respect, the title of *Doomed Love* becomes a definition, as Jonathan Rosenbaum has half-mockingly observed, of *acute cinephilia*, valid for most films by Oliveira ([1981] 1995, 66).

In *Abraham's Valley*, fashion is also one of the main factors responsible for the opacity of representation. It is impossible to detect the time period of the story: costumes, decorations and cars represent different ages, trends and social backgrounds. This lack of referentiality is not compensated by a symbolic level of meanings, but produces a 'third meaning', a 'noise' revealing the medium of film.[9] Fashion as visual excess replaces the narrative and emotional excess of melodrama. This can be considered Oliveira's original discourse on the paradox of fashion revealing the culturally changed female body by covering it. Fashion, as a phenomenon making absence (the body) visible through excess, is a central subject of modernity and, as Baudelaire emphasizes in his *The Painter of Modern Life*, of the new trends in visual representation of women ([1863] 1964, 31–3).

In *Abraham's Valley*, the paradox of the modern woman, moving on, but haunted by the phantoms of the past and that of modern cinema stuck between literary and visual tradition and new narrative technologies, are thoroughly intertwined in a metaphorical relationship. The oscillation between the traditional role of a housewife staying at home and that of the independent, modern woman crossing her boundaries is reflected by still images, *tableaux vivants* that start moving and,

---

[8]   A definition from the *Oxford English Dictionary*, cited by Wilson (2007, 96).
[9]   On the third, non-referential and non-symbolical meaning, see Barthes (1985).

conversely, images of action freezing into stilled movement. The independence of Ema is largely indebted to fashion, as it gives her the sensation of control by creating a 'better self' in a society characterized by hypocrisy and mediocrity. Fashion, glamour and dandyism, in her case, become, as Baudelaire put it, 'the last spark of heroism amid decadence' ([1863] 1964, 28). Fashion is also blurring the boundaries between le monde and le demi-monde, the respectable bourgeois woman and the actresses/prostitutes: the mise-en-scène, the surface exhibition, the pure appearance, that used to characterize the courtesan, aiming to get close to the man who pays her. This oscillation between respectability and immorality is thematized both in Agustina Bessa-Luís' novel and in its film adaptation by Oliveira: Ema's social status as a wife and/or a courtesan is a constant dilemma. This is plastically represented in the film by a contrastive repetition of the image of a family altar, a triptych (as symbol of her religious, conservative education) and a threefold mirror, the same composition, in which she is constantly watching her new, fashionable self. The mirror is used by Ema to construct herself as a *sight* (Berger 1972, 51). The scenes of staring into the mirror do not show the female body and face as an object (of desire), but as an abstraction, an image of an idealized self. Moreover, in one of the last scenes, we see an ageing Ema with heavy make-up, looking into an oval mirror juxtaposed with a photo of her young self. When she moves away, another body becomes visible in the same frame: that of Christ on the crucifix (see Figures 1.1–1.4).

Figures 1.1–1.4 An analogy between the family altar and the mirror in *Abraham's Valley*.

Abraham's Valley is a Portuguese-Oliveirian version of *Madame Bovary*: Flaubert's novel, contemporary with Baudelaire's essay, is also about the role of fashion in the pursuit of happiness and independence. Its protagonist, Emma, tries to set herself free from her small bourgeois lifestyle by buying extravagant clothes and fashion articles which will cause her debts and ultimately leads to her suicide. She cannot escape her traditional role as wife and cannot move on as a courtesan whose debts are paid for by her lover. So, after a short but intense adventure of freedom, fuelled by the desire of happiness, she is regressing to the stillness of death. In *Abraham's Valley*, her difficulty to move on is symbolized by her limp. Just as clothes are meant to conceal this imperfection, the glamorous image is meant to hide the 'motoric imperfection' of narration and is targeting a spectator who wants to get a hold on the image and contemplate it. For Ema, a party scene or a social event often functions as a catwalk: she walks in, not looking at anybody while everybody is watching her, then she stops, posing, as if in front of the voyeuristic, fetishistic gaze of the 'possessive spectator'. In this film, the pose, turning the body of the character into a still image, stands for the 'surprise principle' of the Oliveirian cinema, constantly slowing down and freezing movement to reveal the 'real', painterly and photographic nature of the medium.

Viewed from the perspective of Baudelaire's essay, celebrating the 'double face of modernity', stability and tradition, together with movement and fashion, thus having a prophetic premonition about visual mass culture, *Doomed Love* and *Abraham's Valley* are thematizing some central theoretical issues of cinema, constantly torn between narrative illusion and the magic of the still image. While 'death drive', a Freudian concept applied by Laura Mulvey to melodramas, turns action into stillness, fashion, glamour and pose are delaying cinematic movement and narration, hiding their imperfections. Both films end with the image of water, a symbol, as Laura Mulvey points out, of narrative halt (2006b, 78–9). Only the still image remains, in accordance with Oliveira's declared intention to move spectators without any dissimulation of the artifice.

2

Towards an Oliveirian aesthetics of stillness

At the beginning of the 1970s, after an absence of nearly twenty-five years, Manoel de Oliveira returned to filmmaking and established his international reputation as a strange old man making odd, unbearably long and slow films. The films that marked his return and brought him international recognition are commonly called the 'Tetralogy of frustrated loves,' but the topic of doomed loves and dysfunctional marriages goes far beyond this series, becoming an obsession for Oliveira, and also, as I argued in the previous chapter, a pretext for staging his original philosophy on visual sophistication and narration. At the beginning of the 1970s, this preoccupation was in line with a phenomenon characteristic of films made after the Second World War that showed a tendency to slow down the movement and linger over a static image which became, as Raymond Bellour later remarked, one of the possible figures of cinema (Bellour 2002b, 113). Justin Remes, in an article on the possible theoretical approaches to the so-called 'cinema of stasis', also points out that the 'aesthetic force' of static films can be appreciated in contrast with motion, still normative in cinema, although, according to many scholars, it is just one of the technical possibilities of film, just like sound and colour (2012).[1]

For both Bellour and Remes, as well as for all the ongoing discourse discrediting motion as a par excellence cinematic feature, Roland Barthes' essay on the Third Meaning is a constant reference: according to Barthes, the third or obtuse meaning (identified also with the 'cinematic' or 'filmique') is 'indifferent' and even 'contrary' to the film movement (1985).[2] The subversive attitude of modernist and New Wave films towards a sometimes 'hysterical' pace of spectacle has inevitably implied an increased preoccupation with the sensual qualities and magic effect of the single, static image. Starting from the 1970s, this has also been reflected in a film theoretical interest in spectacle and spectatorship, visual pleasure, the still(ed) image as

---

[1] He refers to a dialogue around 'Defining the Moving Image' between Carroll (2006) and Yanal (2008).
[2] See Remes (2012, 265), Bellour (2002b, 115) and Campany (2007).

28   *The Cinema of Manoel de Oliveira*

attraction versus issues of narration. The magic of the single image, animated by desire and the death drive has since been debated by Laura Mulvey (2006c) and Tom Gunning (1990) in the context of 'a cinema of attractions'. Together with the 'possessive spectator', another type of spectator has been described: the 'pensive spectator'. According to Bellour, the spectator of the classic cinema 'under pressure' made aware of time and consciousness by a still image is replaced with a pensive, contemplating spectator (2002a, 75–80).

As static films 'demand prolonged engagement and meditation in a way that is often encouraged by traditional visual art' (Remes 2012, 266), art history and theory became another direction of researching these films, placing them in the visual cultural tradition of painting and photography. This kind of approach identifies painterly style and composition as a concentration of figurative meanings, corresponding to Lessing's 'pregnant moment' (Bellour 2002b, 119). As Pascal Bonitzer puts it, the 'plan tableau', due to its allusive character of imitation, can reveal a profound secret of the film (1985, 30). He also distinguishes two kinds of film directors: those who believe in reality and those who believe in the image (a typically French distinction, he argues, that can be traced back to Bazin). The directors representing this latter tendency are the opponents of the (narrative) illusionism characteristic of cinema. Instead of narrative illusion, they prefer the 'trompe l'oeil' of the plan tableau and *tableaux vivants* which, instead of reinforcing illusion, are rather de-masking it (1985, 29–36).[3] According to the famous statement of Deleuze, plans are 'the consciousness of cinema' – not only because they are specific to certain periods of cinema, but also because the use of plans is approaching cinema to painting, its past, due to 'framing' or 'décadrage' (Bonitzer 1985). An image-centric approach characterizes the most recent film theory by Thomas Elsaesser and Malte Hagener (2010), associating distinct senses to types of cinematic frames – windows, doors or mirrors – thus realizing a phenomenological meta-theory when introducing a film history 'through the senses'.

This overview of some relevant phenomenological, art-theoretical, cultural-anthropological discourses[4] of the still cinematic image is far from being complete and only serves as a theoretical framework to the interpretation of two films by Oliveira, representative of his peculiar philosophy of cinematic image and motion. He is undoubtedly a director who believes in the magic of the image and although his narrative techniques are not spectacularly subversive, his

---

[3]   Not surprisingly, he takes as examples Godard's *Passion* (1982) and Rohmer's *The Marquise of O* (1976).

[4]   As, for example, Laura Marks has shown it, the 'sensuality' of particular film images can be culturally coded and successfully used in the study of so-called 'intercultural films' as 'trace of memory' and as an alternative to the more widespread 'narrative memory' (2000).

stories either lack actuality, or are unfinished, unbearably slow and stuck in details, merely serving as a contrasting background to a constant experimentation with the aesthetic possibilities of the image.

From narrative and emotional excess to visual excess

The work of Oliveira, one of the longest in film history, extends through both of the above mentioned periods, that of preoccupation with narrative illusion and motion before the Second World War and that of an increased interest in the figurative power of the still(ed) image after the war. The cinema of Oliveira, however, has always been more representative of this latter paradigm. This is why some of his critics, unable to place his work in any narrative tradition, chose to call him a vanguard artist.[5] The adherence of Oliveira to the aesthetics of the image can also explain his puzzling approach to melodrama, a pertinent cinematic genre in both the pre-war and post-war era. Intriguingly, his preference for melodrama does not mean his sharing the tradition of classic or modernist melodrama either. In most cases, he adapts nineteenth-century novels, romantic melodramas, without any actuality in the last quarter of the twentieth century and modernist film. The emotional and narrative excess characteristic of the genre (often reflected in long, passionate dialogues) is transformed into visual excess, manifested in an overwhelming use of frames, mirrors and painterly compositions. As I pointed out in the previous chapter, in these films, the impulse–passivity mechanism regulating the narration of melodrama is translated into a movement – stilled movement dynamics and a preference for *tableaux vivants*.

At the beginning of *Doomed Love*, for example, there is a scene of a duel emblematic of both the basic narrative model of the actual film, the melodrama genre in general and Oliveira's concept of film, conceived as dynamics, a 'duel' between image and narration, stillness and movement. This duel is registered with an intense camera travelling to the right and to the left, following the movement and exchange of swords of the duelists. Then, an unexpected turn occurs, one of the duelists takes out a shotgun and shoots the other: suddenly everybody and everything becomes still, as if in a *tableau vivant*. This scene, a

---

[5] Jonathan Rosenbaum, for example, considers Oliveira's *Doomed Love* a vanguard film (1995, 213–17). His first short documentary, *Douro, Faina Fluvial* (*Labor on the Douro River*, 1931) about the labour on the Douro River, following the Soviet vanguard aesthetics of montage, the work of Dziga Vertov in particular, and also Walter Ruttmann's, *Berlin: Symphony of a Great City* (1927), is like an early ars poetica, in this respect. He has never really moved away from experimenting with the aesthetic possibilities of the static image.

30   *The Cinema of Manoel de Oliveira*

family historical prologue to the romantic melodrama to follow, functions as a premonition of the actual story: after a series of reciprocal insults, Simão, the impulsive protagonist, also shoots his rival, Baltasar, and is then incarcerated, turns melancholic, passive and dies. The sequence also relies on the psychological mechanisms underlying the melodrama genre in general (an increasingly tensioned confrontation of the hero with his circumstances, culminating in a dramatic turn, followed by stillness) and is ultimately playing on the surprising effect of the intense movement turned into stasis. Between still and moving images, in an emotional space between familiar and unfamiliar, canny and uncanny, emerge two qualities of film as medium: the visual and the photographic on the one hand, and the narrative ability on the other. The deepest pleasure of cinema may reside in visual attractions rather than in the way the story is narrated. In the so-called 'melodramas' of Oliveira, instead of melodramatic tensions, strong emotions are created in the interstice between media and different forms of representation, in accordance with Gunning's 'astonishment principle' (1990), which involves 'a subtle shock of subverted expectations' and engenders introspection (Remes 2012, 268).

When approaching melodramas from a psychoanalytical point of view, insisting upon a metaphoric relationship between the Freudian death drive principle and the tendency of cinematic narration and movement to turn still or freeze, Laura Mulvey cites Garrett Stewart: 'Into the (metonymic) chain of continuity, continuous motion, of sequence, of plot, breaks the radical equation stasis equals death, the axis of substitution, the advent of metaphor' (Stewart 2006, 25). Just like the original story of Romeo and Juliet, *Doomed Love*, its Portuguese version starts with the statement of a more or less repressed hatred between the two families, released by the violent temper of Simão and culminating in the act of killing, followed by an irreversible sliding of both Simão and Teresa into inertia and, ultimately, death.

Framed bodies

In *Doomed Love*, *Francisca* or *Abraham´s Valley*, the frequent use of *tableaux vivants* is anticipating the final and definitive stillness of death, narration and cinematic movement. In *Doomed Love*, after a dynamic first part dominated by the actions of an impulsive protagonist, both lovers are incarcerated, Simão in a jail, Teresa in a monastery. Starting from that moment they both become increasingly passive, as if paralyzed by their fate. They are literally 'fading away', growing pale and white, turning the film image into its own negative. This effect is reinforced by a 'fading away' of the very materiality of the medium, too: for this film, Oliveira used 16 mm stock, excellent for poetical purposes but not very enduring. By becoming increasingly aware of the *texture* of the image while contours of things and human figures become blurred due to the precarity of image quality, spectators are actually experiencing the materiality of the image, fading just like the bodies it represents.

As typical of the genre, the characters of Oliveira's melodramas are often trapped between social restrictions, rivalry between families, are reduced to stillness due to illness, are jailed, closed up in a convent or in a house. This is how 'framing' and at times multiple framing becomes another metaphor of entrapment: characters are captured, framed, transformed into pictures and *tableaux vivants* meant to symbolize paralyzing social conventions, mostly related to religion or family roles. In *Doomed Love*, the image of bars becomes a recurrent metaphor of the melodramatic situation, the inability and helplessness to step out of it: the lovers are often shown behind bars, and Teresa is even 'framed' as a conventional picture of Virgin Mary or a Catholic saint (Figures 2.1–2.4).

Figures 2.1–2.4 Frames and grids as metaphors of entrapment and stillness in *Doomed Love*.

The central aesthetic figure of the melodramas *Doomed Love, Francisca* and *Abraham's Valley* is the *tableau vivant*, called an 'oxymoron' by Pascal Bonitzer, a sphinx, a composite monster playing 'guessing games' with the spectator-Oedipe.[6] Steven Jacobs elaborates on this specificity of the *tableau vivant* and tableau shot, emphasizing that 'because of their aestheticization of immobility, they create blockages in the flow of a narrative film that result in a kind of enigma' (2011, 95). The *tableau vivant* has the similar double function of a coded image in *Abraham's Valley*, as both an example of the Oliveirian aesthetics of cinematic stillness and a critique of a rigid bourgeois social order. These tableaux show Ema, the protagonist, in suffocating family reunions, at the church or around dinner tables. She is *beautiful as a picture* – and men are looking at her *as at a picture*, when trying to decipher her enigma (whether she is adulterous or just extravagant) in long, ekphrastic monologues describing her as an image (Figures 2.5–2.6).

In a scene of *Abraham's Valley* that shows Ema, her husband and family friends attending a mass in a Catholic church, sitting on the balcony, the camera angle flattens the image and transforms their group into a photographic *tableau vivant*. But, as Brigitte Peucker suggests, an opposite movement also takes place: with the introduction of the real (living people sitting still), the image is animated and tension is created between the real and the representational (Peucker 2007, 42). The *tableau vivant* appears as family photography, while photography itself is, as Roland Barthes in his seminal book, *Camera Lucida*, stated, 'a kind of primitive theatre, a kind of *tableau vivant*, a figuration of the motionless and make-up face beneath which we see the dead' (Barthes 2000, 32). This *tableau*

Figures 2.5–2.6 Ema 'framed' as a picture in *Abraham's Valley*.

---

[6] 'Le tableau vivant, cet oxymoron incarné est un monstre composite, un sphinx, qui pose de devinettes au spectateur-oedipe. Que veulent dire ces tableaux? Pourqui sont-ils là? A quel mistere, á quel culte secret, á quel crime renvoient-ils?' (Bonitzer 1985, 32).

vivant as a nodal point in the film's representational strategies, revolving around the movement–stillness dichotomy, at the same time historically reconnects the film with the bourgeois tragedy of the eighteenth century and the staged melodrama of the nineteenth century (Peucker 2007, 60). This tableau moment features Ema trapped, 'framed' and slowly killed by rigid bourgeois social rules dictated by appearances. The uncanny inversion of the artistic process (moveshent turning into stillness or the other way around), the oscillation between movement and stillness, is used by Oliveira, in line with the formalist ethic of defamiliarization of modernist cinema, as a metaphor for the tension between life and death, constantly present in Ema's self-destructive lifestyle. Furthermore, the increased interest in duration, time and stillness is also reflected in a kind of sculptural presence of characters: Ema's posing moments are prolonged, and often she appears as distant and cold as a statue.

Due to its invocation of earlier sculptural, dramatic, literary and pictorial models, the *tableau vivant* 'can be seen as an evocation of the repressed memory of cinema' (Jacobs 2011, 101). It is also closely related, due to the stillness–movement illusion, and the play with the frames, to the trompe l'oeil effect also reminiscent from the painterly tradition. Frames and mirrors are constant metaphors of the Oliveirian cinema after the 1970s and they are also often interchangeable in a trompe l'oeil: a door or a window frame can be mistaken for a mirror by the spectator or, conversely, a mirror appears as a frame, opening to another space. This can refer metaphorically to the narration (in the ball scenes from *Francisca* to the illusion of wealth and power of aristocracy, or in *Doomed Love* to the assumption that the lovers watching each other through opposite windows *as if in mirrors* are soul mates) or can become a complex self-reflexive figure of Oliveira's approach to cinema. As Vivian Sobchack puts it, the metaphor of the frame:

> 'is emblematic of the *transcendental idealism* that infuses classical formalism and its belief in the film object as *expression-in-itself* – subjectivity freed from worldly constraint while the metaphor of the mirror entails a critical judgment of the cinema that is as damning as it is descriptive. It condemns the very ontological being of cinema as substitutive (rather than expansive) and deceptive (rather than disclosing)'.
>
> 1992, 17[7]

---

[7] Thomas Elsaesser and Malte Haneger in their, *Film Theory: An Introduction through the Senses* (2010), are taking these metaphors as representative for particular chapters of film theory and are using them as central concepts in their original film theory.

The frequent interchangeability of (door and window) frames and mirrors can be interpreted as an allusion to the curious position of Oliveira's cinema between a classic formalist and a self-reflexive, modernist tradition. Mirrors in Oliveira's films are not only figures of 'pure representation' by simply doubling the characters and scenes, but are constantly revealing the illusionary, 'trompe l'oeil' nature of filmic representation. As mentioned above, one of Oliveira's main concerns is to thematize both the stasis and the motion *in the image* as illusion (the film does not stop running) by halting the action and using *tableaux vivants* as 'pregnant moments' of narration. By doing this, he is seeing time and not movement as the essence of cinema, something that is most fundamental in distinguishing it from photography and painting.

Doomed Love, for instance, presents a neat distinction between the Deleuze-ian movement-image characteristic of the first part of the movie, full of actions and dramatic turning points, as well as the time-image settling in with the incarceration of the protagonists, their turning still, meditative and resigning (Deleuze [1982] 1986, [1985] 1989). Long shots of their frontal images are taking over the scenes of action, while they are reciting the contents of their exchanged letters. As Francis Ramasse points out, in the second part of the film, participation gives place to contemplation, emotion to intelligence and what has been proper melodramatic pleasure becomes intellectual and often 'cinéphilique' pleasure (1979, 66). Posing has a similar time effect in *Abraham's Valley*: for Ema, a party scene or a social event often functions as a catwalk: she walks in, not looking at anybody while everybody is watching her, then she stops, posing in front of a voyeuristic 'obsessive' spectatorial gaze. As Simone de Beauvoir puts it:

> Male beauty is an indicator of transcendence, that of woman has the passivity of immanence: only the latter is made to arrest the gaze and can therefore be caught in the immobile trap of the reflective surface, the man who feels and wants himself activity, subjectivity, does not recognize himself in his fixed image.
>
> 1975, 527–8

In film, a pose is both revealing something of the nature of photography and functions as a *pause*, a sudden emergence of time in a flow of events and actions. In *Abraham's Valley*, posing woman and still image become syononyms with passivity: men (husbands and lovers) are away 'with business', only the placid, feminine image remains 'in the frame', as a prey of the spectatorial gaze. There is no way out, no possibility of change or action for Ema: her sports car, just like her feet and legs, are not vehicles of action, but fetishistic objects, making her appearance more attractive for male collectors.

Feet and legs: Fetishistic image vs narration

As John Berger argues in his *Ways of Looking*, 'A man's presence suggests what he is capable of doing to you or for you,' while, by contrast, 'a woman's presence is manifest in her gestures, voice, opinions, expressions, clothes, chosen surroundings, taste – indeed, there is nothing she can do which does not contribute to her presence.' Or, to put it briefly, 'Men act and women appear. Men look at women. Women watch themselves being looked at [...] the surveyor of woman in herself is male: the surveyed female' (1972, 46–7). Berger's statement, so often quoted by the feminist criticism of visual culture finds, in fact, a paradigmatic representation in film history: in the classic melodrama genre, for example, the action and motion set off by men is often delayed, stopped or derailed by a mesmerizing female appearance, a femme fatale or a vamp.

As already discussed in the previous chapters, in *Abraham's Valley* Oliveira celebrates cinematic stillness through an innovative thematization of fashion. Just like in many other films by Oliveira, the highly artificial quality of the image is meant to counterbalance the 'motoric' imperfections of movement and narration, just as Ema's glamorous appearance is meant to hide her physical defect: she has a limp. While this is part of the magic, the fashionable 'asymmetrical body' making her *appearance* even more disturbing,[8] at times when we see her walking, it appears as a noisy intrusion into the still image. Similarly, narration, the intervention of a voice-over narrator or movement often seems to be disturbing the quiescence of the image. As an alternative, Oliveira is modelling a silent, invisible observer in this film, when one of the female characters, walking bare feet along soft carpets, is making a full circle around the scene that we are watching, without the others noticing her.

In *Abraham's Valley*, the rather fetishistic significance of feet and legs is evocative of some films by Luís Buñuel (*Tristana*, 1970, most evidently) and by one of his disciples, Pedro Almodóvar (his *Live Flesh*, 1997, for example). Although the cinema of Oliveira can be compared to that of the two directors in

---

[8] On the relationship between the asymmetrical body and fashion, see Harvey (2007, 65–94).

terms of a subversive attitude towards the Catholic Church and middle-class morality, as well as body fetishism, the social critique in his films has always been subdued by highly aesthetical considerations regarding the image, movement and narration. Instead of overtly critical representation of social and religious taboos, Oliveira merely uses a vaguely comic or ironic effect, achievable by juxtaposition or comparison of images, as in the case of a contrastive fetishistic and non-fetishistic presentation of feet and legs in *Abraham's Valley*: the naked legs of Ema and of Carlos's first wife as opposed to the feet and legs of Ema's religious aunt, all covered in black trousers and shoes (see Figures 2.7–2.10).

As many times during his career, in the case of this film, Oliveira used the intermediation of a homonymous novel by Portuguese writer, Agustina Bessa-Luís, a Portuguese version of *Madame Bovary*, with an interesting switch: here is not Hippolyte, the stableboy who has a limp, but Ema, the central character. In a scene where Ema approaches the bedroom of her husband with a candle through a long dark corridor (a widely used metaphor of sensual connotations in film history), because of the limp, her face lit by the candlelight appears as if pulsing with desire. In the last scene of the film, in a representation of the death drive as a desire to regress to stillness, we see Ema dressed as her younger self and her limp becomes a euphoric 'floating' through orange trees. On the small pier, she steps on a broken board, falls into the water and ultimately drowns. The death drive associated with the compulsion to repeat – in this case, a moment of youth –

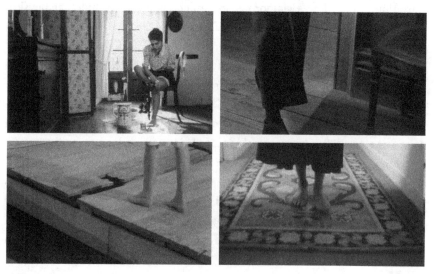

Figures 2.7–2.10 Leg and foot fetishism in *Abraham's Valley*.

leads to stillness that appears as a consequence of a mistaken step (a possible allusion to the adulterous past of Ema), *a bad move*.[9] The film closes with the image of still water marking a point of narrative halt, but also a point 'beyond narratability' that also suggests 'a return of the repressed stillness in which cinema's illusion of movement depends' (Mulvey 2006a, 78–9).

The metaphor of the death drive appears in Oliveira's melodramas as a displacement, 'illuminating another context through refiguration, highlighting certain relations of structural or functional resemblance': a double metaphor or *metalepsis*, defined by Sobchack as a trope of a trope, a scheme referring back to other figurative schemes (2004, 205). In *Doomed Love*, as well as in *Abraham's Valley*, the emotional excess of melodramas is translated into a visual excess of frames and mirrors: the characters are not only trapped by social conventions, regulations, illness or a motoric defect, but their bodies are framed and captured as pictures, as sensual objects exposed to the gaze of a possessive (and pensive) spectator. Images and bodies are interchangeable: the 'decomposing' images of *Doomed Love* are standing for the fading bodies of the unhappy, dying protagonists. In *Abraham's Valley*, the image of Ema's transformation and her transformation of her own image are reversible phenomena. Cinema is not only showing make-up, but *it is the make-up*, 'able to "fix" (in the doubled sense of repair and stasis), to fetishize and to reproduce faces and time as both "unreel" before us' (Sobchack 2004, 50). Accordingly, the limp, both a defect of the body and of narration techniques and moving image, is not only responsible for the anti-diegetic effect, but transforms *Abraham's Valley* into an expression of experience by experience.

---

[9] Donaldson-Evans also refers to an essay by Florence Emptaz about the importance of the role played by feet and footwear in the novel. Emptaz sees in Hippolyte an emblem for Emma's moral claudication, his 'disequilibrium an image of the adulteress's *vertu chancelante*' (Emptaz 2000, 23–81).

3

The trope of the doll

In the cinema of Oliveira, the carefully framed image of a beautiful woman is anchored in the aesthetics of modernity, that, as formulated by Baudelaire in his *The Painter of Modern Life* ([1863] 1964), conceives the artistic creation as an adventure of the gaze turning everything into spectacle, just as fashion and make-up transforms women into dolls and mannequins, passive objects of the (male) gaze. Stillness, doll-ness, 'to-be-looked-at-ness' or 'image-ness' of the female character, a heritage of the impressionist painting (especially Manet, whose paintings are also referred to in his films) is central to Oliveira's aesthetics of the frame, manifesting, as we have seen, in a preference for window- and door-frames, as well as mirrors. The doll (both as toy or as a still, distant woman) is a recurrent fetishistic object that can be considered one of the major, complex clues to the Oliveirian work. While in *A Talking Picture* the toy-doll is a figure of a cultural-political allegory, in other films it appears as the 'inexhaustible object of our desire and our fantasies' (Agamben 1993b, 58). Furthermore, the toy/doll can also represent the frustration of artistic creation: for Baudelaire, for example, 'the toy is the emblem of the relationship – of impenetrable *joy* mixed with stupefied frustration – that *is* the basis of artistic *creation* as of every relation between human and objects' (cf. Agamben 1993b, 57, italics in the original).

A Talking Picture, considered by many critics to be a response to the 9/11 terrorist attacks, is a road movie that follows a historian mother and her daughter on their journey from West to East, from Europe towards India, on boat, with stops at touristic sites emblematic of the encounter with the Muslim world. While Oliveira plays with the possibility of a globalized West where everyone understands each other despite speaking different languages (the guests on the board of the boat do so), his visionary premonition is pessimistic, even ruthless: shortly after the cosmopolitan American captain (played by John Malkovich) gives the little girl a doll dressed in oriental costume, bombs are detected on board and the ship explodes before the girl and her mother (who return to fetch

40   *The Cinema of Manoel de Oliveira*

the doll from the cabin) could escape. The film closes with a freeze-frame of Malkovich's face, lit by the blast and revealing the horror of the Medusa effect: an image turning still, as if petrified. The figurative role of the doll in this film has been neglected so far by critics (some refer to it as a 'gift'); it is, in fact, an object, a product that emblematically and historically concentrates the economic and political aspects of the West–Middle East relationships. According to Giorgio Agamben, the temporality of history is more present in a toy than in historical and archaeological monuments, to which Oliveira's road movie seems to be dedicated:

> For in the toy, as in no other site, can we grasp the temporality of history in its pure differential and qualitative value. Not in a monument, an object of archaeological and scholarly research, which preserves in time its practical, documentary character (its 'material content,' Benjamin would have said); not in an antique, whose value is a function of its quantitative ageing; not in an archive document, which draws its value from its place in a chronology and a relationship of proximity and legality with the past event. The toy represents something more and something different from all these things. [...] What the toy preserves of its sacred or economic model, what survives of this after its dismemberment or miniaturization, is nothing other than the human temporality that was contained therein: its pure historical essence. The toy is a materialization of the historicity contained in objects, extracting it by means of a particular manipulation.
>
> Agamben 1993a, 71

The doll dressed in oriental female costume, wearing a long dress and a veil, bought by the American captain in a bazaar, represents the historical, economic and civilizational exchange between the West and the Middle East, but it also participates in the pessimistic, visionary allegory of these relationships in the twenty-first century. The trip to Bombay, which throughout the film seemed to signify the hope of a cultural continuity and reconciliation, in the last scene turns into a nightmare. The death of the girl and her mother on a ship connecting the two civilizations translates as a gloomy vision of the future of the Portuguese nation in particular, and Europe in general, endangered by a crisis also involving the USA. The toy, or more specifically, the doll, besides its role of 'container' of meanings related to historicity and temporality, especially 'the temporal dimension of a "once upon a time" and a "no more"', as Agamben points out (1993a, 72), in most films of Oliveira acquires existential, psychological content through its abstraction into the aesthetic principle of *dollness*. In *A Talking Picture*, Catherine Deneuve, Irene Papas and Stefania Sandrelli, in the roles of the American captain's guests, bring along their international star *image*, a sort of *dollness*. I argue that a study of figurative occurences of dolls and of 'dollness' throughout the work of Oliveira – from *Aniki Bobó* (1942) to *The Strange Case of Angelica* (2010) – can be helpful in tracking the line of transformations of an emblematic object into a central figure involving a range of psychoanalytical concepts, such as the uncanny, the fetish or the transitional object.

Aniki Bobó and the doll in the window

Considered by many critics to be a proto-neorealist movie, the first feature film of Oliveira, *Aniki Bobó* tells a story spanning over a few days of working-class children based in Porto, the home city of Oliveira. It is a tale played by non-professional child actors and reveals serious dramas that occur on the verge between play and reality, childhood and adulthood, life and death. The daily play of children takes place by the River Douro, between the river and the esplanade, a street with shops looking at the river, an in-between space representing childhood as a transition between nature (represented by the enormous river) and culture/civilization, created and inhabited by adults. This transitional condition, the coming-of-age process, is emphasized by the children's rhyme that the film's title derives from and which is chanted repeatedly by the protagonists: from the rhythm which evokes archaic rites, incoherent words emerge denoting, in turn, animals, musical instruments and biblical figures. The distance between adults and children is apparent from the very first scene of the film: the protagonist is playing with a bibelot (a miniature, a version of the toy) while his mother is preparing him for school, the bibelot breaks and he is slapped instantly by the mother. But this scene is only a premonition of the central topic that also involves conflicts with adults: a doll in a display window triggers a series of anecdotal scenes, being stolen and delivered to the girl the child protagonist is desperately in love with.

The image of the doll in the window is central for other reasons, too: it structures the narrative (on the one hand it halts the action, the intense play of children, who always stop to admire it, on the other hand it marks the turning points in the story) and it becomes an alternative to it, prefiguring the contemplative, visually charged, slow cinema of Oliveira. João Lopes was the first to point out the importance of the scene with the doll in the window in this film, reflecting on the uncanny effect triggered by an unidentified point of view

Figures 3.1–3.2 The doll in the window and the unidentifiable gaze in *Aniki Bobó*.

from behind the doll (Lopes 1981). Indeed, the gaze of the children is paired with a counter-shot coming from nowhere (Figures 3.1–3.2).

Two possible interpretations emerge, without mutually excluding each other: this is a projection of the children's belief in the magic of the toy that, just like in Playland from Pinocchio, can come to life. At the same time, it is a self-reflexive moment, where a disembodied gaze reveals the spectator by staring back.

In *Aniki Bobó*, the trope of the doll in the window is a figuration of the narrative (an emblem of childhood, innocence and magic), but, as we have seen, it also belongs to the domain of the figural, of the artistic discourse independent of a specific narrative and providing a clue to the entire work, as described by D. N. Rodowick in his *Reading the Figural* (2001). There are a few other pieces in the filmography of Oliveira where the doll as object has a figurative and figural role. Besides *A Talking Picture*, where it is both an emblem of the relationships between West and East and a site of historical time, in *The Letter* (*A Carta*, 1999, an adaptation of the French novel by Madame de La Fayette, *The Princesse de Clèves*, 1678) it appears as a metaphor of the heroine (passive and helpless, stuck in the position of a child who promised her mother not to marry the man she loves; Figures 3.3–3.4).

The Letter also evokes the doll-in-the-window effect, the discourse on the (female) image as object of (male) spectatorial desire (the admirer of the princess is repeatedly standing in front of her house, staring at her window). Most intriguingly, this admirer, the Portuguese pop star, Pedro Abrunhosa, playing himself, never removes his dark sunglasses, which makes his gaze unlocalizable. His enigmatic (and exaggerated) star image reveals him, too, as an object of the female (and spectatorial) desire, an icon.

Figures 3.3–3.4 The trope of the doll in *A Talking Picture* and *The Letter*.

The trope of the doll in the window launched in *Aniki Bobó* can be regarded as a signature of Oliveira's visual aesthetics, sublimated in the very recurrent image of the (inexpressive, passive) woman in the window, exposed to a gaze that doubles that of the spectator. In most cases, the woman in the window remains a distant image, the object of a distant longing of the male protagonist. This is also true for the tetralogy of frustrated loves, in which the courtly, purely platonic love for a (dead, rejected, idealized or mystified) person turns characters into carefully framed images, composed as paintings and often reflected in mirrors. The discourse on 'the woman as doll' and 'woman as work of art' overlaps in painterly compositions.

The magic, the desire, the uncanny, the frustration and rejection they cause also make the toy/doll and the work of art comparable, as in Rainer Marie Rilke's words, quoted by Agamben:

> it [the doll] makes us almost indignant at its tremendous and crass forgetfulness; that hatred that, unconscious, has always constituted a part of our relation to it breaks forth, the doll lies before us unmasked like the horrible strange body on which we have dissipated our purest warmth; like the drowned corpse painted on the surface that allowed itself to be lifted up and borne along by the floods of our tenderness, until we would dry up again, abandoning it in some hedge.
>
> Agamben 1993b, 57

Animism, fetishism and belief in the magic of children in *Aniki Bobó* becomes a recurrent topic in Oliveira's films as an infantile wish or belief in the living doll. As Mathias Lavin has already pointed out (2014, 130), both the *Eccentricities of a Blonde-Haired Girl* (2009) and *The Strange Case of Angelica* display the scene from Hoffmann's *The Sandman*, where the young man falls in love with a beautiful automaton. This short story is analysed by Freud as an example of the uncanny experience, consisting of 'doubts whether an apparently animate being is really alive; or conversely, whether a lifeless object might not be in fact animate' (Freud [1919] 2003, 5), as is the case of the impression made by waxwork figures, artificial dolls and automatons. But even beyond that, this trope is a figure of the uncanny effect of still images (paintings and photographs) animated by cinematic movement and of the opposite, of moving images turning still, transforming into *tableaux vivants* and visual objects.

The beautiful automaton

As Agamben has shown, the doll is, on the one hand, 'infinitely lesser than an object, because it is distant and beyond our grasp', but 'it is on the other hand infinitely more, because it is the inexhaustible object of our desire and our fantasies' as 'in it [the doll] we would mix, as in a test tube, whatever unknowable things happened to us, which we would see boil up and turn colors there' (1993b, 58). In Oliveira's cinema, the recurrent voyeuristic scene, in which a man is contemplating a woman in the window (as already remarked by other critics, Cruchinho, 2010, or Lavin, 2014, for example), also recalls children's fetishistic attraction to dolls. But beyond the fetishistic content of the male gaze that transforms the female body into 'an unattainable object that satisfies a human need precisely through its being unattainable' (Agamben 1993b, 33), the doll and dollness become central in the Oliveirian discourse on cinematic ontology, film and modernity, movement and stillness and the cinematic image as ultimate fetish.

Playing an organic part of his life (itself characterized by the duality of inactivity and hyper-creativity, an active sportsman's or artist's life and a contemplative lifestyle in his vineyard, followed by his spectacular return to filmmaking), the cinema of Oliveira is constantly revealing a fascination for both technical innovation and aesthetic tradition, the machine and the statue or painting, respectively. This duality is plastically represented in his *The Cannibals* (*Os Canibais*, 1988), a sinister opera-film displaying the uncanny effect generated by the tropes of the living dead and the automaton: the mysterious and seductive count, whom the female protagonist falls in love with, turns out to be half-human, half-machine, with prosthetic limbs annexed to his body. When he removes these limbs, his body is turned into a torso, a reminder of antic statues: it reveals stillness, movement and technology in the same human body, becoming a complex figure of the myth of modernity. (Figures 3.5–3.6).

Figures 3.5–3.6 The torso and artificial limbs as tropes of the stillness–movement dichotomy in *The Cannibals*.

The same two-facedness of modernity is concentrated in the trope of the doll, or the woman who acts, moves like an automaton. Echoing Degas's painting, *Portrait of Michel-Levy in His Studio* (1879), in which the doll, the artistic prop, is responsible for the uncanny effect (at first, we think it is a woman, the artist's model, just to realize, from the clumsy pose, that it is an object), this motif has become in Oliveira's cinema a figuration of woman as a spectacle. Starting from *Aniki Bobó*, this immobile object of contemplation keeps coming back in a series of films, where the woman is framed as the still object of contemplation: *Doomed Love*, *Francisca*, *The Letter*, *Eccentricities of a Blonde-Haired Girl* or *The Strange Case of Angelica*. The prototype of the silent, numb female body in the window exposed to the male gaze can be found in *Doomed Love*, where the lovers, Teresa and Simão, see each other through the opposite windows of their paternal houses. They will meet only once, in a dark garden, which makes their relationship seem fantasmatic, while its melodramatic circumstances transform Teresa into a passive marionette of destiny.

The same applies to Francisca, who consents to run away with her admirer, is taken to his house and kept there as a beautiful captive, regressing slowly into silence and stillness, to a state of living dead – as suggested by the compositions and light effects that show her as a lifeless doll. This trope is also emphasized by her monotonous way of speaking, symptomatic of her melancholy. In a similar vein, the female protagonist of *The Letter* is like a puppet devoid of own will, all her decisions being animated by the wish of her dead mother not to marry the man she loves. Thus, she becomes a beautiful automaton in the window, admired from a distance, as a puzzling, enigmatic phenomenon, just like the girl from *The Eccentricities of a Blonde-Haired Girl*. This latter film is visually dominated by idealizing frames, portraits of the worshipped, mostly silent woman (observed from the opposite window), and ends abruptly after showing the image of the young woman falling

Figures 3.7–3.8 Variations on 'dollness' in *Eccentricities of a Blonde-Haired Girl*.

apart like a marionette (as Mathias Lavin also points out, 2014, 130) when her husband realizes that she is a kleptomaniac. By letting spectators fall into the abyss of the closing black screen and their unfulfilled expectations – nourished by memories of Hitchcock's *Marnie* (1964) or Bresson's *A Gentle Woman* (*Une Femme douce*, 1969) – Oliveira's artistic choice is that of a detached contemplation that is never disturbed by the obsession of solving the mystery of the woman. The film of Oliveira ends where that of Hitchcock and Bresson begins. The male gaze, transforming the woman into a doll, worships her only as long as she is perfect and idealized: at the first sign of eccentricity and vulnerability, she ends up rejected, like a doll abandoned by children (Figures 3.7–3.8).

The same reference to the infantile aspects of fetishism prevails in *Abraham's Valley*, completed with the magic and the uncanny associated with the image of the female figure in the window. In this adaptation of Agustina Bessa-Luís's homonymous novel, Ema, the main character is a disturbing presence: whenever she appears in the window, car accidents happen in front of their house. Her beauty has a sinister element, linked by Lord Byron with 'the doomed and the damned' (cf. Wilson 2007, 96, 302). But, most intriguingly, she has a limp, which makes her movement uncannily mechanic, automaton-like. Ema's oscillation between the traditional role of housewife staying at home and that of the independent, modern woman crossing her boundaries is doubled by still images, *tableaux vivants* getting on movement, and freeze-action images. This 'imageness' and 'dollness' make her comparable to fashion models, whose facial inexpressivity is due, according to Agamben, to 'the awareness of being exposed to the gaze'. As he argues,

> it is this brazen-faced indifference that fashion models, porn stars, and others whose profession it is to show must learn to acquire: they show nothing but the showing itself (that is, one's own absolute mediality). In this way, the face is

loaded until it bursts with exhibition-value. Yet, precisely through this nullification of expressivity, eroticism penetrates where it could have no place: the human face, which does not know nudity, for it is always already bare. Shown as a pure themselves means beyond any concrete expressivity, it becomes available for a new use, a new form of erotic communication.

2007, 90

The uncanny effect of the expressionless doll-face is often emphasized by its gaze that looks back at the spectator, transforming the motionless body in the image into a disquieting presence. As Manet's *Olympia* (1863) testifies, this is, beyond the presentation of the female body as an object of the male gaze, a self-reflexive thematization of the cinematic representation of the motionless female body. This trope finds a complex autobiographical, media-theoretical and artistic-cultural representation in *The Strange Case of Angelica*, a film rich, as the title suggests, in uncanny effects that transform the beautiful automaton into a transitional object between life and death.

The doll as transitional object

Dramatic circumstances like the death of a young female cousin of one of his grandsons and his advanced age have continuously nurtured Oliveira's preoccupation with death, represented and sublimated over and over in his films about strange cases of deadly, obsessive and pathological passions. Morbidity is a constant poetical source for Oliveira and the death/dying scene in his films often becomes a paradoxical figuration of life, in accordance with Foucault's observation: 'the morbid authorizes a subtle perception of the way in which life finds in death its most differentiated figure. The morbid is the rarefied form of life, exhausted, working itself into the void of death.' Foucault also defines death as 'the lyrical core of man: his invisible truth, his visible secret' (2003, 245).

One of the recurrent scenes of Oliveira's films – *Doomed Love, Benilde or the Virgin Mother, Francisca, Magic Mirror* (*Espelho Mágico*, 2005) and *The Strange Case of Angelica*, to name but a few – that of the death of a young woman, strikes as both painterly due to its composition and photographic in capturing the moment and framing the perfect stillness of doll-like bodies (Figure 3.9).

These two qualities are reconciled in the intermedial figure of the *tableau vivant*. *The Strange Case of Angelica* is further illuminating the inherent

Figures 3.9 An aesthetics of death in *Francisca*.

intermediality of the cinematic image, indebted both to the painterly and the photographic tradition. The film is overtly self-reflexive and metaleptic, bearing numerous autobiographical details, not to mention that Oliveira casts his grandson, Ricardo Trêpa, in the role of the main protagonist. The young Jewish photographer played by him is hired to take photos of a dead young woman, Angelica, a mission that turns to be fatal for him. In the scene of the photo session, we are witnessing a reframing of the image of the beautiful dead girl (who seems alive and even smiling in her death) that results in an intermedial flickering between film, painting and photograph. The film is making the frames, boundaries and crossings visible, thus becoming a whole concentrated history of cinematic intermediality, from painterly composition through photographic freeze-frame to the movement dissolving the stillness. This oscillation presents cinema again as a medium indebted both to modernity and to cinematic modernism that pushed the experimentation with defamiliarizing aesthetic possibilities of the stillness–movement duality to the extreme. In *Angelica*, the painterly composition of the motionless body of the dead girl, reminding one of Pierre-Auguste Renoir's painting of Madame Monet (1872),[1] is being reframed by the camera of the photographer, then blurred, in a reference to the impressionist painting (Figures 3.10–3.11).

But the strange case of Angelica starts when, through the lens of the camera, the girl comes back to life (smiles at the stupefied photographer), in a kind of replay of the fairy tale of Sleeping Beauty. Thus, beyond this short genealogy of intermedial relationships – including sociocultural background, such as the practice of taking photos of dead people, or the framing of the moment, of the atmosphere in impressionist paintings – we are witnessing here a figuration of

---

[1] This reference might not be a coincidence as the painting is in the collection of the Gulbenkian Museum in Lisbon, and Oliveira was most probably familiar with it.

Figures 3.10–3.11 The painterly image of the dead woman in *The Strange Case of Angelica* (2010), echoing Renoir's *Madame Monet Reading* (1872).

the cinematic technology, presented as a miracle that makes the still image move. Following this scene, the photographer becomes obsessed with this girl who is visiting him every night and takes him to fly, in a setting reminiscent of the films by Georges Méliès (using the technique of superimposition), until one morning he is found dead in the boarding house where he lives. This story, that can well be interpreted as an allegory of the fatal attraction between life and death, as well as film and photography, ends by showing the photographic image as the ultimate common denominator of the two technologies. According to Raymond Bellour (2002a), stillness in cinema traditionally serves to represent the non-representable, like birth, death, or miracles of Christianity such as resurrection, immaculate conception and apparitions, topics systematically exploited by Oliveira since the beginning of the 1970s.

Blurring the borders of media and those between movement and stillness, life and death refers to the ontology of photography, and by opposing the stillness *in* the image to the stillness *of* the image, reveals cinematic stillness as a *trompe l'oeil*. In the films of Oliveira, the scenes of dying are represented in very long shots, meant to grab the (almost invisible) moment of passage from movement to stillness, from the cinematic to the photographic.

The same intention to reveal the discreet line between painting, photograph and film can be found in *Benilde or the Virgin Mother*, largely dealing with the representability of the miracle of immaculate conception. Benilde, a young girl, claims she is bearing God's child, which stirs vehement reactions from her household and friends, formulated, in turns, in religious, scientific and laic discourses. During her 'persecution', the photograph of her mother, framed as a painting and repeatedly intercut with the ongoing scene, 'comes to life' in three steps: first her expression changes, then slightly turns towards us and, finally, we

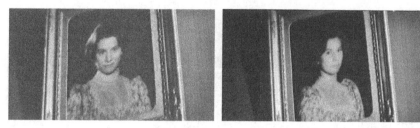

Figures 3.12–3.13 The uncanny effect of the 'living photograph' in *Benilde or the Virgin Mother* (1975).

are witnessing the scene through her point of view, in another example of the uncanny (Figures 3.12–3.13).

What we have here, again, is a concentrated genealogy and a revelation of the technical mechanisms of cinema, of movement achieved as a succession of individual images. This is skilfully modelled in the memorable scene of Angelica when the series of photos of Angelica drying on a rope in Isac's room are animated: a series of stills produce the illusion of movement. In the case of the example from Benilde, an exaggerated slowing down and repeated reframing turns the scene into a real cinephile delicacy. As Belén Vidal argues, the emphasis on framing as artifice and 'instances of temporal and spatial manipulation' such as fixed framings, long takes, slow motion, zooms or superimpositions 'strain the narrative as a whole, drawing our attention to the visual textures of the film. This "overwriting" of the shot throws into relief tensions between discursive and figural dimensions of film' (Vidal 2012, 111). For Oliveira, the magic of cinema lies in its photographic origin: not so much in its ability to make images move, but rather in creating the illusion of stillness. This is a possible interpretation of the inscription 'Foto-génia' on a shop close to Isac's place, giving, as Mathias Lavin argues, a historical approach to the medium specificity of film. By referring to the term 'photogénie' as used by Louis Delluc, Jean Epstein and Jacques Aumont, this inscription emphasizes the attraction provided by the plasticity of plans and their temporality (Lavin 2013, 28).

Oliveira, through the trope of the doll(ness) and automaton not only thematizes intermedial transitions as figurations of movement and stillness, but, as already hinted at earlier, conceives of film itself as a 'transitional object' between the familiar (or the visible and speakable) and the unfamiliar (invisible and unspeakable). The psychoanalytical concept of transitional object was initially used in the description of a developmental stage of infants that has been later extended to the cultural experience of adults. According to its original definition, for a baby, a transitional object such as a blanket, a pacifier, a cuddly toy, serves to relate between the outer and the inner reality, facilitating the child's acceptance of the new. In Donald Winnicott's view, 'no human being is free from the strain of relating outer and inner reality', and transitional objects and transitional phenomena help us negotiate that relationship (quoted by Kuhn 2005, 401). Agamben links the concept of fetish with that of the transitional object that does not belong to the internal and subjective nor to the external, but to 'the area of illusion, the location of culture and play', a 'third area' (1993b, 59). Annette Kuhn, in her 'Thresholds: Film as Film and the Aesthetic Experience' (2005), considers transitional processes in adult life in terms of an aesthetic moment (a term borrowed from Bernard Berenson via Marion Milner), defined as an occasion when time becomes space (that is, concretizes in an object) for the subject. We are stopped, held in reverie, to be released eventually back into time proper (Kuhn 2005, 401).

In the aesthetic moment, the subject then becomes part of that reality, and that reality becomes part of the subject, which reminds us of the phenomenological description of the film experience by Merleau-Ponty saying: 'well, the movies are particularly suited to make manifest the union of mind and body, mind and world, and the expression of one in the other' (quoted in Kuhn 2005, 405). In her essay, Kuhn takes this idea even further arguing that this experience is due to a particular configuration of space within and outside the edges of the film image, the film frame:

> through its organization within the frame of space, time, stillness and motion, film is capable, I would suggest, of replaying or re-evoking certain states of being which are commonly experienced as inner. This, I would argue, is the site of the activity of transitional processes.
>
> Kuhn 2005, 403

This observation is very close to Laura Mulvey's approach to cinematic stillness and film frame modelling 'the longstanding reluctance of the human mind to confront death' (Mulvey 2006, 43). I argue that what makes Oliveira's case special, beyond the aesthetic moment achieved through constant reframing that reconciles images of life with those of stillness and death, is his obstinate clinging to cinema as a unique language – a transitional object – capable of translating the experience of the passage between life and death. Films become the fetishistic object suitable to make this transition smooth, just as the animated image of the dead woman is helping the photographer's passage to death in *The Strange Case of Angelica*. The obsession with the beautiful automaton and photography overlap, just like the obsession with the dead woman and death itself. In this film, containing many autobiographical elements and implying, as Lavin argues, an anachronistic time travel (backwards, 'contretemps' or 'against time') by evoking a more than sixty-year-old family tragedy and reworking a similarly old film script (Lavin 2013, 25), the oxymoron of the Jewish photographer (the Jewish religion, at its origins, prohibited all images, painted or sculpted) serves as a figure for the representation of death as non-representable. At the age of 102, when this film was made, Oliveira chose to delve into the mystery of death through a close study of the photographic image of a dead woman. The strange case of Oliveira consists of an exaggerated cinephilia, an obsession with the aesthetic moment that, according to Kuhn, 'is characterised by a feeling of being, or becoming, at one with a work of art; and this entails a sensation of crossing over a boundary and entering into another kind of reality – and then returning "home," renewed' (2005, 404).

It might not be exaggerated to state that Oliveira is performing the experience of crossing over with the euphoria of the artist directly involved with the moving image. This game with the frames and intermedial possibilities of the medium somehow evokes the experiments of the avant-garde artists of initial times. Because he is not only an eccentric, a cinephile par excellence, but also a *ciné-fils*, to use Serge Daney's playful term, the son of cinema. His stories might appear clumsy, outmoded, uncanny or too simple, but they always serve as background for an experimentation with the still, painterly or photographic image. As Ágnes Pethő puts it: 'still image appears to be "folded" over movement, while the spectator is invited not to a narrative decoding but to a kind of post-cinematic contemplation over individual frames and scenes' (2011, 6). These frames, marking intermedial boundaries, are only partly figurations of the story: Oliveira manages to isolate the still image (of a woman represented as a doll, mannequin or automaton) as a figure of the life and death dynamics, sublimating death anxiety.

References

Agamben, Giorgio 1993a. *History and Infancy*. London, New York: Verso.
Agamben, Giorgio 1993b. *Stanzas: Word and Phantasm in Western Culture*.
   Minneapolis, MN: University of Minnesota Press.

Agamben, Giorgio. 1999. *The Man without Content*. Stanford, CA: Stanford University Press.

Agamben, Giorgio. 2007. *Profanations*. New York: Zone Books.

Baptista, Abel Barros. 2009. '*O Erro de Simão*'. In *Amor de Perdição. Uma Revisão* [The Mistake of Simão. In Doomed Love: A Revision], ed. Abel Barros Baptista, 81–112. Coimbra: Angelus Novus.

Barthes, Roland. 1985. 'The Third Meaning: Research Notes on Several Eisenstein Stills'. In *The Responsibility of Forms: Critical Essays on Music, Art, and Representation*, 41–62. Berkeley, CA: University of California Press.

Barthes, Roland. 2000. *Camera Lucida: Reflections on Photography*. London: Vintage Books.

Baudelaire, Charles. [1863] 1964. The Painter of Modern Life. In *Baudelaire: The Painter of Modern Life and Other Essays*, 1–41. London: Phaidon Press.

Bazin, André. 2005. 'The Ontology of the Photographic Image'. In *What is Cinema?* Vol. 1, 9–16. Berkeley, CA: University of California Press.

Bellour, Raymond. 2002a. '*Le Spectateur pensif*'. In *L'Entre-Images: Photo. Cinéma. Vidéo. Les Essais* [Between-the-Images: Photo. Cinema. Video. The Essays], 75–80. Paris: Éditions de la Différence.

Bellour, Raymond. 2002b. '*L'Interruption, l'instant*'. In *L'Entre-Images: Photo. Cinéma. Vidéo. Les Essais* [Between-the-Images: Photo. Cinema. Video. The Essays], 109–34. Paris: Éditions de la Différence.

Berger, John. 1972. *Ways of Seeing*. Gloucester: Peter Smith Publisher.

Bernheimer, Charles. 1997. *Figures of Ill Repute: Representing Prostitution in Nineteenth-Century France*. Durham, NC: Duke University Press.

Bonitzer, Pascal. 1985. *Décadrages – Peinture et Cinéma*. Paris: Cahiers de Cinéma, Éditions de l'Étoile.

Bordwell, David. 2013. 'Looking at the Fourth Wall'. Available at: http://www.davidbordwell.net/blog/category/directors-oliveira/ (accessed 28 August 2018).

Bukatman, Scott. 2006. 'Spectacle, Attractions and Visual Pleasure'. In *The Cinema of Attractions Reloaded*, ed. Wanda Strauven, 71–82. Amsterdam: Amsterdam University Press.

Campany, David (ed.). 2007. *The Cinematic*. Cambridge, MA: MIT Press.

Carroll, Noël. 2006. Defining the Moving Image. In *Philosophy of Film and Motion Pictures: An Anthology*, eds Noël Carroll and Jinhee Choi, 113–34. Malden, MA: Blackwell.

Cavell, Stanley. 1979. 'Baudelaire and the Myths of Film'. In *Reflections on the Ontology of Film*, 41–60. Cambridge, MA, and London: Harvard University Press.

Costa, João Bénard. 1981. '*Diálogo com Manoel de Oliveira*'. In *Manoel de Oliveira*, 31–46. Lisboa: Cinemateca Portuguesa.

Costa Andrade, Sérgio. 2008. *Ao correr do tempo. Duas decadas com Manoel de Oliveira* [Over Time: Two Decades with Manoel de Oliveira]. Lisboa: Portugália Editora.

54   *The Cinema of Manoel de Oliveira*

Cruchinho, F. 2010. '*A Mulher na Montra e o Homem olhando para ela*' ['The Woman in the Display Window and the Man Looking at Her']. In *Manoel de Oliveira: Uma Presença* [*Manoel de Oliveira: A Presence*], ed. Renata Junqueira, 87–96. São Paolo: Perspectiva.

Daney, Serge. 2001. '*Notes sur les films de Manoel de Oliveira*'. In *La Maison Cinéma et le monde I: Le Temps des Cahiers* [*The Cinema House and the World I: The Time of the Cahiers*], 225–7. Paris: P.O.L.

de Baecque, Antoine and Jacques Parsi. 1999. *Conversas com Manoel de Oliveira* [*Conversations with Manoel de Oliveira*]. Porto: Campos das Letras.

de Beauvoir, Simone. 1975. *The Second Sex*. Harmondsworth: Penguin Books.

Décadrages – Peinture et Cinéma. Paris: Cahiers de Cinéma, Éditions de l'Étoile.

Deleuze, Gilles. [1982] 1986. *Cinema 1: The Mouvement-Image*. Trans. Hugh Tomlimson and Barbara Habberjam. Minneapolis, MN: University of Minnesota Press.

Deleuze, Gilles. [1985] 1989. *Cinema 2: The Time-Image*. Trans. Hugh Tomlinson and Robert Galeta. Minneapolis, MN: University of Minnesota Press.

Donaldson-Evans, Mary. 2005. 'A Medium of Exchange: The Madame Bovary Film'. *Society of Dix-Neuviémistes*, 4 (2005): 21–34.

Elsaesser, Thomas and Malte Haneger. 2010. *Film Theory: An Introduction through the Senses*. New York: Routledge.

Emptaz, Florence. 2002. *Aux Pieds de Flaubert*. Paris: Grasset.

Flaubert, Gustave. 1857. *Madame Bovary*. Paris: Michel Lévy Frères, Libraires-Éditeurs.

Foucault, Michel. 2003. *The Birth of the Clinic: An Archaeology of Clinical Perception*. New York and London: Routledge.

Freud, Sigmund. [1919] 2003. *The Uncanny*. London: Penguin Classics.

Gunning, Thomas. 1990. 'The Cinema of Attractions: Early Film, Its Spectator and the Avant-Garde'. In *Early Cinema: Space Frame Narrative*, ed. Thomas Elsaesser, 56–62. London: British Film Institute.

Harvey, John. 2007. 'Showing and Hiding: Equivocation in the Relations of Body and Dress'. *Fashion Theory*, 11 (1): 65–94.

Jacobs, Steven. 2011. *Framing Pictures: Film and the Visual Arts*. Edinburgh: Edinburgh University Press.

Kovács, András Bálint. 2007. *Screening Modernism: European Art Cinema, 1950–1980*. Chicago, IL: Chicago University Press.

Kuhn, Annette. 2005. 'Thresholds: Film as Film and the Aesthetic Experience'. *Screen*, 46 (4): 401–14.

Lavin, Mathias. 2008. *La Parole le lieu: Le Cinema selon Manoel de Oliveira* [*The Word and the Place: The Cinema According to Manoel de Oliveira*]. Rennes: Presses Universitaires de Rennes.

Lavin, Mathias. 2013. *Manoel de Oliveira: L'Étrange Affair Angélica*. Paris: Scéren-CNDP.

Lavin, Mathias. 2014. '*A palavra*' ['The Word']. In *Manoel de Oliveira. Análise estética de uma matriz cinematográfica* [*Manoel de Oliveira: Aesthetic Analysis of a Cinematographic Matrix*], 123–34. Lisboa: Edições 70.

The Trope of the Doll

Lawton, R. A. 1964. 'Technique et signification de Amor de Perdição'. *Bulletin de Études Portugaises*, Nova Série, tomo 25, 77–135.

Lawton, R. A. 1985. 'Les Peines d'Amour perdues de Camilo Castelo Branco'. *Arquivos do Centro Cultural Português*, 21. Lisbon and Paris: Fundação Calouste Gulbenkian.

Lévy, Dennis. 1998. 'Manoel de Oliveira'. *L'Art du cinema*, 21/22/23: 51–3.

Lopes, João. 1981. 'A Boneca na Montra' ['The Doll in the Display Window']. In *Manoel de Oliveira*, 57–59. Lisboa: Cinemateca Portuguesa.

Marks, Laura. 2000. *The Skin of the Film: Intercultural Cinema, Embodiment and the Senses*. Durham, NC: Duke University Press.

Mulvey, Laura. 1975. 'Visual Pleasure and Narrative Cinema'. *Screen*, 16 (3): 6–8.

Mulvey, Laura. 2006a. 'The Death Drive: Narrative Movement Stilled'. In *Death 24x a Second*, 67–84. London: Reaktion Books.

Mulvey, Laura. 2006b. 'The Possessive Spectator'. In *Death 24x a Second*, 161–80. London: Reaktion Books.

Mulvey, Laura. 2006c. *Death 24x a Second*. London: Reaktion Books.

Oliveira, Manoel de. 2009. 'Acte de filmer et conscience filmique dans mon cas particulier' ['The Act of Filmmaking and Cinematic Consciousness in My Particular Case']. *Trafic*, 7 (Automne): 35–8.

Orr, John. 1993. *Cinema and Modernity*. Cambridge: Polity Press.

Parsi, Jacques. 1981. 'A trilogia dos amores frustrados' ['The Trilogy of Frustrated Loves']. In *Manoel de Oliveira*, 71–8. Lisbon: Cinemateca Portuguesa.

Pethő, Ágnes. 2011. *Cinema and Intermediality: The Passion for the In-Between*. Newcastle upon Tyne: Cambridge Scholars Publishing.

Peucker, Brigitte. 2007. *The Material Image: Art and the Real in Film*. Stanford, CA: Stanford University Press.

Ramasse, Francis. 1979. 'Le Mélodrame en question (Amour de perdition)'. *Positif*, 22 (Octobre): 65.

Remes, Justin. 2012. 'Motion(less) Pictures: The Cinema of Stasis'. *British Journal of Aesthetics*, 52 (3): 257–69.

Rodowick, D. N. 2001. *Reading the Figural, or, Philosophy after the New Media*. Durham, NC: Duke University Press.

Rosaak, Eivind. 2006. 'Figures of Sensation: Between Still and Moving Images'. In *The Cinema of Attractions Reloaded*, ed. Wanda Strauven, 321–36. Amsterdam: Amsterdam University Press.

Rosenbaum, Jonathan. [1981] 1995. 'Doomed Love: A Masterpiece You Missed'. In *Placing Movies: The Practice of Film Criticism*, 213–17. Berkeley, CA: University of California Press.

Rowland, Clara. 2009. 'O Escolho do Romance. In Amor de Perdição. Uma Revisão' ['The Choice of Romance. In Doomed Love: A Revision'], ed. Abel Barros Baptista, 59–80. Coimbra: Angelus Novus.

Sobchack, Vivian Carol. 1992. *The Address of the Eye: A Phenomenology of Film Experience*. Princeton, NJ: Princeton University Press.

Sobchack, Vivian Carol. 2004. *Carnal Thoughts: Embodiment and Moving Image Culture*. Berkeley, CA, and London: University of California Press.

Sontag, Susan. 1978. *Illness as Metaphor*. New York: Farrar, Straus and Giroux.

Steele, Valerie. 2004. 'Femme Fatale: Fashion and Visual Culture in Fin-de-Siècle Paris', *Fashion Theory*, 8 (3): 315–28.

Stewart, Garrett. 2006. *The Look of Reading: Book, Painting, Text*. Chicago, IL: University of Chicago Press.

Vidal, Belén. 2012. *Figuring the Past: Period Film and the Mannerist Aesthetic*. Amsterdam: Amsterdam University Press.

Wilson, Elizabeth. 2007. 'A Note on Glamour', *Fashion Theory*, 11 (1): 95–108.

Yanal, Robert. 2008. 'Defining the Moving Image: A Response to Noël Carroll'. *Film and Philosophy*, 12: 135–40.

Part Two

Camões and Don Quixote

4

The cultural philosophy of Oliveira

In the light of Oliveira's obsessive questioning of the mysterious transition between life and death, one might be tempted to see in his death on the Easter Holy Week in 2015 a final recurrence of this topic. The director's own last *Rite of Spring* appears to connect, once more, to the greatest mystery of Christianity that reveals death and life as synonymous and death not as an end, but as a new beginning. This coincidence, illuminating life as a full circle, completes Oliveira's artistic discourse on God, time and death, where the personal, the national and the universal coexists. The same idea of death as celebration of life is transmitted through his bio-documentary, *Visit. Memories and Confessions* (*Visita. Memórias e Confissões*, 1982), presented, according to his instructions, after his death. Made in the early 1980s, at the age of 72, this film, evoking the eighteenth-century literary genres of memoire and confession (a connection ensured by the writer Agustina Bessa-Luís, the scriptwriter of the film), was meant to be a closure, a testament. Ironically, it marked the beginning of a most prolific career, a 'new life' that continued for another thirty-three years. Surrounded by great expectations and a kind of suspense facing a message from death, this is not, however, a film of big revelations but rather that of small, personal confessions, whispers and memories about the director's private life during the Salazar dictatorship (1932–68), a time of reflections compensating for his withdrawal from filmmaking.[1] The central image of the film is the family house of Oliveira in Porto, the scene of countless events throughout generations, that he had to sell to pay debts. This house, a visual commonplace, a metaphor of subjectivity in classic psychoanalysis, at first appears isolated, and closed, inhabited by spirits that engage in philosophical conversations around topics that will be thoroughly debated in his upcoming films: doubt and faith, the temptation of

---

[1] Apart from premiering in Porto and Lisbon, as well as at the Cannes Film Festival in 2015, this film was not made public, and thus maintained its privacy. The family reserves the right to decide about its commercial distribution.

60   *The Cinema of Manoel de Oliveira*

discoveries and an irresistible attraction to the past and the mythical history of Portugal.

In this film, a kind of guided tour of his private life, memories and future projects, Oliveira reveals that he is currently working on a film entitled, *No, or the Vain Glory of Command* (*Non, ou a Vã Glória de Mandar*, 1990), that became emblematic of a recurrent duality in his work, the coexistence of patriotism with the questioning of the imperial aspirations of Portugal. This paradox is central to a series of films subsequent to *Non* – *Word and Utopia* (*Palavra e utopia*, 2000), *A Talking Picture* (*Um filme falado*, 2003), *The Fifth Empire* (*A Quinta Império*, 2004) and *Cristopher Columbus* – *The Enigma* (*Cristovão Colombo* – *A Enigma*, 2007), just to be retaken in Oliveira's last film, *The Old Man of Belém* (*O Velho do Restelo*, 2014). In this series of films, allegory and parody, as figures of repetition and imitation serve the artistic mission of Oliveira to reframe the national myth of Portugal, largely based on its colonial past. The familiar historical events are, however, often paired with an unfamiliar, strangely static style and an educative tone, filled with pathos, resulting, again, in an uncanny effect. Camões, the author of the national epic poem and Don Quixote, are emblematic figures representing the recurring national identity and memory discourse, as well as the individual fight with illusions (often related to national, cultural identity), respectively. Most characters of films analysed in the chapters of this section are determined to prove a far-fetched theory or carry out an impossible plan at all costs, fuelled by outdated ideals about humanity, nations and human relationships, just like the hero of Cervantes.

The short feature, *The Old Man of Belém*, is an allegorical concentration of the director's views on Portuguese history, in which both Camões and Don Quixote are invoked to thematize the inseparable duality of victory and defeat, the perpetual nature of human efforts, as well as the limits and limitations of artistic creation. The title itself is a reference to a scene from *The Lusiads* by Luís de Camões, the Fourth Chant, in which an old man from Restelo (a neighbourhood of Belém, where the Portuguese navigators used to sail off from), acting weirdly, is isolated from the cheering crowd assisting the departure of the ships: 'A reverend figure / fix'd each wond'ring eye, / And, beck'ning thrice, he wav'd his hand on high, / And thrice his hoary curls he sternly shook, / While grief and anger mingled in his look.' With a long, prophetic monologue he denounces 'the frantic thirst of honour and of fame, / The crowd's blind tribute, a fallacious name,' the 'dreadful woes' that will lead to the loss of Paradise and 'simple innocencence'. Lamenting over the price of these conquests – 'Conquest, and

The Cultural Philosophy of Oliveira

laurels dipp'd in blood, be priz'd, / While life is scorn'd, and all its joys despis'd?' – he ends up coursing 'the man who first on floating wood, / Forsook the beach, and braved the treach'rous flood!'

This chant, also containing the words that gave the title of *Non* ('O frantic thirst of honour and of fame, / The crowd's blind tribute, a fallacious name' and 'Oh! madness of ambition! thus to dare / Dangers so fruitless, so remote a war! / That Fame's vain flattery may thy name adorn . . .'; Camões 1986, 102–22), surprises the reader as a subversive, paradoxical outburst in a work that was meant to praise the historical, political and cultural importance of conquests of new territories. The same contradictory vision haunts the films of Oliveira, raising directly or indirectly the issue of the colonial past, a source of both pride and shame, an opening towards the world and, at the same time, a closure in the national destiny accomplished by colonial wars and the falling apart of the colonial empire.

The message of uselessness of colonial aspirations can also be identified in films not dealing directly with these historical dilemmas. *Eccentricities of a Blonde-Haired Girl* (*Singularidades de Uma Rapariga Loura*, 2009), one of Oliveira's latest films, is also susceptible to a postcolonial, allegorical interpretation. It is the story of a young man, who, in order to gather enough fortune to marry a young girl whom he adores from a distance, is forced by his uncle to work in a colony in Africa, just to find out, after marriage, that his new wife is a kleptomaniac. This story also attracts an allegorical, pessimistic interpretation of all colonial efforts: the sacrifices were useless and served the wrong cause, as the wealth gathered in the colonies could not buy happiness back home. Or, it was *not enough* for the beloved person.

The same pessimistic ideas are reiterated in *The Old Man of Belém*, starting with the titles projected on the image of waves, followed by the invocation to 'remember the big defeats'. Oliveira, the 'old man of Oporto' or, as César Monteiro once called him, 'the fossil of Oporto', in this short film orchestrates a male choir featuring his main actors (Mário Barroso, Luís Miguel Cintra, Diogo Dória, Ricardo Trêpa), as well as recurring characters and historical references: Camões, Don Quixote, Camilo Castelo Branco and Teixeira de Pascoaes. The monologues of these emblematic, static characters, different impersonations of the old man of Belém, formulate aphorisms about the work of art, a 'projection of the fauna and flora created in our intimacy' or evoke personalities who 'develop in volcanic explosions' (like Camilo Castelo Branco impersonated by Mário Barroso, who used to be an actor, narrator and director of photography in Oliveira's films). The Camilian genius is repeatedly invoked through quotations from *Doomed Love* and *The Day of Despair*, together with the evocation of the disastrous defeat of Portugal and Christianity at Alcácer Quibir. This tragic event is illustrated with an insert from *Non* and accompanied by a voice-off reciting the respective fragment from *The Lusiads*.

In a garden trimmed with contemporary apartment buildings that constitute an anachronistic background to these characters and their monologues, Don Quixote, the absolute symbol of the uselessness of human ambitions, of illusions turned into delusions, an 'equestrian statue', a 'Christian centaur', is also invoked through a recurrent scene depicting Quixote's emblematic fight with the windmills, in an intertextual quotation from Grigor Kozintsef's black-and-white version of *Don Quixote* from 1952. The Don Quixote topic first appears in an introductory image of the film, with an etching that serves as illustration for Gustavo Doré's *Don Quixote de la Mancha*, published in Porto in 1876. This image anchors the figurative signification of the character and of his tale in a Portuguese context, elaborated later in the moral reflections about the Battle of Alcácer Quibir. This intermedial repetition not only emphasizes the centrality of the Don Quixote topic, but, by connecting it to different moments of media history – printing, analogue film, digital film – also gives a historical perspective to technologies of representation, or to what Ernst Bloch once called 'the human venturing beyond the limits' (Bloch 1986, 51). As Bloch points out, Don Quixote, just like Don Giovanni, Odysseus or Faust, 'on the way to the perfect moment, in utopia which thoroughly experiences the world, warns and demands, in dream-monomania, dream-depth' (Bloch 1986, 50). The recurrent image of the allegorical representation of this delusion (Figure 4.1) resonates with the critique of useless conquests and the question that closes the film: 'What victories?'

Figure 4.1 The recurring etching of Don Quixote, an illustration of the uselessness of human efforts.

The stubborn repetition of human aspirations defeated by their own utopian illusions, thoroughly documented in cultural products, is often thematized in films of Oliveira. This personal discourse is reflected in a series of films that conceive of cultural identity as a result of fatal (historical) repetitions (the Battle of Alcácer Quibir and the colonial wars), religious and cultural profanations (re-enactments, parodies, farces), cultural and transnational interactions, doublings, imitation (or 'mimicry'), as well as self-othering processes.

In the following chapters, relying on recent writings on Oliveira's journey films, seen as reflections of his transnational views,[2] I will first tackle the phenomenon of historical/cultural allegory described by Ismail Xavier ([1999] 2004). This figuration is very susceptible to moralization and educational purposes, typical of the films proposed for analysis: *Non, or the Vain Glory of Command, A Talking Picture* (*Um Filme Falado*, 1997) and *Cristopher Columbus – The Enigma* (*Cristóforo Columbo – O Enigma*, 2007). The second chapter focuses on 'profanations' of religious mysteries and miracles, seen by Giorgio Agamben as a loss of aura and a return to use, and parody as a unique way to approach mysteries (Agamben 2007, 46–78) in *Rite of Spring* (1963), *The Divine Comedy* (1991), *The Uncertainty Principle* (2002) and *Magic Mirror* (2005). Finally, the third chapter turns towards the topic of cultural identity, Portugal's position in Europe, its geopolitical liminality that triggers an urge of 'mimicry' of the Western cultural, especially French colonizing models that goes hand in hand, according to Homi Bhabha, with an ironical distanciation (Bhabha 1994). This latter topic will involve the discussion of the 'French connection' of these films (represented by actors, locations, production, adaptations and other art references), as well as the many other references connecting them to the wider European (visual) culture. The films referred to here – *The Satin Slipper, Anxiety, The Letter, Voyage to the Beginning of the World* as well as *Gebo and the Shadow* – are all representative of a Portuguese cultural identity seen by Oliveira as 'the other' of Western European values and identities.

Historical allegories and identity quests

The idea of double in every shape and degree is one of the main sources of the uncanny in the cinema of Oliveira. As Freud points out in his seminal essay, the

---

[2] See on this Overhoff Ferreira, *Portugal, Europa e o mundo* (2012).

uncanny or *Unheimlich* mostly thrives in the constant recurrence of similar situations, which is the case of love triangles, the impossible, frustrated romantic relationships, historical events and defeats in Oliveira's films. The trope of the double also appears as the repetition of the same face (the recurring actors throughout several decades, or the same actor playing two different roles in the same film, in *Non*, the casting of his grandson, Trêpa, of a striking physical similarity with his young self in many of his films), or of a character trait (great receptivity to romantic illusions, idealism, even delusions in his films depicting a decadent bourgeoisie and the historical dramas presenting monomaniac characters). In terms of historical dramas, uncanny repetition is present in the recurrence of the twist of fortune (in the glorious colonial history of Portugal), a repeated crime (the disasters caused by the 'frantic thirst of honour and of fame', predicted by the old man of Belém), or a name invoked throughout several consecutive generations (the name of Dom Sebastian, 'the hidden one', in connection with the utopia of the Fifth Empire). All these types of repetition reveal a feeling of helplessness, paired with a stubborn wish to understand and make understood historical connections – this is one of the main preoccupations of Oliveira in the context of a sociocultural and national identity crisis subsequent to the decades-long Salazar dictatorship. In fact, as a unique case of a cinematic overview, the oeuvre of Oliveira is constantly retrieving past events. This is an urge that can be interpreted as a self-assumed responsibility of the artist to contribute to the national memory work and to deal with the crisis induced by the regime change. Herbert Kitschelt, in a study on methods of a comparative analysis of post-communist regimes, emphasizes the role of cultural 'entrepreneurs' in difficult, confusing times:

> In periods of societal crisis, people are capable of activating their long-term memory and scan its content in order to interpret their strategic options under conditions of uncertainty. Moreover, technical and institutional memory enhancers (scripture, literacy, media of communication, education, professionals in charge of preserving memories) and (...) 'cultural entrepreneurs' (...) extend the capacity of human actors to retrieve and process information over lengthy periods of time.
>
> 2003, 62

Oliveira assumes this artistic responsibility by bringing seemingly anachronistic stories to the present, with the aim to convey new meanings to them. This gesture might seem moralizing, reminiscent of what Xavier calls the 'rhetoric of pedagogical allegory, an elegant illustration of a priori, worn out ideas' ([1999]

2004, 344). But, considering the low spectator rates at movie theatres and the subsequent poor distribution of his films in Portugal, Oliveira is far from indulging himself in the role of an 'educator' of the nation. Instead, it appears that the highly figurative language he uses, his preference for allegories, on the basis of which his cinema has been labelled elitist and aristocratic, needs to be seen in the wider context of a European cinematic discourse, in which, according to Xavier, allegory becomes a 'key notion in the evaluation of culture of modernity', while national allegory functions as:

> a sign of a new consciousness of history where the appeal to analogies and to a vivid memory of the past is now taken not as the celebration of an identity connecting past and present, but as an experience able to teach us that repetition is always an illusion, and that old facts, like old signs, lose their 'original' meaning when looked at from a new perspective.
>
> [1999] 2004, 349

Instead of a pedagogical rhetoric, the allegories of Oliveira form a kind of 'rhetoric of temporality', described by Paul de Man as the impulse to memorize and identify with a previous moment (of history, of a personal life), 'that ends up communicating the sense of crisis and separation from the irretrievable past' (cf. Xavier [1999] 2004, 349).

The films analysed below can be seen as national allegories typical of periods of sociopolitical transition – in this case, from the isolation during the dictatorship to membership of the European Community – characterized by an intense identity quest, detectable in a preoccupation with the national character and stereotypes, the reflection of big historical movements in individual destinies, as well as a wish to find the place of Portugal among the other nations of Europe.

The spirit of negation: *Non* and *The Fifth Empire*

Changes of regime and the transition process to a new political order are often animated by an urge to settle with the past. This tendency can be identified in an intense memory work dealing with tensions, traumas and frustrations, as well as the intention to draw conclusions and start off with a new page. Moreover, as the case of post-dictatorial societies proves, the bigger the crisis of transition, the bigger the need to reach a new order of shared national and social values. In the

66   *The Cinema of Manoel de Oliveira*

case of Oliveira, the fall of the Salazar regime marks the beginning of a new, prolific artistic era, that completely neglects the representation of the long period of dictatorship. Instead, in a quest for a common ground for social values and national identity, he returns to the times *preceeding* the instauration of dictatorship: the nineteenth century and the fin de siècle become points of reference for a new, anachronistic romanticism in films like *Doomed Love, Francisca, Anxiety, The Cannibals*, all representing an idealism that contrasts the decadent values of a bourgeoisie depicted in *Past and Present, Abraham's Valley* or *The Uncertainty Principle*. Most of these films are melodramas, a popular genre susceptible, according to Xavier, to allegorization ([1999] 2004, 338–40): in them, the destiny of a young couple usually reflects a sociohistorical crisis of a patriarchal, hierarchical order exhausted by empty fights for privileges. This order is unable to back up an erratic generation blinded by exaggerated illusions about love, lacking a solid vision of future and unable to engage in a long term, responsible relationship. In *Francisca*, this figurative connection between the topic and the depicted historical moment is the most evident: the romantic melodrama about a couple that manages (unlike the protagonists of *Doomed Love*) to flee from home, but, left alone, are unable to start a new life, unfolds with a historical background renowned for political and societal crisis in Portugal (the first part of the nineteenth century), signalled in intertitles at the beginning of the film. In fact, this introductory text establishes a direct connection between Big History and the individual drama, considering political circumstances responsible for the emergence of a disillusioned generation:

> The independence of Brasil generated an atmosphere of instability and despair in Portugal. The death of D. João VI left a kingdom divided between the followers of his sons D. Pedro and Don Miguel who engaged in anatgonistic movements of liberalism and absolutism. A group of youth, who in the civil war in 1847 saw its traditionalist ideas lost, ended up to represent a sceptic type, susceptible to frustrated passions.
>
> (Author's own translation)

In addition to these links to a not very distant past, Oliveira returns to the foundational myth of Portuguese national identity through a series of films in focus in this chapter: *Non, Cristopher Columbus, The Fifth Empire* and *A Talking Picture*. While meant to (re)place Portugal on the map of a new, united Europe, these films also keep interrogating the myth based on glorious discoveries and the dream of a Christian, Fifth Empire, opposing it to human sacrifices and the horror of wars. In this respect, Oliveira's approach to history follows that of Walter Benjamin focusing on the notion of disaster and represented, most accurately, by the narrative figure of historical allegory. As Xavier emphasizes, 'allegory tends to interact with historical fractures and violence, especially when observed from the point of view of the defeated. It brings to light the tension between the impulse to totalize and its inevitable incompleteness' ([1999] 2004, 345–6).

The series of films participating in Oliveira's discourse on the national myth of Portugal starts with a categoric 'Non' to a colonialist politics. 'It is a terrible word, a "non", says the motto, attributed to Father António Vieira, the protagonist of another film on the Fifth Empire, *Word and Utopia* (*Palavra e utopia*, 2000). In a detailed analysis of *No, or the Vain Glory of Command*, Xavier argues convincingly that this film is the personal reading of Oliveira of Father Vieira's particular sermons that refer to the 'non' in various contexts: the non of Providence to the change of the divine will with respect to the Portuguese will, the difficulty to resist demands and orders given by state authorities with the formulation of a 'don't want' or 'can't' and the 'non' in the context of the relations between the human and God, in what is fair or unfair (Xavier 2013, 194–202).

No, or the Vain Glory of Command starts with a type of scene that in film history traditionally signals the induction into another state of mind, or a different level of consciousness: people under motoric inhibition are being taken, with a means of transportation, to unknown territories. Credits appear on military vehicles loaded with soldiers, sitting quiet, only engine noise and an extradiegetic, dissonant percussion music can be heard, while a very long shot shows the top of the trees they leave behind in an African landscape. The point of view corresponds to that of a moving observer, an outsider, who, keeping distance, doesn't want to get involved. It is a point of view that can be attributed to any of the soldiers sitting on the truck, their impassive faces shown in a semi-close, frontal, long shot. This scene is representative of the whole film about individuals who are taken, as if in a hypnosis, by the machinery of the big history to places and actions they do not know and understand and are reluctant to participate in. While advancing in the African landscape, an opposite movement is taking them back to their homeland: they confess they are yearning for their land, their village. The same question arises repeatedly: 'Why are we here?'

The very nature of film, the coexistence of an illusionary stillness with an illusionary movement, the 'here and now' of the single frame with the series of images preceding it can be seen as a figuration of history, where every isolated

68 *The Cinema of Manoel de Oliveira*

historical event is both consequence and cause of other events. Due to this opposition – between the motoric inhibition of talking, conversing protagonists and the dynamism of events recounted – this film is more than a moralizing, educational allegory. It rather belongs to the category called 'reflexive allegory' by Xavier, implying a higher consciousness of film language, visible in the horizontal and vertical montage, as well as the tableau-like images. The close-ups and semi-close-ups of talking, intrigued faces, accompanied by the disrupting noise of the engine of the military vehicle are also figures of the above mentioned inherent paradox of cinema: an apparent stillness produced by the constant movement of the reel. Non-diegetic music participates in a vertical montage that is meant to localize narration and to communicate anxiety (the percussions invoking the rhythm of Africa, an unknown territory for the European soldiers), later ensuring the transition between the present of the historical lesson narrated by Lieutenant Cabrita and the representation, as a historical costume drama, of the narrated events. It is non-diegetic music and not the voice-over narrator that connects past and present, creating an uncanny effect with the discrepancy of the images of a historical reconstruction and contemporary instrumental music. This choice, to use music as a link between the present time of narration and the past events instead of the voice of the same narrator, is explicable with another detail, the uncanny doubling of the present-time narrator and protagonists in the narrated historical stories, in which they also feature as main characters. They appear in historical scenes that proved crucial for the national identity of Portuguese people: the fight of Lusitanes against Rome, decided by the murder of Viriato, the emblematic Lusitane leader (a scene in which the noise of battle is merging with a melancholic extradiegetic music mourning over an immense loss), the battles against the Muslims, the wedding of Don João Pedro and Dona Isabel, the accidental death of the latter and his burial ceremony.

As Xavier points out, this preference for ceremonies, closely related to theatricality and an iconography of still compositions, always has to do with a closeness of death in the cinema of Oliveira (2013, 193). So does the baroque artificiality of images: the dreamlike, overdecorated images of conquered territories that appear in *Non* as Paradise on Earth, with naked children and nymphs, are in striking contrast with the image of conquerors, dressed in black, messengers of death and destruction.[3] The otherworldly, baroque music of this

---

[3] See Randal Johnson's analysis of this scene, unique in terms of not relying on historical facts, in *Manoel de Oliveira* (2006, 65–6).

scene alternates with the moralizing lamentation of the present, over the Paradise Lost, the antihumanitarian nature of conquests, as in the favour of humanity, would be 'what is being given' and not 'what is taken away'. Historical incursions alternate with personal confessions of the soldiers about homesickness (in fact, the more complex notion of 'saudade', also meaning 'longing', 'desire'), women and fidelity. Their attitudes define a national character that includes patriotism, national pride, sense of guilt, frustration over loss and a subsequent, constant melancholia. The dramatism of the battle itself, delayed by long conversations, is due to the encounter with the 'other', the colonized black man. Hesitation, triggered by this encounter, causes the injury of Lieutenant Cabrita and ultimately his death. The two temporal dimensions, the heroic past and the present, collapse into each other in the hallucinatory dream of Cabrita at the hospital, in which Dom Sebastian, the Portuguese king defeated by the Moors at Alcácer Quibir appears covered in blood, with a mutilated hand that symbolizes powerlessness and defeat. Ironically, an absence, a missing king, became the founder of 'sebastianism', the national myth of an imperium revigorated by a powerful and visionary leader. Messianic and historical narratives are thoroughly intertwined through a central character of a national allegory. Xavier calls this personification: a single character, one-dimensional, dominated by an obsessive neurosis that is not susceptible to any negotiations, is taken as standing for the entire nation ([1999] 2004, 340).

Besides the narrative of salvation, the reflection of individual stories and destinies in large-scale historical and social processes make of *Non* a contemporary national allegory of the defeated. The cut from the bleeding mythical character to the dripping blood at the hospital ensures, as critics have already argued, the continuity between Dom Sebastian and Cabrita.[4] The parallel maintains, however, the tension between the two messianic images: that of a maniac leader, animated by grand plans of political extension and that of the everyman, dying for the sins of others, in a redemption story emphasized by the written statement of his death on the day of the Carnation Revolution in April 1974. The final scene at the hospital does not give a comforting answer to all the questions raised throughout the film: it only emphasizes the uselessness of human sacrifice projected against a huge and confusing historical fresco. Oliveira, like Walter Benjamin, does not see history as a progress, where all efforts and sufferings make sense. That is the historical vision of the conquerors, of the leading nations of the Western world. From the point of view of the nations

---

[4] See on this Xavier (2013, 205), Overhoff Ferreira (2009) and Alvarez (2009).

70   *The Cinema of Manoel de Oliveira*

that see themselves at the borderline of the European community, history is nothing but a repetition of distressing events, a fragmented narrative with uncanny situations and encounters. The unsettling music score at the beginning of the film reveals, in this sense, a presentiment of the soldiers who, with the Portuguese history in mind, are already projecting the outcome of their expedition. As Xavier observes, the gazes in this film are typical of men facing death: those of the conversing soldiers, that of the tragic hero Viriato, the perplexed gaze of Dom João at the funeral of his son, whose marriage would have saved the kingdom, that of Dom Sebastian before the battle and, finally, in a Buñuelesque image, the huge single eye visible in the bandaged face of the soldier at the hospital.[5] The sinister effect of the familiar–unfamiliar is rooted here in what Freud singles out as the main factors turning something fearful into an uncanny thing: the attitude to death, the fear of castration, darkness and losing the eyes (Freud [1919] 2003, 14).

Directed at the age of 82, *Non* could easily be considered an artistic testimony of a leading national intellectual, the Master, as many used to call Oliveira. Not without educational overtones, this film uses allegory as a figure connecting past and present, compensating a fragmented history with the unbroken myth of a powerful nation and the utopia of the Fifth Empire. Almost fifteen years later, in 2004, Oliveira returns obsessively to Dom Sebastian, in *The Fifth Empire* (*O Quinto Império: Ontem como Hoje*, based on a novel by José Régio), an ostensibly static film, deconstructing a mythical character by continuously contrasting his grandiose dream of Portugal's leading role in the creation of such an empire with the warnings and realistic advices of his counsellors. The setting, the interiors of a castle, functions, in turn, as a background for ideological and political debates and a claustrophobic, expressionist décor for grandiose, at times hallucinatory, dreams. The young king (played by Trêpa, the grandson of Oliveira) is haunted by voices and divine instructions, while he makes plans ranging from illusion to delusion about new military expeditions and conquests against the Muslim world. This film adds to the number of Oliveira's talking pictures – *Word and Utopia, A Talking Picture, Non, Mon cas* – in which words, dialogues and monologues often overflow the frame, creating a tension between static scenes, with sitting and standing bodies and the words evoking intense mobility, energetic activities and an immense desire to conquer new territories. The concept of the Fifth Empire, propagated first by Father Antonio Vieira as a global

---

[5] See Xavier (2013, 185, 207) and Johnson (2006, 68).

The Cultural Philosophy of Oliveira 71

spiritual empire, led by the Portuguese nation, seen by Fernando Pessoa as the empire that followed the Greek, Roman, Christian and European empires, is added a new dimension in *The Fifth Empire* by the political context in which it has been released. It can be referred to the European Union (EU), that underwent new substantial enlargement in 2004, when a number of Central Eastern European countries joined, triggering the re-evaluation of the position of the other countries.

The re-emergence of sebastianism, of the myth of Portugal's central role among European nations can also be interpreted as a critique of any political ambition of 'extension' (hence the significance of the subtitle in Portuguese: 'Yesterday as Today'). As mentioned above, in *The Fifth Empire*, the indoor, theatrical setting points at the impossibility to move on, contrasted with a huge ambition and motivation. The initiative of Sebastian is depicted as a personal, lonely undertaking, also illuminating Oliveira's artistic position: at that time aged 96, still active professionally but aware of his physical and spiritual limitations to help the mission of 'Il Encoberto' to ensure Portugal's central position among the European nations. This projection of the personal in the historical and national appears in Oliveira's choice to cast his grandson, Trêpa, as the visionary king. This gesture will be retaken in *Cristopher Columbus – The Enigma* (*Cristóvão Colombo – O Enigma* 2007), a film in which national myth and personal identity quest thoroughly merge.

Spectres of nostalgia: *Cristopher Columbus – The Enigma*

After the implicit goal of *Non* to (re)place Portugal on the map of Europe and its critical overtones regarding the excesses of the colonial past, in *Cristopher Columbus – The Enigma* Oliveira goes one step further in his ambition to advocate the contribution of Portugal to the foundation of a New World and a subsequent global culture. In a sort of version of *The Convent* (*O Convento*, 1995), in which an American researcher visits Portugal in order to prove Shakespeare's Spanish and Jewish origin, this film explores the possibility of the Portuguese origin of Cristopher Columbus. Both films' narratives are structured by a quest and scientific research meant to defuse an enigma based on legends, non-official data, oral tradition and historical speculations as opposed to the official national history on display in *Non*. But while in *The Convent* the visit of the foreign couple (played by John Malkovich and Catherine Deneuve) reveals an external gaze contemplating Portugal as a source of exoticism, eroticism, occultism and mysticism, ultimately leading the characters into Faust-like contracts signed in Buñuelian circumstances (Figures 4.2–4.3), in *Cristopher Columbus* the quest is related to a personal identity, inseparable from national identity.

The quest is made personal by casting Oliveira's grandson, Trêpa, in the role of a young Portuguese emigree to the United States in 1946, who dedicates his life to prove the Portuguese origin of Columbus. The narrative evoking the efforts of Don Quixote, blinded by illusions, unfolds in a circular way, starting with the journey of the protagonist to the United States as an immigrant and his repeated return, first as a young man to Portugal and then as an old man to the Island of Porto Santo, part of the Madeira Archipelago. Here, trying to trace the hypothetical stations of Columbus's life, he visits the museum dedicated to the great navigator. At the origin of this quest is a hypothesis that links the fifteenth-century village Cuba in Alentejo to the place discovered and named by Cristopher Columbus (possibly Colon, from the Greek phallic letter, related to the protection of travels and causes). Further speculations see Columbus as Salvador Fernandes Zarco, the son of Isabel Goncalves Zarco and the biological son of Don Fernando, first duke of Beja, who only later changed his name to 'Colon'. Following the images of the wedding of the protagonists in the Sé of Oporto and a visit to the Beja castle, with a big leap in time and space, we find Oliveira and his wife in New York, in 2007, in front of an inscription commemorating the landing of Columbus and his crew, just before heading to the Museum of Maritime Navigation and Communication. The fact that the protagonist as an old man is played by Oliveira himself (his wife, Dona Isabel, playing the wife), in a most explicit way presents Trêpa as a double, an alter ego of the director, a form of repetition that reveals the director's attitude in

Figures 4.2–4.3 The external gaze on 'Portugueseness' attracted into Faust-like contracts in *The Convent*.

The Cultural Philosophy of Oliveira

front of his imminent death. As Freud points out, doubling is a form of preservation against extinction, that has:

> sprung from the soil of unbounded self-love, from the primary narcissism which holds sway in the mind of the child as in that of primitive man; and when this stage has been left behind the double takes on a different aspect. From having been an assurance of immortality, he becomes the ghastly harbinger of death.
>
> Freud [1919] 2003, 9

Melancholia, the mourning over an unspeakable or imminent loss (of identity, home or life), characteristic of the individual consciousness, in this film intertwines with nostalgia, a feeling of longing for a home, a lost community and a ceaseless desire to return in time to a utopian unity and national greatness. This merger of the personal with the national, illuminates the complexity of the Portuguese word *saudade* that Svetlana Boym defines as 'a tender sorrow, breezy and erotic, not as melodramatic as its Slavic counterpart, yet no less profound and haunting' (Boym 2001, 28). This content of *saudade* is epitomized by the two scenes with Dona Isabel singing a song. On the boat, after singing about the 'great lady with a torch', the Statue of Liberty in New York, she suddenly turns to Manoel and asks him directly whether he truly loves her. This unexpected question infuses the scene with a touch of romantic longing and quiet happiness about still being together at such an advanced age. The second singing occurs at the end of the film, during the visit to the memorial house of Columbus in Porto Santo (that preserves the relic of Portuguese discoveries, to which, according to their guide, played by Miguel Cintra, Portugal has not paid much attention). Standing at the window opening on the ocean, with a boat passing on the horizon, Dona Isabel sings: 'This word – yearning / Whoever coined it / Must surely have cried / when they first said it.' Indeed, nostalgia cannot be overcome with philosophical or scientific argumentation, rationalization (the method of the researcher protagonist of the film). It is more on the side of expression and seduction rather than conviction, as Boym would argue, hence the preference for elegiac poems, songs and personal confession in this film.

Cristopher Columbus is both about the 'nostos' (the image of a stable, welcoming home) and 'algia' (the constant, unsatisfiable yearning for what is lost) aspect of the nostalgic feeling. It reveals nostalgia as connected to both time and space, and, in the light of Boym's categorization, is both restorative and reflexive: it aspires to a coherent, grand national narrative, that is deconstructed, however, by the revelation of its fragmented, repetitive and speculative aspects

(2001, 28). To the nostalgic longing for a distant home and the possibility of a glorious national history, revealed in *Non* and *Cristopher Columbus*, adds the point of view of the outsider, the immigrant returning home to prove, once again, the respectable place of his nation among other leading nations of the world. As Boym puts it:

> It is not surprising that national awareness comes from outside the community rather than from within. It is the romantic traveler who sees from a distance the wholeness of the vanishing world. The journey gives him perspective. The vantage point of a stranger informs the native idyll. The nostalgic is never a native but a displaced person who mediates between the local and the universal.
>
> Ibid., 27

However, da Silva's return home, disguised as a scientific quest, does not appear as an emotional rediscovery of the old places or refamiliarization, but rather as a peculiar way of sublimation of an unspeakable yearning. The personal theory of Columbus's Portuguese origin is not only a pretext to return home, but also a discourse rationalizing his feeling of loss, by turning it, with distanciation, from a deeply personal case into a national mission. This urge to rationalize feelings appears in a striking contrast with the free flow of feelings, epitomized by Dona Isabel's emotional behaviour and singing. The repeated occurrence of an allegorical figure, a woman wearing Portuguese national colours who goes unnoticed by the main protagonist and can be seen only by the spectator, is more than a tool of allegorical didacticism, it can also be interpreted as the figuration of the same, overtly emotional, patriotism (Figures 4.4–4.5).

The alternative to this 'disguised' quest of identity (which corresponds to Boym's argument about nostalgia's tendency to manifest itself 'sideways', 2001, 28) is the deliberate, overtly assumed need to return to the origins and childhood

Figures 4.4–4.5 Allegorical personification of Portugal in *Cristopher Columbus – The Enigma*.

in *Voyage to the Beginning of the World*. In this film, the two travellers, the middle-aged French actor (played by Jean-Yves Gautier) in search of his relatives in a remote village that his father left behind and the elderly director (Marcello Mastroianni in his last role) revisiting the places of his youth, represent two different interpretations of nostalgia: for the actor, it means a return in space, to a place of origin (just to realize that this involves a time travel, too), while for the director it is a journey through time, highlighted by the ruins of a lost childhood. Both quests culminate in reflexive nostalgia that prioritizes the 'algia', the constant pain of yearning that always postpones homecoming. It also emphasizes the doubts of the modern man about stability and its preference for details, fragments and repetitions.

The road to a transnational identity: *Voyage to the Beginning of the World*

Oliveira's 1996 film, probably one of the most internationally acclaimed (partly due to its international casting and self-reflexivity, with Marcello Mastroianni as the alter ego of the director), dwells extensively on the topic of *saudade*, with several approaches and definitions differentiated along gender and age differences. The wordplay of the title, giving a temporal dimension to a spatial movement, completed with the double meaning of the Portuguese word 'princípio', which, as Randal Johnson observes, means both 'beginning' and 'principle' (Johnson 2006, 122–6), anticipates the philosophical, inner nature of the journey. This is an aspect that clearly distinguishes the European genre of journey films from their American counterparts, mostly thematizing evasion from a restrictive society, as well as the subsequent danger and adventure. As David Laderman points out in his book, *Driving Visions: Exploring the Road Movie*, in European road movies, the exploration of psychological, emotional and spiritual states becomes more important:

> Overall the European road movie associates road travel with introspection rather than violence and danger. Put differently, traveling outside of society becomes less important (and perhaps less possible) than traveling into the national culture, tracing the meaning of citizenship as a journey. With smaller countries sharing more national borders, the European road movie explores different national identities in intimate topographical proximity. Therefore, these non-American road movies tend toward the quest more than the flight,

and imbue the quest with navigations of national identity and community – navigations that often take on sophisticated philosophical and political dimensions.

2002, 248

The rationalizing attitude in this film is sustained by a tight dialogical form enabled by the journey, the intimacy of travelling together in a car, a recurrent topos of road movies. An old director, a Portuguese actor (played by Diogo Dória) and an actress (Leonor Silveira), as well as a French actor are travelling together, taking a break from a filmmaking process. As we find out, the director sets off with the aim to revisit the scenes of his childhood and the French actor wants to find his Portuguese roots in a remote village in North Portugal. The discussion unfolding between the protagonists would never be possible on the film set. But in the heterotopia of the car, reuniting different nationalities, ages and sexes, a variety of attitudes and roles become possible, unfolding during the three stops of the first part of the journey, concerned with the director's memories.

The topic of different European nationalities travelling together, further developed in *A Talking Picture*, beyond illustrating the topographic proximity of European nations and their quest for identity, can be interpreted as an allegory of the European Community. Transnational mobility does not involve considerable changes in the characters' identities, as everybody speaks French, the official language of a cultural Europe. The Portuguese spoken by people in villages (at times with a Spanish accent) does not impede communication either, as there is always somebody around translating into French (an illustration of the adaptability of people from geographically and/or politically liminal countries of Europe to a cultural centre). From the safe interior of the car, where travellers are engaged in philosophical discussions, the world outside the European Community seems chaotic and inhuman. While the director expresses his concern about the ongoing Balkan War, the Portuguese actor takes it further to a universal, then a cosmic level by affirming that 'Sarajevo is everywhere in the World, Apocalypse, now!' Beyond the geopolitical approach and humanism of Oliveira praised by the critics of this film,[6] this hyperbolization of human suffering paradoxically takes off the edge of this remark and becomes a gesture of distanciation from suffering and responsibility. Accordingly, the reference to

---

[6] See, for example, Overhoff Ferreira (2013), Rovai (2010) and Viegas (2014).

Coppola's film on the Vietnam War alienates the disaster unfolding at the borders of the EU as a spectacle, a film or a series of TV news, watched helplessly by EU citizens growing gradually insensitive at the mediatized sight of destruction. At the same time, speaking about Sarajevo at the ruins of the Grand Hotel of Pezo, the travellers contemplate war from a civilizing and temporal perspective, as a mechanism that only precipitates the process of disappearance orchestrated by time. As Mauro Ruiz Rovai points out, the intertwining of a personal history with a historical event at the ruins of a building is a statement about the passing time that not destroys individual lives and bodies only, but victorious nations and countries as well (Rovai 2010, 87).

As an allusion to the 'driving visions' of European modernism, more precisely Bergman's *Wild Strawberries* (1957), the interior of the car becomes a claustrophobic, a bit uneasy scene orchestrating various voices that reflect upon the 'age that isolates'. Accompanied by a disturbing music of percussions (by Emmanuel Nunes and similar to that at the beginning of *Non*), the rear windshield of the car shows, just like in the film of Bergman, in a very long shot, the image of the road left behind. This image brings together, again, the journey towards a destination and a travel back in time.

The young Portuguese actress, Judite, is overtly flirting with the director Manoel, who willingly participates in the new game, inverting the roles: the actress, dressed and acting like a cheeky schoolgirl, a sort of Lolita, is the one who constantly questions and reflects upon the director's words. This role play culminates during the first stop, by the Douro, 'a river of Gold', where the group contemplates the Jesuit school where Manoel was educated, visible on the other bank.

With its three stops, the film exemplifies what Laderman calls the 'campfire approach' of road movies, 'where soul-searching discussion occurs in mobility's pauses' (Laderman 2002, 253). Indeed, it is during the first stop that Manoel confesses, 'I don't know what I am', and his memories about his childhood seem more vivid than his perception of reality. Speaking in French, he also complains about the feeling of being cut off from his memories – the French word *souvenirs*, that also means 'gift', is an allusion to the possibilities and physical-psychological competences of youth, now lost. While conversing, he uses a binocular to see the old school better, that is, to bring the past closer: the optical device participates in the allegorical language of memory. The 'campfire situation', however, while ensuring an intense cerebral mobility, carries the risk of becoming too educational and aphorismatic. The concluding sentence of Duarte, the

Portuguese actor, 'between eras there lies a time which becomes present', sounds like a pretentious definition. The biblical allusion to Judith and Holofernes, in connection with the relationship between the young Judith and the elderly Manoel also seems to reveal too much from the figurative potential of the film. Fortunately, Manoel only tells the story about a young woman killing the leader of a hostile tribe in order to defend her own town, without further explanations, leaving to the spectator the choice of whether or not to apply the biblical story to the actual situation. Ultimately, Judith-Leonor Silveira's inquisitive behaviour can be seen as epitomizing 'women's power', be it sexual or intellectual, traditionally illustrated with famous female 'castrators', Salome or Judith. This applies to almost all roles of a female seductress played by Silveira, including *Abraham's Valley*, *Anxiety*, *The Uncertainty Principle*, *Magic Mirror*, *Porto of my Childhood*, *The Convent* and *Party*. On a metanarrative level, this reference also points at Silveira's position as a fetish-actress in the whole work of Oliveira.

The second stop of the journey is all about male power, with the statue of Pedro Macau, 'who is carrying a pole' as illustration of a trapped male identity, of a man 'small but tough' who, bent beneath countless responsibilities, became a 'hero against himself' (Figures 4.6–4.7). In this allegory of the crisis of a patriarchal society, in which 'maleness' is an increasing load, both Afonso and Manoel recognize themselves: Afonso is carrying the weight of the mission to return to a family once left behind by his father in an enormous effort to survive. He is, in fact, filling a gap that his father failed to fill, as he never returned to Portugal. Manoel, in his turn, is struggling with the ruins of his past and the closeness of death that urges him to make a final balance. At the end of the film, Afonso's statement, 'You are another Pedro Macau, Manoel,' is addressed to both Manoels: the one in the film, played by a terminally ill Marcello Mastroianni,

Figures 4.6–4.7 The statue of Pedro Macau, illustrating the burdens of masculine identity in *Voyage to the Beginning of the World*.

and the one behind the wheel (of the car, as sometimes we manage to glance Oliveira playing the role of the driver) and behind the film itself.

The next stop at the Grand Hotel in Pezo, accompanied by the same dissonant piano music, is the scene of an elaborate discussion around *saudade*: it is first defined as 'nostalgia of the past', then, after Pessoa's *Saudade and the Fallen Land*, as 'a fallen land in a dreaming heart'. *Saudade* also appears as closely related to age: while the discussion is mostly orchestrated by Manoel, who confesses, in yet another definition of this longing, that he knows his own history 'as if in another life', Judite, the youngest member of the group, shows a nonchalant attitude. Resonating with Manoel's confession in a contrasting way comes Afonso's statement that he, in turn, knows his father's story 'as if it happened to him'. It is at this point, halfway through the film, that the focus turns to the quest of Afonso. At the arrival at his aunt's house, the translation is not enough any more to (re)establish an intimate relationship between family members. This will happen in the small hut, by the fire, a version of the 'campfire situation', only that this time philosophical thoughts are replaced by a welcoming ritual. The cemetery they all visit is just another heterotopia that reflects upon the society of the living ones, as well as the mechanisms of remembering and nostalgia. The silent stroll of Manoel-Mastroianni between tombs (visionary in terms of his imminent death) illustrates the personal confession of Oliveira about an increasingly distant own life and a closeness of own death.

The topic of human suffering, lack of solidarity and its globalized representation in television (the 'evil's work') recurs in this final visit, too. The same topic of reflection of private story in history is at the centre of a more elaborately allegorical film, *A Talking Picture*, depicting a European Community and identity trapped in a globalized World Order. Both films are also about the fear of dying before having seen something (the places of youth and the place of origin in the case of *Voyage*) or before having seen the places that have to be seen (the emblematic places of European culture in *A Talking Picture*).

Places to be seen before you die: *A Talking Picture*

While *Journey* is probably the most widely known film of Oliveira due to its international cast, the late modernist topic of the journey and its self-reflexivity, *A Talking Picture* remains the most analysed opus by both Portuguese and international critics focusing on its geopolitical, transnational and allegorical

80   *The Cinema of Manoel de Oliveira*

message.[7] In this film, the car reuniting travellers of different nationalities, ages and sexes is replaced by a boat, called by Michel Foucault the heterotopia par excellence:

> a floating piece of space, a place without a place, that exists by itself, that is closed in on itself and at the same time is given over to the infinity of the sea and that, from port to port, from tack to tack, from brothel to brothel, it goes as far as the colonies in search of the most precious treasures they conceal in their gardens.
>
> Foucault 1986, 27

As such, the boat has not only been the great instrument of economic development over the centuries, but 'has been simultaneously the greatest reserve of the imagination' (ibid., 27). The ship, instead of being represented as a means of mobility (as would happen in an American road movie), in this film becomes a static image, *a figure*. This resonates with Ira Jaffe's observation regarding the shots of the ship:

> One recurring image is a close shot of the ship's prow moving through water, which could be anywhere. No camera movement is detected, and the prow's position in the frame does not change. The result is an impression of static rather than dynamic motion – or of stillness in motion.
>
> Jaffe 2014, 106

Stillness, a central feature of slow cinema, favours discourse to the detriment of mobility. In this film about the journey on a ship of a historian mother and a daughter to Bombay, where they are to join the pilot father, with stops at emblematic places of European cultural history, the ship appears as a place that engenders a series of allegories: that of cultural memory, communication between distant cultures, transmission of cultural values, as well as the relationships inside the European Community.

As Xavier points out, this tendency of allegorization is characteristic of world cinema, with films that now share a common historical ground that encompasses a language of crisis, presented by dramas that are 'typical in periods of transition and accelerated technical-economic changes which enforce people to revise their views of identity and shared values'. Bringing examples from the cinemas of European countries that either economically or politically face crisis or are in a marginal position – Balkan, Eastern European countries, but also Portugal – he

---

[7]   See, for example, the writings of Johnson (2006), Pianco and Panini (2010), Overhoff Ferreira (2013), Lavin (2008), Xavier (2013) or Jaffe (2014), as well as Viegas (2014).

discovers 'a new trend of story lines involving multinational encounters of protagonists who belong to distant cultures but are led to an unexpected interaction, most of the time of a clearly private nature' (Xavier [1999] 2004, 360). The international meeting on the ship board has been interpreted by critics as a figure of Portugal's outsider position in the European Union: while mother and daughter are invited to the table and discussions, it is only Portuguese that is not spoken or understood by the others. Moreover, as Wiliam Pianco and Juliana Panini argue, there is another hierarchical structure, in the global – European relationship, represented by the American captain (played by John Malkovich), who considers all the ladies gathered around the table to be his guests. But cultural differences are reduced to a common 'ground zero' by the bomb placed on the ship, an evident allusion to the 9/11 attacks. It is allegorically referred to by the song 'Neranzoula', about a cold wind from the North that destroys the fruits of a fragile orange tree, sung by Helena (Irene Papas), the Greek member of this international team (also featuring Catherine Deneuve and Stefania Sandrelli).[8]

This is not the first film of Oliveira loaded with acts of speech (monologues, dialogues, polemic discussions), but the power of spoken language and its signification – figurative or referential – are permanently questioned in this film, as already anticipated by the synthetical title emphasizing the prominence of speech over image, of *what is said* over *what is seen*. The English translation of the title – replacing 'film' with 'picture' – also adds a historical dimension to the syntagm by evoking the 'talkies', the era when cinema was mesmerized by its own voice, but also the figurative potential of the silent image that can signify or 'talk' without words. As Mathias Lavin argues, this film is about the evocative power of the spoken word instead of its invocative or convocative role (this latter, epitomized by *Non*, where the word ensured the passage between the event narrated by another professor of history, Cabrita, and its representation; Lavin 2003, 38). But this power is not sufficient to compensate for the absence of events, places, monuments, rituals and ceremonies lost in time, in the absolute past ('ilo tempore'), constituting what Jan Assmann calls 'cultural memory': a mediated memory of a mythical, primordial time by specialized carriers, texts, iconic representations and performances (Assmann 2008, 117). The effort of the mother to make historical events understood is all the more frustrating because all she can provide are evocative descriptions, confronted by the little girl's ceaseless questioning. For Maria Joana, the superb monuments of antiquity

---

[8] On the allegorical meaning of the song, see a detailed analysis in Pianco and Panini (2010, 97–126).

appear as lifeless ruins and 'human nature', responsible for wars and destruction, an enigmatic syntagm. As Ira Jaffe rightly puts it, the mother Rosa Maria's explanations often bear on absence and loss, both material and emotional. Her example about a doll taken away to illustrate the lust for power of the human race and the cause of wars has been often cited as anticipatory of the final scene of the film: 'Suppose you had a doll and someone tried to take it away. You'd hold it tight to keep it.' Maria Joana's reply, 'But if I had a doll, would they try and take it?' betrays sheer anxiety. As Jaffe points out, 'It is perhaps the first time in *A Talking Picture* that the daughter evinces inner concerns – and that the threat of physical assault becomes intensely personal' (2014, 110). The passage from historical to personal is made possible by the figure of a toy, something that also illustrates the manipulative value of (cultural, economical) objects.

Shortly after the cosmopolitan American captain gives Maria Joana a doll dressed in oriental costume, bombs are detected on board the ship and it explodes before the girl and her mother (who return to fetch the doll from the cabin) can escape. The film closes with a freeze-frame of Malkovich's face, lit by the blast and revealing the horror of the Medusa-effect: turning still, as if petrified.

The reference to the 9/11 events turns the trope of the doll into another allegory of American–European economic relationships based on manipulative interest-configurations that have contributed to the European–Middle East conflicts. Through the doll, cultural memory is actualized as communicative memory of a traumatic event that continues the line of conflicts thought as lost in distant, historical and mythical times. Just like in *Non*, in this film, Oliveira manifests an artistic responsibility to warn next generations of an uncanny repetition of similar historical events. The horrified face of the captain witnessing the death of innocent people is frozen in a still image, but also as a materialization of an elementary and uncanny fear (of death). The line of many temporally distant, stereotypical historical stories evoked by monuments, perfect examples of non-places – touristic places that are transitional and only temporary, accessible for a certain type of Western traveller according to Marc Augé (2009) – culminates, just like in *Non*, in a unique and useless event of personal sacrifice. In the next chapters, I will focus on a contrary movement, revelatory of another aspect of the cultural philosophy of Oliveira and the uncanny aspects of his cinema: the profanation, that is, the repetition of an individual, initial sacrifice (Christ's Passion) or of another sacred (miraculous) event, in *Rite of Spring*, *Magic Mirror* or *The Divine Comedy*.

5

Profanations

The Passion of Christ according to Oliveira

As Freud observes in his essay, there are many more means of creating uncanny effects in fiction than in real life. According to him, effacing the distinction between imagination and reality is a solid base of the uncanny effect in every fiction (Freud [1919] 2003, 18). Ever since *Douro, faina fluvial*, the systematic deconstruction of borders between the real and imaginary, reality and fiction, archaic and modern becomes the artistic signature of Oliveira and a fertile source of his much praised irony. César Monteiro emphasized Oliveira's Catholicism that is inseparable from a transgressive filmmaking and a violent, subversive gaze that makes the separations visible (Monteiro 1996, 421). According to Giorgio Agamben, the separation between the human/everyday use and divine/sacred is orchestrated by sacrifice, which is the basis of all religion (Agamben 2007, 73). The sacrifice of Christ ensured the divinization of a human body on which the Christian allegory of salvation is based. As Xavier points out in his treatise on allegory, salvation endows human history with internal logic, and becomes the master narrative for all providential fictions, re-presentations and re-enactments ([1999] 2004, 341–2). Oliveira's *Rite of Spring* is a paradigmatic example of the human imitation/repetition of divine acts, re-presenting, re-mediating on film the mystery play of Christ's Passion in the village of Curalha, based on the late medieval, dramatic-religious text of Francisco Vaz de Guimarães.

One of the main issues raised by this film's criticism is its genre, oscillating between documentary, fiction and a self-reflexive auteurist cinema, a multiplicity, a millefeuille effect (as Serge Daney has put it), formally realized by a montage structure, suggesting the perpetual alternation of being inside and outside the play (Daney 1977, 35). What Oliveira represents is, in fact, the process of profanation of a divine act: from this standpoint, the play of the villagers and the

84   *The Cinema of Manoel de Oliveira*

act of filmmaking are two versions of the same human urge to return the sacred to use. This inevitably triggers, according to Agamben, the loss of aura of the object represented: as he puts it, 'profanation [...] neutralizes what it profanes' (Agamben 2007, 77). I argue that the filming of the mystery play at the beginning of the 1960s is an act of profanation of a biblical narrative, not only in the spirit of Benjamin's thesis on the loss of aura, uniqueness of the work of art in 'the age of mechanical reproduction' (the film of Oliveira was released, distributed, presented at festivals, cinemas, now is accessible on the internet, too), but also by turning it into a *spectacle*. The archaic mystery play is represented as a unique event, an *attraction* for the tourists arriving from the cities. For the film crew, it is an exotic, rare phenomenon that needs to be preserved for the future. But the film goes far beyond the cultural responsibility of an intellectual making ethnographic films: it represents the passage from the sacred to the profane in a form that Agamben labelled as 'an entirely inappropriate use (or, rather, reuse) of the sacred': a play in both the dramatic and ludic sense of the word (2007, 75).

The tripartite structure of the film, following the form of the classic dramatic play, has often been targeted by critical analysis. As Ana Isabel Soares points out, for example, to this triade correspond three different modes of narration, characters and even texts, creating multiple readings, described by Daney with the syntagm of multilayered history (2013). The three parts do not simply correspond to introduction, a presentation of the characters and preparations, followed by the play itself and then a moralizing closure. The montage ensures from the very beginning an interplay between the semantic layers responsible for the figurativity of the film. The different types of texts invoking different temporal dimensions establish a complex, matrix-like net of significations with the images: the voice-over biblical quotation about the afterlife happiness of those poor in spirit connected to the images of the archaic form of labour of villagers, alternates with the scene of the villagers reading and commenting on the journal article about the landing on the Moon and the advertising poster of the upcoming Easter celebrations. The juxtaposition of the quotation from the New Testament about an afterlife happiness and the futuristic narration about the landing on the Moon contrasts two different concepts of history – a religious one conceiving it as a continuous aspiration towards the divine and another, a laic one that sees it as progress. This is another example of profanation opposing an afterlife, imaginary heaven to the Galaxy as 'real' space that can be conquered by humankind. In this respect, the illustration with the labour on the fields translates the controversial syntagm 'poor in spirit' as lacking devouring aspirations, ambitions and frustrating desires: self-sufficient, content, strongly rooted in the present and the land. All three texts – the biblical, the journalistic and the advertisement – are anchored and reflected upon with images of the labour and the crowd reading the texts and distanciating them with laughter.

Laughter at both miraculous events – the Passion and the landing on the Moon – adds a new dimension to the process of profanation: that of the parody. As Agamben argues, there is an 'intimate solidarity' between mystery and parody: 'In approaching a mystery, one can offer nothing but a parody; any other attempt to evoke it falls into bad taste and bombast' (Agamben 2007, 46). According to him, parody is an artistic choice to represent the unnarratable, the unattainable: as such, it becomes the liturgy of the mass, the representation par excellence of the modern mystery (Agamben 2007, 46).

Parody can also be conceived of as a tension between the universal and the particular, grammar and own language, language and dialect, paradigm and variable. In this respect, made two years before Pasolini's, *The Gospel According to Matthew* (1964), *Rite of Spring* represents the same 'serious parody' displaced, according to Agamben, 'onto its contents, giving it the weight of a metaphysical signification'. It also stages the conflict between the universal narrative and its local interpretation as an opposition between cinematic language and particular cultural, archaic visual models and traditions (Agamben 2007, 46 and 101). Both films oppose the universal narrative to long shots and compositions evoking a pre-cinematic, painterly tradition. The frontal, ceremonial images and the iconography of the Passion – for example, Veronica's scarf, the crucifixion, the removal from the cross and burial of Christ – ensure in the film of Oliveira, just like in that of Pasolini, the transition from the theatrical to the visual/pictorial and ultimately the filmic. Steven Jacobs, in his historical overview of the *tableau vivant*, emphasizes the intensifying role of this intermedial form as the culmination of the drama, rooted in the eighteenth-century play and accomplished in early Passion films, as well as in many religious films. As he argues:

> This reliance on tableaux vivants in religious films is no coincidence since these subjects had strong ties to an age-old iconographic tradition in the theatre and visual arts. In many cases, it seems to have been sufficient to make vague references – the spectator simply had to be aware that the shot compositions were based on paintings without the need to recognise them.
>
> 2011, 96

Ceremonial costumes, decoration and declamatory style are not paired, however, with the frontality of religious icons (a type of composition that would later become a signature of Oliveira's visual style, starting with *Doomed Love*). The characters are not looking into the camera, as if avoiding all connection with the spectators, closing themselves, as it were, in the 'here and now' of the oral representation, the play. This predominance of immediacy over intermediacy – the refusal to acknowledge the presence of the camera – is reflected, as Soares points out, not only by the gazes directed *beyond* the camera and cinema, but also by the repeated gesture of characters *turning their backs* to the camera (2013, 75). These alienating effects of Oliveira's 'serious parody' epitomize Agamben's remark about the 'intolerable reality' of its object that needs to be kept at a distance: 'To fiction's "as if", parody opposes its drastic "this is too much".' The spectators of the mystery play, tourists arriving in fancy cars and other villagers, are not alter egos of the future spectators of the film: they are an organic part of the Passion, the way onlookers are traditionally part of the visual, pictorial representations of this prominent biblical narrative. The uncanny effect is the result of a familiar narrative that is alienated through the medium of film: its spectators are not participants, nor witnesses, but passive onlookers, voyeurs of re-enacted scenes of the greatest mystery of the Christian faith.

The coda of the film, of about three minutes in length, shows images of human destruction – war, the mushroom cloud of the atomic bomb – on which the image of a suffering Christ is superimposed. This transforms the film into a discourse on the paradoxical – constructive and destructive – nature of human creativity. In the documentary, black-and-white images resonate in a contrastive way with both the news about the landing on the Moon and the mystery play celebrating the possibility of redemption of humankind, metaphorically illustrated with the renewal of nature in Spring. As Soares argues, the choice of the word 'Spring' instead of 'Passion' reflects Oliveira's personal interpretation of a real resurrection, while the closure serves as a neat delimitation of the play itself from its 'frame' in order to emphasize it as an autonomous entity, and not a simple adaptation of a dramatic text (2013, 78). This last montage also reflects on Oliveira's film as a creative act that shows a similarity with Ernst Bloch's views on the power of a work of art 'to complete the world without the world being exploded as in the Christian religious anticipatory illumination, and without disappearing apocalyptically'. As Bloch puts it, it is only art that 'drives world figures, world landscapes to their entelechial border without causing their

Profanations 87

demise' (1986, 72). The same idea is transmitted in another Oliveirian approach to the human re-enactment of the divine, in his *A Divina Comédia*.

The comedy of the alienated: *A Divina Comédia*

Despite its title, this film does not establish a direct intertextual relationship with Dante's poem, rather being, as the title suggests, only one of the many imitations of the divine, building on textual encounters across space and time, just like Dante's classic. Biblical narratives and characters, Fyodor Dostoevsky's *Crime and Punishment*, *The Karamazov Brothers*, Nietzsche's thoughts and José Régio's play, *A Salvação do Mundo* (*The Salvation of the World*, 1954), are brought together in an intertextual dialogue on God's existence, salvation and sacrifice, the philosophical concepts of womanhood, music and writing. In an interview, Oliveira denied the intercultural relevance of these texts, that he considered stemming from the same problem of resurrection and the absolute nature of values that regulate human acts.[1] Contrasting ideas represented by antagonistic characters – the Prophet and the Philosopher, the Saint/Virgin and the laic woman, Alyosha and Ivan Karamazov, Man and Woman – are framed by play, a par excellence form of profanation of the sacred and parody. In this respect, the title can be interpreted as an oxymoronic description of profanation of the sacred, an earthly imitation of the divine characteristic of all human undertaking, including artistic creation.

The setting – the house of the Alienated, an insane asylum, gathering characters with strong delusions about their identity (hence another reference to the spirit of Don Quixote) and their relationship to God – is a common psychoanalytical topos of personality, its personal and culturally conditioned 'layers' being represented here by voices of prominent characters and personalities of European culture in general and Christianity in particular. Taking into account the fact that it was made after the death of his grandson, David – to whom it is also dedicated – this film can be seen as a particular, personal act of mourning that activates and reconsiders the cultural heritage (religion, literature, music) that might be helpful in the process of consolation. God's existence and the possibility of redemption are invoked repeatedly, but are also questioned by the Philosopher who, representing the sheer anger of the survivor, is in denial,

---

[1] See the interview by Jean A. Gili, 'A Mental Conception of Cinema', in Johnson (2006, 142).

88   *The Cinema of Manoel de Oliveira*

and even calls himself the Antichrist. 'God? What is God? – he asks – the artist is God, music is God.' At the end of the film, he voices the dreadful loneliness of those without God: 'God? I don't know what it is. Terrible.' Next to denial appears the promise of afterlife and resurrection: the same 'happy are those poor in spirit, because heaven is theirs' is uttered by the Christ-imitator resident, from the top of the piano, where Maria João Pires plays classical music. Whenever music starts, the residents of the asylum stop acting and struggling with their delusions: in a demonstration of art's therapeutic power, they all gather in silence around the piano, and the Philosopher-Antichrist discovers the divine nature of music.

The two competing discourses related to the grieving process – the angry subversive one represented by the Philosopher-Antichrist and Ivan Karamazov, and the acceptance and hope guided by faith, embodied by the Prophet, Sonya and Alyosha Karamazov – are illustrated by the various scenes enacted in the film by the characters. Raskolnikov's dream about the killing evokes, as Randal Johnson observes, the style of German Expressionism, with distorting optical solutions and a hallucinatory (uncanny) doubling of the character, while the meeting between Alyosha and Ivan, 'supervised' by the doctor, opposes two confessions of faith, the former's devotion and the latter's stubborn, 'I don't understand and don't want to understand,' both presented in frontal shots. The presence of the doctor reinforces the 'house as personality' metaphor, by establishing an analogy with the superego, that observes and interprets the ongoing psychological processes manifest as dreams, monologues and play. The personal, autobiographical character of this figurative representation is emphasized by Oliveira's acting the role of the doctor in the meeting scene between Alyosha and Ivan, replacing Ruy Furtado, who fell ill before the completion of the shooting. The film director's appearance – probably the longest in his career – in his own film as the director of the asylum, as a modernist, self-reflexive trope thematizes the filmmaker's role as a Master who orchestrates the heterogeneity of characters, ideas and methods, real and imaginary elements. His confession made during his reconciliating conversation with the Karamazovs (If God exists, there is only one of him, so there is no reason to argue) strikes us as a desperate one, closer to that of Ivan than to that of Alyosha: 'I don't believe in God, nor in men.'

The discourse of hope is represented by the re-enactment of the miraculous resurrection of Lazarus and the allusion to another one, in Ivan's poem, that of a little girl. The first appears at the beginning of the film, as a parody of the

Profanations 89

inconceivable mystery of the miracle: one of the residents lies down in a coffin, the respective text from the New Testament is read by Raskolnikov and Sonya utters the sentence, 'I am the resurrection and the life.' The others gather around the coffin, the resident playing Jesus has a speech that includes the sentence, 'happy are those poor in spirit as heaven is theirs', and after the presentation of two more biblical scenes (Jesus teaching about prostitutes and thieves), Lazarus takes the coffin and leaves.

Besides these two contrasting attitudes about religion, faith and death, there is another central line of ideas in this film, persistent in the entire work of Oliveira: the one revolving around the woman as mystery. The many aspects of the same feminine principle – sensual, seducing, angel or saint – are all present in the female characters played by Leonor Silveira and Maria de Medeiros. This puzzling duplicity of the feminine, instigating the male protagonists to irrational, Don Quixote-like actions, appears in many other films of Oliveira, becoming central, for example in *Abraham's Valley*, *The Uncertainty Principle* and *Magic Mirror*, all featuring Oliveira's fetish-actress, Leonor Silveira, as main protagonist. Moreover, all three films thematize the aspiration towards an ideal (family, happiness, femininity), considered sacred by religious norms, but turned into a series of parodic imitations by a bourgeoisie stuck in a web of exhausted social formalities.

Imitations of life: *The Uncertainty Principle* and *Magic Mirror*

Feminine mystery is often conceived by Oliveira as a duality between the saint and the worldly, the Virgin and the cocotte or promiscuous woman. In a most prominent example, Ema from *Abraham's Valley* oscillates between the roles of a middle-class wife and mother who attends Mass regularly, and that of a luxury prostitute. In a bold gesture of profanation, she exchanges the family altar, a triptych, for a similar mirror, in which she constantly contemplates her narcissistic self. Sacred and worldly images of the woman are conflicted since *Doomed Love*, where Teresa, the female protagonist, obeys her father's wish to go to a convent instead of fighting for her love. When her father communicates his decision, she appears in a blue veil, a common attribute of the Virgin Mary's iconography. Similarly, as an example of chivalresque courtship, her lover Simão's emotions are fuelled by the unattainability of their object. The same mechanism appears in *Francisca* (in which the virginity of the female character becomes a central question for her husband) and in *Benilde or the Virgin Mother*. This latter is a re-enactment of the biblical narrative of the immaculate conception, the reiteration of questions related to miracle and the 'sacralization' of the female body, as well as the story of the sacred family, about a man marrying a woman who became pregnant under miraculous circumstances.

The Holy Family is the ideal towards which the protagonists of *The Uncertainty Principle* also aspire. In a recurrent scene, we see Celsa (Isabel Ruth), the maid of the Clara family, praying in front of a painting of the Virgin with the Child. She does everything in order to preserve the domestic equilibrium around her: as we find out, she had exchanged one of her sons with the stillborn baby of Rutinha (Cecília Guimarães), her employer, in order to save her from too much pain. She is also responsible for the marriage between her son, António, raised 'upstairs' by the wealthy Clara family, and Camila (Leonor Baldaque), even though she knows about the romance between the latter and her other son, José Luciano, raised by herself. Camila, whose father went bankrupt due to his passion for gambling, makes the sacrifice of a marriage of convenience in order to save her family. At first, she appears as an innocent girl with religious inclinations, emphasized by her mysterious visits to the old chapel (one of them is the opening scene of the film). The door of the chapel remains closed until the last scene. She is also shown in *tableaux vivants*, enacting the role of the Virgin with the Child, that alludes to the painting in front of which Celsa regularly prays, as well as to the baroque iconography in red and blue of the topic (Figures 5.1–5.2).

Although Camila shows indifference at Vanessa's intrigues (the mistress of her husband and business partner of Luciano, played by Leonor Silveira), she gradually develops an ambivalent behaviour, as if, as Randal Johnson argues, she would internalize the dark side of the feminine, represented by the cynical

Figures 5.1–5.2 Painterly references to a religious family ideal and values in *The Uncertainty Principle*.

Vanessa.[2] The interactions between the two women clearly show the characteristics of a fight for dominance over men, where Camila's apparent passivity and goodness facing open attacks subverts a narrative based on causality and the good–bad conflict, thus undermines the spectator's solid position in taking sides and drawing conclusions. In this respect, the title also reflects upon this destabilized spectatorship, facing a narrative where nothing is what it seems to be. Johnson considers this an illustration of Heisenberg's uncertainty principle, meaning, 'The more precisely the position is determined, the less precisely the momentum is known in this instant, and vice versa,' without, however, further elaborating on the meaning of this sentence or applying it more closely to the film under analysis (Johnson 2006, 23). In addition to the already mentioned spectatorial position, constantly challenged to revise presuppositions, I find that this principle also characterizes the upper middle-class, with an apparently well-determined position in society, secured by appearances, but constantly menaced by the revelation of well-kept secrets and lies.

Based on Bessa-Luís's novel, *O Princípio da Incerteza: Jóia de Família* (*The Uncertainty Principle: Family Jewel*, 2002), the film exposes in a paradigmatic way a recurrent narrative strategy of Oliveira, namely blurring the lines between truth and appearances, between *what is* and *what is seen*. Social class critique and artistic ingeniosity instigating to look for details, hidden signs and connections overlap. Stylistically, the posing of characters (that of a femme fatale or an innocent girl) represent this duplicity. Camila herself confesses that she is no good, only well mannered, which reveals another middle-class constraint: 'I don't hurt anyone, it's a question of discipline, like covering your mouth when you yawn.' The central figure of the psychological mechanism of concealing secrets and taboos is the chapel that opens to us in the final scene, as part of a delaying narrative strategy. We find out that it was a cobwebbed statue of Jeanne d'Arc that Camila (now left alone, as a sole heir to her husband's fortune) was praying to regularly during her fight for independence and – as we get to know by now – power. But the Virgin of Orléans is not a simple guardian angel for Camila: she rather identifies with her (there are a number of instances in the film comparing her to Jeanne d'Arc) in an evident demonstration of a disproportionate vanity, somehow reminding of Ema's constant looking into the mirror in *Abraham's Valley*.

---

[2] Johnson also refers to António Cabrita's Camila/Eve, Vanessa/Lilith opposition (2006, 123).

92   *The Cinema of Manoel de Oliveira*

The 'vanity fair' recurrent in Oliveira's films about the upper middle-class[3] goes hand in hand with the self-deceptive illusion (or delusion) of both male and female characters. The representation of these desired images (of the self, of a supernatural entity) is a difficult task that all artists are confronted with. As Agamben puts it in his *Profanations*:

> To communicate one's desires to someone without images is brutal. To communicate one's images without one's desires is tedious (like recounting one's dreams or one's travels). But both of these are easy to do. To communicate the imagined desires and the desired images, on the other hand, is a more difficult task.

> Agamben 2007, 53–4

As we have seen in *The Uncertainty Principle*, Oliveira communicates Camila's desire through concealment and delay, as a hidden aspiration towards an ideal that makes her behaviour ambivalent in the eyes of other characters. The issue of Camila's character is reiterated in the continuation of this film, *Magic Mirror*, an adaptation of Bessa-Luís's novel, *A Alma dos Ricos* (*The Soul of the Rich*, 2005): Luciano, imprisoned at the end of *The Uncertainty Principle* as a suspect in the murder of António (Camila's husband), is now released, but not before being profoundly disturbed by accusations calling Camila 'a pervert'. He is struggling to prove that Camila is a saint by revealing miraculous events that happened with her and describes the hypnotic effect that she had on everybody since her childhood. He is not denying his strong attraction to her, but he becomes visibly anxious when he discovers the uncanny excesses in Camila's behaviour: the familiar is recontextualized as unfamiliar, demonic. In this respect, Camila's character is comparable to that of young Ema from *Abraham's Valley*, the simple appearance of whom caused accidents on the street. This bitter revelation explains Luciano's new reverence for another woman, Dona Alfreda, obsessed with an ideal, the Virgin Mary, whom she hopes to meet one day.

After being released, the brother of Luciano finds him a workplace at a wealthy house, where he becomes the servant of the childless Alfreda, engaged in constant philosophical and theological discussions with priests and scientists about the possibility of her desire coming true. In the film, the mirror becomes a central trope in the visual communication of this delusionary longing: Oliveira is playing trompe l'oeil games with the spectator by repeatedly showing the

---

[3] Johnson gathers a series of films under the title of 'Bonfire of Vanities' (2006, 62–94).

reflection in the mirror first, and then revealing the scene itself, thus emphasizing the perception of reality by the female protagonist (played by Leonor Silveira) as a double, a mere reflection of the ideal. This is epitomized in a series of scenes, in the dialogue between her and her sister, the scenes of her deathbed (where she is shown doubled for a moment) and the final images, reflections in a mirror, of the murals with a biblical theme of the Venetian Saint Marc Palace. The lake in which Mme Alfreda regularly swims is also perceived as a mirror of mysterious apparitions, paired with voices that cannot be distinguished from the voice of Luciano calling her during this rêverie. As Alfreda herself formulates, the mirror is a reflection of time, and this effect can be healed only by the visit of the Virgin. Only this would restore the sacred in the profane, the boring everyday life of the rich.

Repetitions and long, tedious monologues and dialogues have an unnerving effect on the spectator. The story of the previous film, *The Uncertainty Principle*, is summarized in the opening scene in the prison, then the events that happened between the actions of the two films are revealed by Celsa, who visits the tomb of her son, António. At the castle, visitors are repeatedly debating the same theological ideas – until something unexpected occurs. A forger (played by Miguel Cintra) proposes to Luciano to stage the miraculous meeting of Senhora Alfreda with the Virgin. According to David Bordwell (who confesses to like about a half of Oliveira's films), this gesture of profanation saves this particular film for spectators, 'restoring the faith in cinema and audiences': from this moment on, 'things get stranger and more elliptical', producing the uncanny effect that binds spectators to their seats. Without this effect, this film would just be a visually accomplished work, in which 'the etched, enamelled images make every texture pop out at you', as Bordwell warns (Bordwell 2006). Intriguingly, the role of the fake Virgin Mary is enacted (for money) by the same Leonor Baldaque playing the role of Camila in *The Uncertainty Principle*, creating a double that communicates in a reflective way with the previous saint image. If that was a pose, a well-controlled behaviour, this is a constructed, manipulated image of the same feminine ideal (Figures 5.3–5.4). This time, the forger Senhor Filipe and the fake Virgin Mary become a couple at the end of the film, following the death of Alfreda. Filipe tells her the unfinished love story between Luciano and Camila, revealing another duplicity: Camila married a lawyer who looks much like Luciano.

Compulsive repetitions of the same story point at 'unfinished businesses', the source of psychopathological problems embodied by Oliveira's

 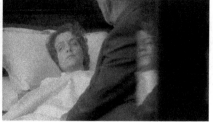

Figures 5.3–5.4 Multiple mirrors as figure of delusion and the forgery serving it in *Magic Mirror*.

upper-middle-class characters: delusions, narcissism, depression and paranoia. Luciano's faith is not restored at the end of the film, he is alone again, back to the beginning, with another memory of an ambivalent relationship, another unfinished business with Mme Alfreda, who apparently loved him pretty much (according to Filipe), but whom he could not save or help, in an uncanny repetition of the story with Camila. His relationship to women is thus similar to that of other male romantics in Oliveira's work, for example *Doomed Love, Francisca, Benilde, Abraham's Valley, Eccentricities of a Blonde-Haired Girl* or *Angélica*: a distant, cavalieresque and ultimately helpless reverence.

The stubborn return to the same type of romantic relationship and woman (an eternal Dulcinea), although put in different cultural (philosophical, religious) contexts and iconographies, points at Oliveira's own unfinished business with the eternal feminine, his own anima. Accomplished in his male roles both in his private life (a patriarch of a big family, with many children and grandchildren) as well as professionally, this may reveal a well-hidden fragility that cannot be said, only shown and figurated. The urge of sublimation adds a new dimension to the various ways of search for identity through repetition, nostalgic and melancholic return and profanation, meant to identify and legitimize the unique, the personal and national in a global, transnational, intercultural context. While the modes of imitation discussed so far were meant to place Portugal on the map of the world, there remains another strategy of personal, national identity quest through repetition and imitation: cultural mimicry as both aspiration to the centre (of the European Community) and for an affirmation of Portuguese's own 'otherness'.

6

Cultural mimicry

Co-productions, collaborations: The French connection

In the work of Oliveira, the insider's point of view of their own cultural position, represented by repetitions, re-enactments of Portuguese historical events or universal (Christian, philosophical) topoi, is often conflicted with an 'adopted' external position examining own 'Portugueseness' through the lens of another culture. I argue that Oliveira's extensive French connections (represented by friends, constant collaborators, actors, producers) add to his cinema a 'double vision' that can be described with Homi Bhabha's term of cultural mimicry. This is defined by Bhabha, relying on Freud and Lacan, as a camouflage, a form of resemblance with a cultural (monumental) model, that becomes, however, 'a discourse between the lines', a desire that reveals so little but makes a big difference (Bhabha 1994, 89). As Bhabha points out, the final irony of the partial representation called 'mimicry' is that it serves the intention to appear as authentic. The little difference, the own detail called 'the metonymy of presence', discloses the ambivalence of the discourse, mocks the power of the monumental model and thus subverts its authority (ibid., 88). As such, mimicry is one of the figures of farce, besides trompe l'oeil, irony and repetition. This tendency can be identified in Oliveira's adaptations of French literature, but also in other references to classics of European literature, like the works of Dostoevsky in *A Divina Comedia* or Goethe's *Faust* in *The Convent*.

This latter also presents an external point of view, a colonial gaze attracted by the exoticism of the South: the English couple arrives to a remote monastery in Portugal to prove the Portuguese origin of Shakespeare, the emblematic figure of the British cultural supremacy. This intention to 'legitimize' Portugal as a worthy member of the European Community is comparable with that presented in *Cristopher Columbus*, only that here it appears as an *external recognition* of Portugal as a source of cultural values, turned later, in the other film, into a

96   *The Cinema of Manoel de Oliveira*

nostalgic, idealistic, windmill effort of an 'insider'. Both members of the couple (played by John Malkovich and Catherine Deneuve) are mesmerized by their Portuguese hosts, and the film becomes a farce, loosely repeating the topic of *Faust* – the Doctor falling in love with the candid librarian of the convent and his wife is sensually attracted by Baltar, the devilish administrator. Finally, they disappear 'without a trace', in a disruptive closure that mocks both the models of Western culture and its efforts to reconnect with its alienated members, its own 'others'. Once again, the familiar cultural topos of Faust is being subverted by an unfamiliar artistic perspective, resulting in an uncanny effect.

In the light of this line of thought, all international collaborations of Oliveira can be regarded as participating in this double – external and internal, respectful and subversive – vision of own cultural, national identity. These collaborations, organic parts of the artistic creation, have started with the Paulo Branco era in Oliveira's work, opening it, through the presence of star actors like Catherine Deneuve, Marcello Mastroianni, Michel Piccoli or John Malkovich, to an international audience. As Pedro Maciel Guimarães points out, their presence also attracts a special characterization of the actors related to their origin, their previous roles, native tongue, their way to speak (or not to speak) French, Portuguese or other languages (the case of John Malkovich), in comparison with Oliveira's Portuguese actors (first of all, Leonor Silveira and Miguel Cintra; Guimarães, 2010, 101). The production of an 'accented cinema' – characterized by either an exaggerated imitation, a too neat, academic use of French or, on the contrary, a propagation of own language through an accented speech (the case of Mastroianni, Cardinale, Malkovich) is yet another signifier of the colonial mimicry.

In the oeuvre of Oliveira, the wish to reveal differences of nuance coexists with a tendency to dissolve cultural borders and a creation of a new image of a director 'bigger than the country', according to César Monteiro (1996, 37). This image was constructed by international, mostly French co-productions that enabled a local and a transnational approach to cultural production and identity. The directorial vision of Oliveira is strongly marked by the French influence and arthouse-cinema trends in terms of visual figuration and acting. All his above mentioned (some of them recurrent) actors bring with them their acting persona that consecrated them in memorable films of the European cinematic modernism and the French New Wave. In this respect, Oliveira's collaboration with Paulo Branco is crucial in the director's cultural mimicry. Although Guimarães does not consider this cooperation as closely belonging to the artistic creation (2010, 74–5), I argue that its role in the mediation between an original authorial vision and a certain European arthouse cinema is very important. This argument is supported by an undeniable similarity with the visual styles of other directors coming from a geopolitically liminal position, who worked with Branco – the Lithuanian Sharunas Bartas and the Chilean Raúl Ruíz, for example – and who also found their way to a highly intermedial trend in European cinema with painterly stylization, a preference for tableau-like images and *tableaux vivants*.

As I argue in Part One of this book, Oliveira, just like the other two authors, share the tradition of the late cinematic modernism, greatly relying on an intermedial visual language represented by Jean-Luc Godard, Derek Jarman and Peter Greenaway. The French-Portuguese co-productions of Oliveira appear, in fact, as heterotopias, defined by Michel Foucault as 'places in-between', where different cultural discourses are reconciled and intermediality becomes a figuration of intercultural translation.[1] Co-productions as heterotopias are also reflecting, sometimes in a distorting or exaggerated way, the intercultural relationships they involve: cultural differences, language issues, as well as relationships of economic dependence, supremacy or subordination. These issues are often thematized in the films themselves, casting Portuguese and non-Portuguese (French, Italian, Greek, American, etc.) actors playing characters involved in intercultural misunderstandings, miscommunications or attractions (for example, *The Convent*, *The Letter*, *Voyage to the Beginning of the World*, *I'm Going Home* [*Je rentre à la maison*, 2001], *A Talking Picture*). Moreover, as Guimarães observes, these international actors are at times playing with their own star image (Malkovich and Deneuve in *The Convent* and *A Talking Picture*, for example), not to mention the self-reflexive reference to the participants of the filming/staging process in *I'm Going Home* (2001) and *Voyage to the Beginning of the World* (with Michel Piccoli and Marcello Mastroianni, acting, respectively, as alter egos of Oliveira; Guimarães 2010: 125).

The visual sophistication of films made together with Branco, but even those made after the conclusion of their collaboration, are typically fulfilling the expectations of film festival audiences by connecting to a wider European artistic or Christian heritage, thus imposing on himself a 'self-colonizing gaze'. A key figure of the mediation between the own and French culture is Jacques Parsi, Oliveira's adviser in all his French co-productions, who authored a monograph on him (2002), conducted numerous interviews (Parsi and de Baecque 1996),

---

[1] See Ewa Mazierska's essay on cinematic co-productions as heterotopias (2012, 483–503), based on Michel Foucault's concept from, 'Of Other Places' (1986).

98   *The Cinema of Manoel de Oliveira*

supervised the diction of his non-French actors, translated scripts, functioned as the French interlocutor of the director, and was all in all significantly responsible for the creation of the director's external image and of his self-othering/ colonizing gaze.[2] While apparently making his persona accessible for the international, larger audience, Parsi also contributed to its mystification and exoticism (by presenting it with sheer admiration as a distant, secretive phenomenon that has to be interpreted). He also acted as an agent of the French culture when providing readings, interpretations and synopses of French literary works in the adaptation process, thus imposing, to a certain extent, his own point of view, later adopted, in a rather carnivalesque gesture of appropriation and subversion, by Oliveira.

French literary adoptions

The colonial mimicry is also present in another aspect of Oliveira's French connection, the adaptations of few literary classics, Paul Claudel's *The Satin Slipper* (*Le Soulier de satin*), Gustave Flaubert's *Madame Bovary* and Madame de La Fayette's, *The Princesse de Clèves (La Princesse de Clèves)*. These adaptations, often analysed by critics as reflections of the local Portuguese in the European or global and the other way around, offer themselves easily to Homi Bhabha's definition of cultural mimicry defined as a desire for a reformed, recognizable Other that is 'almost the same but not quite (not white)'. As Bhabha argues, turning the 'high ideals' to low literary effects is the most elusive and effective mimetic strategy, that ensures the transformation of the colonial man from an object of regulatory power into the subject of racial, cultural and national representation (1994, 91). In the case of Oliveira, however, this subversive gesture revealing the own through imitation does not consist of 'low literary' effects (Bhabha does not explain this term either), but rather of an uncanny effect resulting from excess, image–word discrepancy, interruptions and repetitions.

As the next section of this book will be concerned in more detail with Oliveira's 'disturbing adaptations', in this chapter I am focusing only on the discourse of a 'colonial man' hidden 'between the lines' of imitations of French literary models. While the attitude of Oliveira (representing a nation of former colonial rulers) towards the colonial past of Portugal is both nostalgic and critical, his relationship with his French literary texts (from the point of view of

---

[2] On the many roles of Parsi in the cinema of Oliveira, see Guimarães (2010, 340).

Cultural Mimicry

99

a culturally 'colonized' subject) reflects a similar duality of idealization and subversion. The two attitudes coexist in his monumental adaptation of *The Satin Slipper* (1985), of a length of about seven hours: praised for its fidelity to its pre-text by Paul Claudel, it is exactly this excessive fidelity (its literalness) that makes it subversive. More than an adaptation, a technical transfer of the narration into another medium, it is rather an *adoption* of the literary text to Oliveira's own authorial discourse on Portuguese national identity, that will become, as we have seen, a recurrent issue in films following *The Satin Slipper*. As Randal Johnson observes, this adaptation, taking cinematic narrative to its very limits, mediates between two major preoccupations in the cinema of Oliveira: the topic of frustrated loves and that of the colonial past and its consequences (Johnson 2006, 44). Being made at the moment of Portugal's adherence to the European Community, this film can also be read as a symbolic work, marking the beginning of Oliveira's preoccupation with the place of Portugal in this organization (cf. Guimarães 2010, 383).

The Satin Slipper is about an unfulfilled love story in a colonial context between Donna Prouhèze (Patricia Barzyk) and Rodrigue (Luís Miguel Cintra), who stay apart (also geopolitically) even after they have a chance of a life together after the death of Prouhèze's husband. Beyond the allegorical reflection of Big History in the private life of the couple, the topic of excessive fidelity (retaken in *The Letter*) metaphorically doubles that of the film to the play of Claudel, or even more, that of cinema to theatre. As this film epitomizes, despite their fatal attraction and proximity in terms of representation, the fusion between film and theatre is never complete: by pushing the theatre–cinema interaction to its limits (with static, tableau-like scenes, frontal monologues, studio décors and lighting), Oliveira aimed to mobilize the spectator, to force him to take an active attitude, different from the one prescribed by Claudel's play. The imperialist and Catholic grandeur of this latter is broken down to private monologues and dialogues reflecting, between the lines, the defeated history of European imperial aspirations against the Islamic world. Preserving carefully the structure and most of the dialogues from the original text, Oliveira subverts it from the interior, in a Don Quixote determination to adapt – he, a Portuguese director – a play considered 'inadaptable' by French filmmakers. Finally, in a symbolic gesture of appropriation/adoption, he framed the whole, faithfully rendered story in a self-reflexive revelation of the theatrical and cinematic dispositive, his own authorial signature.

Despite the uproar of the Portuguese public caused by *The Satin Slipper*, with Oliveira being accused of 'propagating' French culture with Portuguese funds, a few years later the director embarked on another mission impossible, that is, the adaptation of the French literary classic, Flaubert's *Madame Bovary*. He was not completely dissuaded by the fact that Claude Chabrol's adaptation of the same novel, with Isabelle Huppert in the leading role, was due in the same period of time. With another Don Quixote move, instead of giving up, he chose not to adapt Flaubert's text, but to *adopt* it, make it a Portuguese story, that is, to appropriate it through Agustina Bessa-Luís's original screenplay based on the homonymous novel, *Abraham's Valley*. As I will argue in the next section focusing on Oliveira's 'irregular' adaptations, in a close analysis of this film, Flaubert's novel is one of those literary works that are impossible to adapt, exactly (and paradoxically) due to their visuality and proto-cinematic effects. The numerous descriptions of tableau-like or film-like scenes, of the act of looking, of colours and lights, can work as a trap of the 'too easy' for the cinematographer who is tempted to translate all this into visual effects. But instead of opting for a servile imitation, Oliveira rather adopts Flaubert's authorial attitude towards a literary genre or text: while Flaubert deconstructs the literary trend of romances, Oliveira thematizes Flaubert's novel as an intertextual quotation, as a pre-text responsible for Ema's image as 'the little Bovary' (a Bovarinha), a kind of copycat of Flaubert's heroine. Ema is reading a Portuguese translation of Flaubert's novel (Figure 6.1), which contributes, just like the romances read by Emma in Flaubert's novel, to her fall.

Figure 6.1 Presentation of the act of reading as revelation of the French influence in *Abraham's Valley*.

Cultural Mimicry 101

Other aspects of colonial mimicry in *Abraham's Valley* include narrative and stylistic differences and thematic slippages that reflect subversively not only on the original literary work, but on all its 'faithful' adaptations as well. First of all, Oliveira's film is neither a costume drama, nor a heritage film that would, with a mannerist excess, attempt to reconstruct the figurative style of the literary work and establish connections with the contemporary spectator. Costumes, interiors and cars used in Oliveira's film are not representative of a certain period of time, a detail that reinforces the moralizing, generalizing undertones of its narration. Narration in this film is, however, the biggest authorial invention: as Guimarães very aptly points out in his book, the voice-over and *voice-in* interaction, as well as the effect of this interaction on the images of the film represent its most original aspect. Oliveira puts Mário Barroso in charge for both the photography of his film and the voice-over narration, and in this way models the authorial function that André Gaudreault calls, 'le grand monstrateur/imagier'.[3] The voice-over actually manipulates the image, regulates it, makes it move or freeze, interrupts the voice-in, reflects on the prescriptive power of the words of the literary text in cinematic adaptations, on the role of the omniscient narrator, but also on the crippling effect that an impersonal, external discourse of societal norms and attitudes has on the individual. The slippage occurs, for example, in the creation of the figure of the female protagonist: Ema Paiva has a limp (in Flaubert's novel, the pharmacy assistant had a clubfoot), in this sense she is both less (the one 'm' in her name might be a signifier of the one leg), and more than Emma Bovary (she is different, the limp makes her sensual, special in the eyes of her lovers).

The same attitude of adoption is retaken in Oliveira's third French adaptation, *The Letter* (1999), from Madame de La Fayette's, *The Princesse de Clèves*. In this film, based on another story about an unrealized love affair, set in contemporary locations, Oliveira performs the subversive gesture of the colonial subject towards an idealized cultural model primarily by casting Pedro Abrunhosa, the Portuguese pop star in the role of the seductive Duc of Nemours. According to Guimarães, this choice might be explained by the lyrical content of Abrunhosa's music, but I find more plausible Oliveira's explanation that by choosing Abrunhosa instead of Leonardo di Caprio, he actually wanted to stage the attraction of the contraries.[4] Indeed, Abrunhosa's noisy intrusion into this adaptation (with concert screenings) serves as a metaphor of the popular–classic opposition. The

---

[3] About this, see Guimarães' chapter on this film (2010, 404–22).
[4] See ibid. (106), and his chapter dedicated to this film (358–61).

platonic love story between the non-professional actor and singer's gangster style (black sunglasses, black suit and a hat) and the marble statue-like, aristocratic figure of Madame de Clèves (played by Chiara Mastroianni, descendant of emblematic actors of the European arthouse cinema, Catherine Deneuve and Marcello Mastroianni), is also about the incompatibility between cultures, social classes, past and present, words (the song lyrics) and images (of the expressionless beauty) and, ultimately, literature and film. The section on Oliveira's adaptations will contain a separate chapter concerned with the representation of the letter-writing and reading scene and the next chapter will focus on intermedial figurations of the cultural dialogue. Regarding the adaptation of Madame de La Fayette's novel, it is sufficient to pinpoint here Oliveira's double vision – subversive with regards to one of the most powerful cultural influences in Europe, and self-ironical at the same time, when confronting Portuguese song lyrics to a formal (spoken) French preserving the traces of the original novel, in a remarkable example of colonial mimicry.

Intermedial figurations of interculturality

In the films of Oliveira, one often comes across the manifold roles of intermedial references, ranging from narrative and poetical to more sophisticated, philosophical, ideological or discursive ones. These mainly pictorial or sculptural references to either individual, recognizable works of art or a certain visual art (painting, photograph, sculpture) as system (colours, lighting effects, composition, style), besides their immediate figurative role in the respective narrative, tend to function as separate, autonomous discourses of the artistic creation and often the sociopolitical context of the film in question. As such, they often appear as an excess to reality, revealing something that cannot be said or narrated, only shown, disturbing the narrative with their figurative load.

Intermedial references in Oliveira's work can often be evaluated as related to the same sense of liminality and aspiration towards a Western European cultural and spiritual centre. Beyond a series of films that are dealing directly with the place of Portugal in the world, discussed above, many films of Oliveira are treating intermediality as figuration of intercultural exchange and a reflection on that very exchange. In this respect, Ágnes Pethő's remark about the intercultural signification of art references is applicable to Oliveira's use of visual art references:

these films manage to dissolve the cultural boundaries between East and West through connecting to particular, universally known references to Western art, as well as through their affinity with more widespread trends in arthouse cinema (while sometimes maintaining their distinctively local, historical reference frames), thus operating a new, complex system of 'liminalities'.

2014, 64

Art references as strategies epitomizing the colonial mimicry of the Other Europe often have the role of reflecting metaphorically on the story and its moral background: for example, in *The Letter*, the group of statues in the public garden where the two protagonists go, without, however, meeting or speaking, seem to concentrate the story of a love triangle marked by social and moral pressures (Figures 6.2–6.3). This work of art is retrospectively a metaphor of the recurrent topic of frustrated love in Oliveira's cinema, placed, at the same time, in a universal context and a French literary tradition.

In a subsequent shot, we see Portuguese pop star Pedro Abrunhosa playing the role of the admirer of Mme de Clèves, framed by, or rather embedded, in the same statue (Figures 6.4–6.5). Besides reflecting on Abrunhosa's expressionless

Figures 6.2–6.3 The group of statues in the Parisian park as representation of the melodramatic situation of the novel.

Figures 6.4–6.5 Pop star Pedro Abrunhosa framed by a statue representing the core dramatic situation in *The Letter*.

posing throughout the film, rigid and motionless like a statue, a parody of a pop-star image, this décadrage singles out the irony in Oliveira's adaptation, by creating a series of slippages between past and present, classic art and pop culture, French and Portuguese culture, colonizer and colonized. The 'intrusion' of a Portuguese element in a French composition on the one hand localizes and actualizes the universal story, while on the other it ironically destabilizes, confronting it with the cultural hegemony represented by the work of art. Abrunhosa shortly poses like a statue, but does not let himself be 'framed' by a 'high' cultural pattern: he continues his walk in the garden. In this film, the topic of frustrated love unfolds in an intercultural context, reflecting upon an uneven cultural relationship, an inconsolable yearning for the aristocratic beauty of the colonizer.

A similar role of statues can be identified in *The Uncertainty Principle*, where the symmetrically set, classical-style statues have a series of figurative roles: they are meant to reflect on the topic of the scene, emphasizing, at the same time, the director's objectifying vision of characters, reminiscent of Bresson's model theory that strongly influenced modernist cinema. The juxtaposition of antique, Greco-Roman-style statues with the motionless bodies reflects on the film's position between the eternal values of classic art and the contingency of the moving image, opposing an antique, classic culture and a local, Portuguese story, while also bringing together and erasing the difference between the animate and inanimate (Figures 6.6–6.7).

As already analysed above, in *The Uncertainty Principle*, a film about an arranged marriage in a morally ambivalent middle-class milieu, a recurring painting about the Virgin and the Child, representative of Western Christianity, is referred to in a *tableau vivant* showing the protagonist with a baby. This scene remains a mere imitation, an imperfect version of the paradigmatic image of

Figures 6.6–6.7 Statues emphasizing the animate–inanimate, eternal–contingent (values) opposition in *The Uncertainty Principle*.

Christian motherhood, opposing the moral uncertainty to absolute faith and a purely formal, staged Catholicism to its ideal.

Tableau-like compositions alluding to specific paintings represent another opportunity for Oliveira to connect with Western European, especially French, painterly tradition. His intermedial references to the French Impressionism are striking examples of the colonial mimicry: the differences, the excesses and gaps open these images towards metanarrative discourses on cinema and modernity, the issue of the gaze and the fourth wall, the stillness–movement dichotomy and the death drive of the narrative. This is the case of the intermedial reference to the painterly genre of so-called 'beautiful horizontals' in *The Strange Case of Angélica*, recalling, among others, Renoir's painting of Mme Monet that can be found in the Gulbenkian Museum in Lisbon. Beyond the gesture of appropriation through remediation and modification, Oliveira uses this reference to elaborate on the ontology of cinema, its affinities with painting and photography, exposing, at the same time, his personal approach to death.

Similarly, the reference to Édouard Manet's *Déjeuner sur l'herbe* (1863, itself a reference to a Titian painting) in *Anxiety* (*Inquietude*, 1998) without the Nude that generated controversies at the time of its exhibition, adopts the subversive attitude of the Impressionist painter in at least two respects: it refuses to represent characters or use colours and perspective in a traditional way and cuts brusquely to a plain air scene from a studio setting. But with these deliberate modifications, Oliveira also personalizes the remediated image: he omits the second female figure, and thus transforms it into an image modelling the love triangle of his many stories of frustrated relationships (Figures 6.8–6.9). Once again, the tableau offers, on the one hand, a blueprint of the big picture, an important

Figures 6.8–6.9 Adopting, through a painterly reference, a subversive artistic attitude in *Anxiety*.

chapter of European cultural tradition, before, on the other hand, cutting back to the individual story.

As already discussed in the previous chapters, interculturality, transnationality, Europeanness and the French cultural connection are overtly thematized in *Voyage to the Beginning of the World*. In this self-reflexive and autobiographical film presenting the travel both in space and time of an international crew of a Portuguese-French film co-production, the discussions unfolding in French are amounting to a nostalgic discourse about a united Europe, where the Balkans, a Sarajevo torn apart by civil wars also belongs to, and where racial, language and religious differences do not count. The founding principle of the world for Oliveira is the one formulated in the memorable scene of the meeting between the French actor and his relatives at the end of the world, in a remote Portuguese village where time has stopped. This scene is framed as a tableau with a chiaroscuro effect reminiscent of the works of seventeeth-century paintings by masters such as Caravaggio or Georges de la Tour, but also Dutch painters (Figures 6.10–6.11).

The same stylistic effect is repeated in the scene shot in the dark, cave-like hut, only lit by the fire, where the welcoming ceremony with the ritual handing over of the bread takes place. Obscurity, the use of natural lights, the chiaroscuro effect is common in Oliveira's films. Writing about the specificities of the Oliveirian image, Guimarães refers to the memories of Renato Berta, his photographer, about the director complaining about 'too much light' during the filming of *The Uncertainty Principle* (2010, 270). Guimarães also considers the obscurity of the image a speciality of Portuguese cinema, explained by the directors themselves as an advantage of liminality: far from the mainstream cinema, they don't need to conform with its standards and regulations (ibid., 269–70). Paradoxically, by assuming their liminality, Portuguese directors,

Figures 6.10–6.11 The chiaroscuro effect as figure of 'the moment of truth' in *Voyage to the Beginning of the World*.

including Oliveira, are reconnecting with another artistic practice, the use of chiaroscuro in painting. Traditionally, this effect, achieved by lighting with a candle or a fireplace in a dark interior, had the symbolic role to reveal something, to unmask somebody, to 'shed light' upon the represented scene. This is the case of de la Tour's paintings (*The Dice Players*, 1650–1, for example), or Caravaggio's *Supper at Emmaus* (1601), the composition of which haunts in the above mentioned scene of encounter from *Voyage*. Caravaggio's painting about the failure to recognize Jesus, followed by revelation, is restaged in this scene: the aunt does not recognize the nephew until a fundamental truth (the principle of the world) is formulated: language is not important, only origin and identity counts. In this scene, Western art reference emphasizes local, Portuguese social issues related to the effects of migration on families and communities.

The same figurative role of the chiaroscuro effect appears in the last long feature *Gebo and the Shadow* (*O Gebo e a Sombra*, 2012, based on a play by Raul Brandão, featuring, besides Oliveira's 'regulars' Miguel Cintra, Leonor Silveira and António Trêpa, Jeanne Moreau and Claudia Cardinale), in which the long conversations about the whereabouts of a prodigal son, his concealed feelings and thoughts, as well as the truth regarding the missing money, are performed around a table lit by a single oil lamp (Figures 6.12). Without aiming at faithful imitations of specific paintings, through these references Oliveira's films model another journey, too: that of the film to its own origins, painting and theatre.[5]

Figure 6.12 The chiaroscuro effect as figure of the quest for the truth in *Gebo and the Shadow*.

[5] On Oliveira's painterly framings, see Ruy Gardnier's inteview with the director (2006, 156).

108 *The Cinema of Manoel de Oliveira*

Allusions to paradigmatic works of European art (both literary and visual) in the films of Oliveira can be either regarded as parts of allegorical discourses about endangered European values or as a self-colonizing vision that serves the reconnection with European cultural tradition and its literary, mythical, biblical or historical narratives. This latter standpoint, comparable to the mimicry of the colonized described by Homi Bhabha, is subversive, as it makes visible the individual and the local in the gaps, excesses and slippages of the re-mediations and appropriations of texts, paintings or statues. The very local, battered statue of Pedro Macao in *Voyage to the Beginning of the World*, that had changed place but is still holding its beam, also reflects on the burdening task assumed by Oliveira. This task consists of moving and translating between cultures in a quest for national and individual identity, inspired, as his last film, *The Old Man of Belém*, summarizes, by two emblematic figures of the European culture: Camões and Don Quixote.

References

Agamben, Giorgio. 1993. *Stanzas: Word and Phantasm in Western Culture*. Trans. Ronald L. Martinez. Minneapolis, MN: University of Minnesota Press.

Agamben, Giorgio. 2007. 'Parody'. In *Profanations*, 37–52. New York: Zone Books.

Alvarez, José Mauricio Saldanha. 2008. '*O 'Non' de Manoel de Oliveira: Uma Fábula Cinematográfica*'. In *Aspectos do Cinema Portugues*, eds Jorge Cruz, Leandro Mendonça, Paulo Filipe Monteiro and André Queiroz, 49–85. Rio de Janeiro: Universidade do Estado do Rio de Janeiro (UERJ).

Assmann, Jan. 2008. 'Communicative and Cultural Memory'. In *Cultural Memory Studies: An International and Interdisciplinary Handbook*, eds Astrid Erll and Ansgar Nünning, 109–18. Berlin and New York: Walter de Gruyter.

Augé, Marc. 2009. *Non-Places: An Introduction to Supermodernity*. London: Verso.

Bhabha, Homi. 1994. 'Of Mimicry and Man: The Ambivalence of Colonial Discourse'. In *The Location of Culture*, 385–9. London: Routledge.

Bloch, Ernst. 1986. *The Principle of Hope*. Cambridge, MA: MIT Press.

Bordwell, David. 2006. 'Movies that Restore your Faith in Cinema and Audiences'. In *Observations on Film Art, 2006*. Available at: http://www.davidbordwell.net/blog/2006/10/03/movies-that-restore-your-faith-in-cinema-and-audiences/ (accessed 19 December 2021).

Boym, Svetlana. 2001. *The Future of Nostalgia*. New York: Basic Books.

Camões, Luíz Vaz de. 1986. *The Lusiads*, 102–22. London: Penguin Books.

Daney, Serge. 1977. '*Notes sur les films de Manoel de Oliveira*'. *Cahiers du Cinéma*, 276, May.

Cultural Mimicry

Flaubert, Gustave. 1857. *Madame Bovary*. Paris: Michel Lévy Frères, Libraires-Éditeurs.

Foucault, Michel. 1986. 'Of Other Spaces'. *Diacritics*, 16 (1): 22–7.

Freud, Sigmund. [1919] 2003. *The Uncanny*. London: Penguin Classics.

Gardnier, Ruy. 2006. 'An Interview with Manoel de Oliveira'. In Randal Johnson, *Manoel de Oliveira*, 154–60. Champaign, IL: University of Illinois Press.

Gili, Jean A. 2006. 'A Mental Conception of Cinema: An Interview by Jean A. Gili'. In Randal Johnson, *Manoel de Oliveira*, 141–54. Champaign, IL: University of Illinois Press.

Guimarães, Pedro Maciel. 2010. *Créer ensemble: La Poétique de la collaboration dans le cinéma de Manoel de Oliveira*. Paris: Éditions universitaires européennes.

Jacobs, Steven. 2011. *Framing Pictures: Film and the Visual Arts*. Edinburgh: Edinburgh University Press.

Jaffe, Ira. 2014. *Slow Movies Countering the Cinema of Action*. London: Wallflower Press.

Johnson, Randal. 2006. *Manoel de Oliveira*. Champaign, IL: University of Illinois Press.

Johnson, Randal. 2008. 'Manoel de Oliveira and the Ethics of Representation'. In *Dekalog 02: On Manoel de Oliveira*, ed. Carolin Overhoff Ferreira, 89–109. London: Wallflower Press.

Kitschelt, Herbert. 2003. 'Postcommunist Regime Diversity'. In *Capitalism and Democracy in Central and Eastern Europe*, eds Grzegorz Ekiert and Stephen E. Hanson, 49–88. Cambridge: Cambridge University Press.

Laderman, David. 2002. *Driving Visions: Exploring the Road Movie*. Austin, TX: University of Texas Press.

Lavin, Mathias. 2003. 'Devant la Parole'. *Traffic*, 48: 38–44.

Maia, Catarina. 2010. 'O eterno retorno: memória e identidade em Non, ou a Vã Glória de Mandar'. In *Olhares. Manoel de Oliveira*, eds Michelle Sales and Paulo Cunha, 93–106. Rio de Janeiro: Edições LCV/SR3/UERJ.

Mazierska, Ewa. 2012. 'International Co-Productions as Productions of Heterotopias'. In *A Companion to Eastern European Cinemas*, ed. Anikó Imre, 483–503. Oxford: Wiley-Blackwell.

Monteiro, César. 1996. 'Le passé et le présent, un nécrofilm portugais de Manoel de Oliveira'. *Positif*, no. 421.

Overhoff Ferreira, Carolin. 2013. 'Portugal, Europa e o mundo'. In *Manoel de Oliveira – Novas perspectivas sobre a sua obra* [*Manoel de Oliveira: New Perspectives on His Oevre*], ed. Carolin Overhoff Ferreira, 213–42. São Paulo: Editura Fap-Unifesp.

Overhoff Ferreira, Carolin (ed.). 2009. *Dekalog 02: On Manoel de Oliveira*. London: Wallflower Press.

Parsi, Jacques. 2002. *Manoel de Oliveira*. Lisbon: Fondation Calouste Gulbenkian.

Parsi, Jacques and Antoine de Baecque. 1996. *Conversations avec Manoel de Oliveira*. Paris: Cahiers du Cinéma.

110   *The Cinema of Manoel de Oliveira*

Pethő, Ágnes. 2014. 'The *Tableau Vivant* as a "Figure of Return" in Contemporary East European Cinema'. *Acta Universitatis Transylvaniae, Film and Media Studies*, 9: 51–76.

Pianco dos Santos, Wiliam and Juliana Panini. 2010. '*A canção como alegoria histórica em um filme falado, de Manoel de Oliveira*'. In *Olhares. Manoel de Oliveira*, eds Michelle Sales and Paulo Cunha, 97–126. Rio de Janeiro: Edições LCV/SR3/UERJ.

Rovai, Mauro Ruíz. 2010. '*Dois percursos da memória em* Viagem ao princípio do mundo'. In *Olhares. Manoel de Oliveira*, eds Michelle Sales and Paulo Cunha, 83–92. Rio de Janeiro: Edições LCV/SR3/UERJ.

Sales, Michelle. 2010. '*Territórios e fronteiras no cinema de Manoel de Oliveira*'. In *Olhares. Manoel de Oliveira*, eds Michelle Sales and Paulo Cunha, 126–36. Rio de Janeiro: Edições LCV/SR3/UERJ.

Soares, Ana Isabel. 2013. *Ação* renovada in *Acto da primavera*. In *Manoel de Oliveira – Novas perspectivas sobre a sua obra* [*Manoel de Oliveira: New Perspectives on His Oevre*], ed. Carolin Overhoff Ferreira, 63–80. São Paulo: Fap-Unifesp.

Viegas, Susana. 2014. '*Itinerários Oliveiranos*'. Dialogos (Maringá. Online), 18 (3): 235–49.

Xavier, Ismail. 2003. *O Olhar e a Cena*. São Paulo: Cosac & Naify.

Xavier, Ismail. [1999] 2004. 'Historical Allegory'. In *A Companion to Film Theory*, eds Robert Stam and Toby Miller, 333–62. Malden, MA, and Oxford: Blackwell Publishing.

Xavier, Ismail. 2013. '*A Morte do alferes Cabrita e a paixão Portuguesa*'. In *Manoel de Oliveira – Novas perspectivas sobre a sua obra* [*Manoel de Oliveira: New Perspectives on His Oevre*], ed. Carolin Overhoff Ferreira, 183–211. São Paulo: Editora Fap-Unifesp.

Part Three

Doomed loves

7

Disturbing adaptations

The majority of the films of Oliveira are literary adaptations – these remediations, as already discussed in the previous sections, celebrate the myth of modernity by orchestrating a dialogue between literature as classic art and the new technology of film. The adaptations of Oliveira show an intermedial complexity, involving painterly, sculptural and theatrical references brought in play to ensure, by figuration and stylization, the 'literary' effect. The emergence of a well-known and popular literary classic in a different medium always triggers the resistance of the readers and spectators as well – the uncannily static, slow and long adaptations of Oliveira had lost some of the Portuguese audience since the disappointment caused by the adaptation of Camilo Castelo Branco's *Doomed Love*.

Although more than forty years have passed since the release of the TV adaptation, then feature film version of this popular romantic novel, the Portuguese public and even the critics are still treating the adaptations of the director with a certain amount of scepticism. The main reason for this is the disturbing effect that resulted from a complex intermedial relationship between the popular nineteenth-century literary work, a heavily poetic cinema of frames and still images, and the fragile, visually inadequate, present-time medium of television, at that time black and white in Portugal. The outraged Portuguese public accused Oliveira of blasphemy and even insinuated that he, being too old (aged 70 at that time), had lost his mental faculties. But ageing means the birth of long-term memory, a kind of resurrection of the past in the case of Oliveira and his relationship with literature: for him, literary works function as memory props, both individual and cultural reminders of a heritage not yet fully understood and processed. The case of the controversial reception of *Doomed Love*, I believe, is an exaggerated illustration of what Belén Vidal calls 'the business of adaptation':

> However the business of adaptation is never a straightforward operation of transposition. Instead, the adaptation trades (as Christopher Orr and John Ellis

114   *The Cinema of Manoel de Oliveira*

have pointed out) with something altogether more diffuse: the memory of the literary referent and the fetishistic attachments of both critics and spectators.

Vidal 2012, 8

Doomed Love became paradigmatic in the work of Oliveira, its title and topic standing emblematically not only for the discourse on the impossibility of a 'faithful' relationship between literary work and film, text/word and image, but also for the tormented relationship with its public and a very select gathering of cinéphiles 'falling in love' with it. Jonathan Rosenbaum, for example, called it 'the masterpiece you had missed' and, according to Serge Daney, few films in film history 'have pushed the exploration of what is shown and what is seen this far' and consequently, 'as all big films, it is very slow but, at the same time, of an incredible rapidity' (Daney 2001, 225).

The exquisite aspects of Oliveira's adaptations offer themselves for cinéphile expectations, corresponding to those of Raymond Bellour's 'pensive spectator', who proposes to himself to see and understand all that is shown in these films (2002a). And this is a difficult task, because the visual delicacies displayed are not spectacular, but sometimes almost subliminal, hidden in tiny details of the setting, decor or compositions. To this difficulty adds sometimes the poor quality of the 16 mm films, which were excellent for poetic purposes, but proved to be less enduring, thus affecting the resolution of the image. The result are blurred, almost 'decomposing' images, perfectly matching the recurrent topic of death (most of the time of a young woman, in *Benilde*, *Francisca* or *Magic Mirror*), and the cadaveric appearance of the characters due to their extreme passivity, stillness and a peculiar effect of natural lighting. Some of these films have never been released on DVD or remastered, representing now an aesthetics of the poor image that, according to Hito Steyerl, 'tends towards abstraction: it is a visual idea in becoming' (Steyerl 31), that is, the idea of materialized memory (represented by the literary work) meant to bridge the gap between past and present.

The process of slowing down, repeating or stilling the image, allows hidden details to emerge within a film sequence or a previously insignificant moment. The disturbing effect of interruptions with stillness or slowness are related in cinema in general and Oliveira's adaptations in particular to extraordinary moments or the unrepresentable. These are obsessively recurring in the chosen literary works seeking answers (words and images) to cultural taboos or the dogmas of the Christian faith: death and resurrection (*The Divine Comedy*), the Annunciation (*Magic Mirror*) or the mystery of the Virgin Mother (*Benilde or the Virgin Mother)*. The most eccentric features of Oliveira's adaptations have to do with his obsession with the frame, also in its figurative sense: the screen, the (pictorial) image, the narrative, as well as the literary and cultural tradition.

(Re)framing literature

Past and Present, Doomed Love, Francisca, Benilde, Abraham's Valley, Magic Mirror and *Eccentricities of a Blonde-Haired Girl* with their *tableau vivant* compositions, constantly posing characters creating an effect of in-betweenness between theatre and cinema, painterly and sculptural references, bear the main feature of the contemporary literary film, that is, according to Villasur, 'the hyperreality of the frame':

> The frame then becomes the privileged site of analysis, exposing the memory *of* the film text rather than the memory *in* the text determined by the strict mimesis of the narrative. In particular, the use of period painting (usually read as a cultural sign that triggers the memory of the literary past) becomes part of the intertext of the film in ways that resist symbolization.
>
> Vidal Villasur 2002, 9

This is the case of *tableaux vivants* evoking Greek mythological scenes in *Doomed Love*, of the Biedermeier-style tableau-like compositions in *Francisca*, or reflections in mirrors in *Magic Mirror*, photographic framing of groups of people in *Abraham's Valley* (where the stilled movement of the painterly image in Oliveira's films is interfering with the cultural history of the photographic image, that of the *pause and pose*). As already mentioned above, Oliveira is bound to choose literary texts that allow him to explore the aesthetic possibilities of the visual rendering of the unspeakable: in *Benilde or the Virgin Mother*, the innocence of the pregnant girl and the Catholic Dogma of the Immaculate Conception or in *Magic Mirror*, the miraculous apparition of the Virgin to the female protagonist. The effort of the characters in both films to re-present (and thus to understand) the miracle results in a tension between words, endless dialogues meant to understand the inconceivable and the figurative meaning of carefully framed images. Intriguingly – and here lies Oliveira's lesson on cinematic representation – the more they want to see and understand, the more they talk and the more they lose their connection to life and reality. The female protagonists in *Benilde* and *Magic Mirror* fade away, fall sick and ultimately die,

116 *The Cinema of Manoel de Oliveira*

while the camera sublimates the melancholia of the resultless quest in carefully framed images: in *Benilde or the Virgin Mother*, after exhausting discussions, the camera backs out from the room, where she is lying, while also framing, in a mise-en-abîme composition, the priest and the fiancé immobilized by confusion and bewilderment. *Magic Mirror* closes with the image of the heroine on her deathbed, refracted in a mirror. In creating this gap between words and images, or overwriting words with images, Oliveira comes very close to Eric Rohmer's *La Marquise d'O*, that can be regarded as one of Oliveira's modernist models in terms of 'refracting' words into images. As Angela Dalle Vacche points out in her analysis on Rohmer's film: 'Refraction here means a mirroring or a duplication that also contains a reversal across different signs and that never collapses into a perfect identity but instead thrives on the very otherness of word and image' (Dalle Vacche 1996, 86). It is also true for Oliveira's other adaptations (*Doomed Love, Francisca* or *Abraham's Valley*) that while characters are often reciting the literary text with expressionless faces, what they think or feel is not expressed by words, but rather by the 'visual spaces: gestures, poses, objects, expressions – that exist between the ordinary and polite sentences they offer to each other' (ibid., 86).

Beyond the topic of pregnancy surrounded by mystery in *Benilde* and *La Marquise d'O* (which in Oliveira's film is thought to be a repetition of the Immaculate Conception, with the suspicion of rape by a mentally ill servant, while in Rohmer's film rape is taken for fact) and its clarifying process bringing in play the word–image discrepancy, Oliveira's adaptations share many other characteristics of the 'literary film', termed by Alexandre Astruc and epitomized by Rohmer's film. In *Benilde, Magic Mirror, The Uncertainty Principle, Past and Present* or *Abraham's Valley*, theatrical, painterly, architectural and sculptural signifiers meet to reveal psychological processes, intimate thoughts and feelings that words fail to express. While Oliveira is often taking a moralizing standpoint in the presentation of a Portuguese upper-middle-class hiding secrets, taboos and social dysfunctions behind empty forms and poses, his interest in humanity goes well beyond a social critique. He is a moralist (just like Rohmer, as Dalle Vacche argues, quoting Rohmer himself) in the original French sense of the word: 'someone who is preoccupied with what is going on inside a man' (Dalle Vacche 1996, 84, quoting from Rohmer's *Monaco: New Wave*, 292). Just like in Rohmer's film, in *Benilde* words are not for the mind, as traditionally defined by Lessing in *Laokoon*. They do not support understanding: characters have either difficulties to speak (the old maid, who saw Benilde growing up and suspects the

Disturbing Adaptations 117

pregnancy and has convoked the meeting with the doctor and the priest, doesn't know how to start and express her doubt), repeat themselves (the aunt who keeps asking Benilde who the father of the child is), get entangled in dogmatic theses (scientific and religious, the doctor and the priest), are confused and emotional (the fiancé). Painterly solutions (framing, compositions, lighting, the use of repoussoirs) in the theatrical space of gestures, sounds and poses become filled with meaning, while words do not bring us closer to the understanding of mysterious events nor to the emotions of characters.

The obsession with words (that never degenerates into verbosity, just like in Rohmer's film) is counterbalanced by the meaningful minimalism of staging and visual details: the changing compositions with three and four arguing characters illustrate the struggle between faith and knowledge as a power relationship. While triangular composition seems to be out of balance (leaving one of the participants alone with his/her standpoint), the scenes with a quadruple confrontation are meant to create a balance between faith and knowledge. As in many Oliveira films (and, again, similarly to Rohmer's period film), characters struggle between rigid social (and religious norms) and self-evaluation (Dalle Vacche 1996, 88).

In *Benilde or the Virgin Mother*, all characters end up defining themselves in relationship to Benilde's mysterious pregnancy on which they need to take a standpoint. They are brought in a very difficult situation to assume their faith or scepticism in front of others. The contents of their minds hover in visual spaces, their gestures and poses. Benilde, dressed in blue (the conventional colour used in the pictorial depiction of the Virgin), poses like Catholic saints and the Virgin in painterly representations: gazing upwards, as if in *extase*, with praying hands. Other pictorial conventions include the fireplace illuminating the faces of the priest, the doctor and the maid in the dark kitchen, signifying, just like in paintings of George de la Tour, the truth for which they are desperately looking. At the beginning of this opening scene, the moving camera that took us to this artificially created space through the labyrinth behind the theatrical stage, zooms in to a framed picture on the wall, a deserted landscape that functions as both an artificial window to the outside world (which we never see throughout the film, and only overhear its elements as loose, heavy rain and wind, creating an apocalyptic atmosphere) and a metaphor of the state of faith in our times. Still life elements – the plate with golden apples in the kitchen and the vase with a big pink bouquet of flowers – also serve as repoussoirs, helping us to see depth in the image (and thus the issue of faith at hand) and to express the feelings of

118   *The Cinema of Manoel de Oliveira*

characters. Golden fruits, figures of Benilde's blessed condition, also direct our gaze to the storm behind the window frame, metaphorically offering faith represented by the piece of still life as a solution of tormented existential condition. Similarly, the bouquet of pink flowers, another source of light in the dark living room, stands as long as the dialogue between Benilde and her aunt is peaceful: but as soon as doubt occurs and the aunt keeps interrogating her about the father of the unborn child, the storm enters the room, making the vase topple over, together with the fragile emotions of trust and understanding. Finally, these repoussoirs direct our attention beyond the foreground of the image, or rather beyond the surface of things, by figurating the depth of faith.

Staging creates the link between the literary work and its adaptation: actors, their gestures and poses reveal theatricality as a connection between the film and the world outside, its role plays, structures, convictions and value systems. The artificial space of action, entered through a labyrinthine horizontal move of the camera appears as an abstraction, as a mental space beyond the stage, that is, a crisis of faith beyond religious formality. It is a crisis filled with terror emphasized by the offscreen wailing, a tool of the horror genre, together with the unidentified gaze represented by the wandering camera. Just like in *La Marquise d'O*, the lack of point-of-view shots (except from that of the dead mother, looking down at Benilde from the portrait) stands for the refusal to enter the mental state of the characters, represented, instead, by the space, dark and austere interiors and the menacing off-screen voices and sounds. The discrepancy between words and images – words that do not bring us closer to understanding the miracle and images that figurate meaning beyond the unspeakable – also reveals the literary text as a female body 'a(du)ltered' by adaptation. But while, as Angela Dalle Vacche argues, Rohmer's film presents adaptation 'as form of intellectual rape' (Dalle Vacche 1996, 89), Oliveira's film rather appears as a more peaceful reunion between arts, meant to multiply the layers of signification.

Interiors as mental spaces

A similar use of the architectural – mostly interior – space as mental space appears in *Past and Present*. The introductory sequences featuring the credits of the film are lingering long on one decorative detail of the massive gate columns in front of the house where almost all the action takes place: an hourglass pointing at the central topic of the film, that is, obsession with the past and the

Disturbing Adaptations 119

inability to live in the present. The story of a charmed princess living in a luxurious upper-middle-class house, who can only love the husband who is already dead, is imprinted in every spatial and architectural detail of the setting, camera movement, costumes and sound design. Moreover, all the characters, the husbands and frequently visiting friends assisting to the main female character's psychosis, appear as decorative, elegant details of this mental space, symptomatic of compulsive thinking and behaviour. Wearing dresses matching the colours of the décor (blue, brown, gold) and the background, characters themselves become ornamental elements in a fresco of a morally superficial high society. While spaces are filled with mirrors, reflecting the characters, visual and verbal forms of self-reflection are completely missing: the social scenes are superficial encounters marked by flirting, lack of eye contact (often one of the interlocutors watching an art album during the conversation), a purely formal use of words and constant posing. The visual, theatrical figuration of a pathological, repressed atmosphere hiding secrets and taboos of a social class relying on anachronistic moral and hierarchical values (like in *The Uncertainty Principle* or in *Abraham's Valley*) is conveyed by multiple door frames surrounded by lush curtains, letting in and out the characters, who are stepping on the scene and have their monologue filled with pathos (but not genuine emotions) or dialogue, as if on the stage of a theatre.

The observation of Angela Dalle Vacche regarding the spaces in Rohmer's film is valid to *Past and Present*, too: 'box-like shots of corridors, doors, gates, windows and walls set in motion a dynamic of open and closed, stable and fluid spaces' (Dalle Vacche 1996, 104). Horizontal camera movement accompanying, together with classical musical excerpts (mostly from Felix Mendelssohn's *Wedding March* from 1842), the characters along the corridors, between the rooms as stages of social life, functions as a signifier of a lonely subjectivity, lost in the labyrinth of lies, deceit, unfaithfulness and forms without content. The same horizontal camera movement appears in the outdoor scene in the graveyard, following from a distance the disturbed woman and her group of friends, on their way to commemorate the death anniversary of the previous husband. While horizontal camera movement stands for societal norms and interactions, the vertical ones, following the characters moving up and down the stairs connecting social and private spaces, become signifiers of changes in emotional intensity (anxiety, fear, confusion). Again, similarly to Rohmer's film (but also to *Abraham's Valley* and *The Uncertainty Principle*), the decorative, architectural details, the period furniture and heavy, ornamental design, represent the

120   *The Cinema of Manoel de Oliveira*

antiquated self-image of the social class. Dalle Vacche's analysis of Rohmer's film also applies here:

> the lives of characters punctuated by neoclassical busts, columns, statuettes, pilasters. These decorative objects are there to remind them of how they are supposed to behave, while making even wider the gap between ideals and realities, duty and impulse.

> 1996, 97

Decorative objects, books and accessories also serve as cues to untold emotions and mental states. In a scene evoking the tale of Sleeping Beauty, the unhappy and powerless husband walks around the bed of his wife, whose enigmatic persona is stressed by veil-like curtains moved softly by the wind. The title of the book on the table (a directorial gesture recurring much later in *Angelica*), *L'Amour plus fort que la morte* (*The Love more Powerful than Death*), summarizes the central idea of the film story, together with the letter-knife beside it, instigating, for a moment of rage, the desperate husband to kill the heartless woman, who is cruel and indifferent with the living husbands. In a similar vein, the cheesy bibelot in the living room, a putto-like figure with an arrow, counterbalances the deadly passions figurated upstairs, in the bedrooms, with an allusion to the superficiality of repeated flirting scenes in the social space. Multiple, in-depth framing of doors in the hallways and corridors, functioning as passages between private and communal spaces, between the individual and social, as well as repoussoirs (flowers and decorative objects), relate in a contrastive way to the flatness of dialogues and gestures, poses obligatory in this environment. It is a decadent, isolated world, stuck in the past, in which discussions about death – own and of others – resonate with framed photos and painted portraits of dead husbands put on pedestals and cyclically restructuring relationships in the house.

In this world of appearances, secrets and repressed emotions, peeping and eavesdropping becomes only natural, giving way to pictorial references, especially the seventeenth-century. Dutch genre painting, in which multiple-framing, in-depth composition with an eavesdropping character in the foreground draws attention to the unspeakable events in the background, that can be heard but cannot be seen or spoken about. The emblematic image showing the eye of the maid through the augmented keyhole, peeping in on her mistress is more emphasized (lasts longer) than what she actually sees: the naked mistress, holding on her lap the oil portrait of the late husband. In this case, the emphasis on peeping

Disturbing Adaptations

and secrecy highlights the pathological nature of her love and peculiar form of infidelity. In both *Benilde* and *Past and Present*, just like in *Francisca*, *The Uncertainty Principle* or *Abraham's Valley*, interiors appear like a prison, a metaphor of hypocritical aristocratic or (upper-)middle-class environment. Multiple door- and window-frames do not work as thresholds towards the outer world, but as figures of concealment and entrapment inside the suffocating milieu of the house. These openings thematize the gaze rather than action, in line with Julianne Pidduck's argumentation regarding British heritage films and costume dramas. Her observations regarding gendered interior and exterior space at work (Pidduck 1998, 381) in Jane Austen adaptations also apply to Oliveira's adaptations, in which interiors work as a 'panoply of detail and patriarchal laws of inheritance, strict codes of comportment' (ibid., 385).

The recurring moment of the woman at the window that 'captures a particular quality of feminine stillness, constraint and longing', characteristic of costume drama adaptations, apply to bourgeois environments depicted in *Benilde or the Virgin Mother*, *The Uncertainty Principle*, *Eccentricities of a Blonde-Haired Girl*, *Francisca* and *Abraham's Valley*. While men move freely beyond the safe frame of home and family, for women the same movement is considered dangerous and (self-)destructive: in *Benilde*, the female protagonist is a sleepwalker leaving the house during the night, when, according to some of the characters, she might have been raped by the mentally ill servant. In a similar vein, the blonde girl of *Eccentricities* can be 'safely' admired as long as she stays behind the window, inside the house. As soon as she gets out and away from her parents' custody, her desires cannot be controlled any more. Visually dominated by idealizing frames, portraits of the worshipped woman, this latter film ends abruptly after showing the image of the young woman falling apart, when the male protagonist realizes that she is a kleptomaniac and leaves her. Similarly, Ema's moral downfall in *Abraham's Valley* begins when she starts leaving the house: the central figure of the newly acquired, self-destructive mobility is her sports car, overcompensating for her socially and physically imposed immobility (motherhood, social status and her limp).

As Pidduck argues, frames as signifiers of an imagined social space and human possibilities, emphasize the psychological role of what Deleuze calls *hors-champ* to describe 'what is neither seen nor understood, but is, nevertheless, perfectly present' (Pidduck 1998, 393; Deleuze [1982] 1986, 16). Framing, by containing and excluding narrative and figurative information, has a decisive role in organizing the image as a text susceptible for cultural, psychological interpretation. As a visual, painterly (pre-cinematic) tool, it fits perfectly the thematic anachronisms of the Oliveirian adaptations, using books and stories from another era to connect past and present with allegorical, critical and sometimes didactic purposes.

Adaptation and/as anachronism

Past and Present is emblematic of all adaptations of Oliveira in that it posits adaptation, through its many art references – pictorial, theatrical, musical, literary – as an anachronistic act, a practice meant to show the gap between the past and the present, and to use it as a critical or didactic tool. Painterly compositions and theatrical gestures, poses and mise-en-scène are obsolete signifiers that ensure the link between film and literature, providing, at the same time, a cultural continuity between painterly, photographic and film images. In this way, in his adaptations, Olivera is repeatedly restaging the early cinematic connections between the camera, the stage and traditional Romantic painting. As Anne Hollander argues in her *Moving Images*, in cinema, the Dutch-style composition with window, the dramatic repoussoir, the mythical overtones, facial types, bodily attitudes, groupings and lighting, are all internalized pictorial conventions set in motion (Hollander 1989, 441–3). In the adaptations of Oliveira, the obsolete, romantic, nineteenth-century topic of doomed loves as results of outdated social restrictions is conferred by similarly anachronistic elements of mise-en-scène, narrative, as well as excessively artificial décor, costumes, acting and sound. The re-presented historical period is often stated at the very beginning, on the opening images (in *Doomed Love*, *Francisca* or *Benilde*), accompanied by a dissonant musical score, signifying anguish when facing time and history that can never be completely understood, only its effect can be felt and acknowledged.

These films have nothing to do with the nostalgia stirred by British costume dramas: literary adaptation for Oliveira is a memory prop, as Iain Chambers puts it, an occasion to circulate art with the tool of anachronism, that is, to represent 'the present drawn into and reconfigured by a negated past that we can never fully recover nor know' (Chambers 2017). By doing so, he rather expresses criticism of obsolete social and moral attitudes that persist over time as just another manifestation of the Freudian uncanny: something repressed that returns. Thus, adaptation becomes the model of an anachronistic infatuation

Disturbing Adaptations 123

with the past, a doomed love from the outset. Dying of tuberculosis and unfulfilled love, becoming pregnant by a miracle, falling in love with the dead husband or committing suicide are the various forms of the same repressed desire and fear to live in the present. Following the mechanism of repression, these emotions re-emerge in each film of the tetralogy of frustrated loves: although apparently different stories, they all provide an anachronistic (that is, pictorial and theatrical) stylization of a female passivity caught in the web of a purely formal upper-middle-class morality, marked by Catholic religious formalities. As a member of this social class himself, Oliveira, just like Agustina Bessa-Luís, whose novels he is adapting (*The Uncerainty Principle* [based on *Joia de Familia* / *Family Jewel*], *Magic Mirror* based on the novel, *A Alma dos ricos* [*The Soul of the Rich*] and *Abraham's Valley*), has the insider's privilege to reveal, and thus sublimate the destructive effect of petrified transgenerational conventions.

The protagonists of these films seem to live in a time capsule: their environment, the objects surrounding them, their tastes, family rituals and poses have changed little over time. The décor of interior spaces, signifier of social relationships, is very similar in *Doomed Love*, *Francisca* or *The Uncertainty Principle*. The characters seem to wear the same elegant clothes that are not characteristic of any particular fashion – their costumes and accessories (fashion items and cars) are just as obsolete, like their habits, gestures, discussion matters (philosophical treatises about love, romantic relationships or death in *Abraham's Valley* and *Past and Present*). While set sometimes in the second half of the twentieth century, Ema from *Abraham's Valley* still uses candles when visiting her husband's rooms and dresses up like a girl before committing suicide as a mature woman. This time travel by anachronism can be identified in images merging pictorial and photographic conventions: for example, images of family reunions or parties, photographic group images lit only by natural light or candlelight. The merger of cinematic, photographic and pictorial in the same image stresses the organic relationship between image and time: or, as Georges Didi-Huberman argues, 'Whenever we are before the image, we are before time' (2003, 31). This also means that: 'The image often has more memory and more future than the being who contemplates it' (ibid., 33). It is only natural to discover a correspondence between the represented trangenerational, repressed issues and transmedial relationships, that is, the return of the (repressed) pictorial and photographic image in the moving, cinematographic image.

124   *The Cinema of Manoel de Oliveira*

The overt aesthetic and temporal disjunction in the adaptations under analysis can also be interpreted as an authorial attitude of distanciation and criticism. As Elena Gorfinkel points out in her article on the role of cinematic anachronisms, 'outdated' historical periods and objects invite spectators to engage affectively, though not necessarily uncritically, with history (2005, 153). As we have seen, in the case of *Doomed Love*, the Portuguese public was not ready to take this distance and relate critically to the excesses of late romanticism, unconventionally represented by Oliveira in the form of endless monologues recited frontally, with expressionless face and body, to the spectator. The regression to a theatrical and an earlier cinematic tradition (that of Robert Bresson, for example) stirred the resentment of the public expecting a spectacular representation of emotions, following in the footsteps of the previous adaptations by Pallu and Ribeiro (that will be discussed in the following chapters of this part). Instead of adapting a love story, Oliveira adapts an authorial attitude in representing a historical moment of fragmentation, bringing along the end of a historical period (the Romantic era) seen as an unbreakable unity, and with it, the birth of a new, modern subjectivity assuming its fragility. By re-presenting by literary texts with anachronistic topics an aristocracy and upper-middle-class stuck in the past, Oliveira makes visible the gap between past and present, as well as the unmendable fissure on the whole of what these historical social classes represent. This is how the artistic use of anachronism works – as Chambers emphasizes: 'It is only by breaking apart the image of a presumed whole and origin that it is possible to release fragments into the present' (Chambers 2017, 2).

The viewer of literary adaptations is always caught between different periods – that of the literary and of the filmic text. The uncanny about Oliveira's adaptations is that even when set in the present and based on more recent literary works (like those of Bessa-Luís or Vicente Sanchez, in the case of *Past and Present*), the past persists in the present, prompting the spectators to take a critical standpoint towards their own present. Instead of conjuring up a gap between past and present social attitudes, these films emphasize, through remediation and organization of a cycle (of *Doomed Loves*), the persistence of past social attitudes in a still very hierarchical and authority-based Portuguese society. The moral, behavioural and characterological descriptions of anachronism ascribed by Thomas Greene (1986) can be directly applied to Oliveira's adaptations, often displaying characters disoriented by outdated moral dilemmas and manifesting typical, historically determined behaviours (see the

Disturbing Adaptations 125

recurrent characters of priests and doctors). From the five types of anachronism listed by Greene (naive, abusive, serendipitous, creative and pathetic-tragic), Oliveira seems to practice most the last one, defined as 'an estrangement from history, which is mired in decline' (cf. Gorfinkel 2005, 156). Thus, the affect channelled through anachronistic topics and obsolete representational practices is rather a melancholia related to fetishized cultural objects of the past (including the literary works in question) and historical referents, in narratives about loss and failure (ibid., 164–6). For example, in *Abraham's Valley*, the antique wooden home altar is a cultural and historical fetish-object, channelling a transgenerational melancholia and a multiple loss: that of the mother, grandmother and ultimately faith. Flaubert's *Madame Bovary* (1857), the book Ema is reading, also becomes an example of an anachronistic cultural object, triggering, by repetition, an anachronistic lifestyle, behaviour and melodramatic failure in her obsession for romantic love.

Flaubert in Portugal: From Emma to Ema

As already referred to in the previous chapters tackling the affinity of the films of Oliveira with modernity and tradition, *Abraham's Valley* is a cross-cultural remediation of Flaubert's *Madame Bovary*. On the one hand, it 'colonizes' the original text (to use Leitch's terminology, 2007, 109–10), imposing new cultural meanings on it, such as the image of the modern woman in a pseudo-modern, moralizing, patriarchal society. On the other hand, the film subversively reveals, with the Portuguese intermediation of the literary text *Vale Abraão* by Agustina Bessa-Luís, the narratological and spectatorial mechanisms of the medium.

In an analysis dedicated to adaptations of Flaubert's novel, Robert Stam pointed out that no film director has attempted to realize the relativization of the narrator's position in *Madame Bovary* (Stam 2005). Moreover, apparently the equivalent of the famous statement, 'I am Madame Bovary' – which Robert Stam interpreted as Flaubert's attitude towards the sentimental literature to which Emma is addicted (Emma's death is a metaphor of this ritual break with a literary tradition and the omniscient narrator) – is also missing from existing adaptations. However, Oliveira's *Abraham's Valley*, besides conferring a Portuguese cultural interpretation on the story, seems to incorporate this contradictory relationship (both respectful and subversive) between the film and the 'old' medium, which Stam suggested. Intriguingly, the criticism of the film, including interviews with the director, emphasized the effort for complete fidelity to the literary text, the novel of Bessa-Luís, which due to its obvious and numerous intertextual connections to Flaubert's novel, can be seen as a Portuguese version of *Madame Bovary*. But the excessive fidelity of the film to the novel, manifested in an intrusive voice-over narration, turns subversive as a result of the extremely long shots and the film's length of more than three hours. The voice-over stops the action repeatedly and unexpectedly, characters freeze in their positions, and the moving picture is turned into a *tableau vivant*. This authoritarian gesture not only works as a metaphor of a traditional, hierarchical and patriarchal society, but also functions as an allegory of the feminine picture ('the picture as woman') being controlled by the male, omniscient narration, an ekphrasis repeating the myth of Philomena.[1] The same mechanism of ekphrasis works in the frequent monologues of different men who analyse Ema's beauty. During these descriptive monologues (often in voice-over), Ema appears as a blank surface, an expressionless, statue-like entity, in many respects similar to Bressonian models onto which the male characters project their views on women, Ema and femininity in general. The protagonist's puppet-like appearance is emphasized in every aspect of the narration: she looks like the mannequins in the European shops, turning, at the end of her life, into an 'antiqued mannequin' (Bessa-Luís 2000, 13–15, 48).

This is not only a cinematic alternative to Flaubert's narration technique – Emma appears as *she is seen by different men* – but also an act revealing the medium in the striking contrast between the aggressive, noisy voice-over (male) narration and the passive, placid and silent (female) picture. Ritinha, Ema's deaf-mute servant, a Portuguese beauty whose story is told by the same narrator, represents the same ekphrastic principle. As Ema emphasizes, Ritinha is a constant presence in her life, who has been with her since childhood, ceaselessly washing the laundry in an old stone pool by the house, while nothing escaped her attention. At the same time, she is obviously a literary topos, representing the adulterous mistress's consciousness, washing the laundry (or spots of shame). The secret life of images revealing unexpected cultural connotations is beyond the control of the big narrator,[2] as they become a symbolic, mythical story of femininity, resisting the male gaze. Her father finds Ema 'a bit frightening', men

---

[1] According to the legend, Philomena represented the story of the rape on a white silk cloth she had woven herself, which became the silent accusation against Tereus, the perpetrator, who loudly propagated another version of the story.

[2] André Gaudreault uses the term 'grand narrateur', along with 'grand imagier', in his *Du Littéraire au Filmique* (1988).

think that she is too gorgeous and try to avoid her, and in general she triggers a 'sudden inquietude' in others (Bessa-Luís 2000, 217 and 279).

The thematization of the visual uncanny – recalling the myth of the Medusa – is a recurrent topic in both the novel and film. Ema, for example, is not a perfect object of desire because she has a limp. This fault obviously disturbs male contemplation, and as an unconventional cinematic representation of feminine beauty, becomes the 'uncanny' making the medium visible. Pedro Dossém, one of her lovers, turns his eyes 'as if seeing a nude', when Ema lies down on the sofa revealing her defective leg (ibid., 206). This subversive detail recalls Impressionist paintings, especially those of Manet that represent women in bizarre, often puppet-like positions and settings,[3] and specifically his *Baudelaire's Mistress, Reclining* (1862), which depicts poet and art critic Baudelaire's semi-invalid mistress, Jeanne Duval (Figure 7.1). Duval lounges like a stiff doll, her left foot oddly protruding from her oversized skirt (Søndergaard 2006, 140, 247, 272). The narrator in both the novel and the film repeatedly depicts Ema as a *tableau vivant*, posing as an odalisque or even as a movie star/character – Lola Montes, Greta Garbo or Marlene Dietrich – representing the vamp or femme fatale. Interestingly enough, the same narrator does not forget to mention that Ema's hands *were not beautiful* – a detail recalling, again, the sketchy, unconventional representation of Duval's hands in Manet's painting.[4]

Figure 7.1 Édouard Manet, *Jeanne Duval, Baudelaire's Mistress, Reclining* (*Lady with a Fan*), 1862, a painting echoed by the character of Ema.

[3] See Søndergaard (2006, 11–28).
[4] For a detailed analysis of this portrait, see Strauber (2006, 99–131).

128 *The Cinema of Manoel de Oliveira*

Ema's limp is, at the same time, an obvious allusion to that of the horseman Hippolyte from the novel *Madame Bovary*, who underwent surgical intervention carried out by Emma's husband.

According to Mary Donaldson-Evans' interpretation of *Madame Bovary*, at that time, a limp was considered a sign of increased sexual drive, and thus would be nothing but an allusion to Emma's sensuality through transposition and her last effort to control it by encouraging her husband to do the surgery.[5] In Oliveira's film, this is the only sign of Ema's predilection to promiscuity, contrasting with her expressionless, rather innocent look. The limp becomes a crack, both in the image of the woman and in the medium, revealing the (imperfect) body of the female character and of the medium as well.[6] In other words, both the modern woman (as opposed to the mythical feminine) and film, as a modern medium aspiring to the perfect illusion of movement, are flawed. (Not irrelevantly, the imperfection of Ema's body is carefully put in an intercultural context in both the Bessa-Luís novel and the film by allusions to other physically imperfect mistresses, such as La Vallière or the Lady of the Camellias.) To illustrate and further reinforce this subversive gesture, in one of the *tableau vivant* scenes, depicting a dinner and the moment when everybody rises for a toast, the characters freeze as if waiting for the voice-over narrator to finish his overwhelming monologue, and Ema (because of her limp) makes a tiny movement, sufficient to break the hypnotic effect.

The influence of the Impressionists, Manet in particular, on Flaubert's writing has been pointed out several times. The work of Flaubert is not only impressionistic because of the detailed descriptions, but also because of his ability to convey the *visual effect* of the scenes through light and colours. The BBC adaptation of the novel (by Tim Fywell, 2000) created the same effect with Emma's strikingly yellow dresses that function as a source of light and a constant attribute of hers. Besides preserving this 'dress code' and an impressionistic style, Oliveira's film, relying on the Portuguese novel, also adapts the subversive gestures of both Flaubert's and Manet's art, producing a noise in representation. As Susan Strauber pointed out, Manet's portrait of Jeanne Duval is also 'Manet's dialogue with Baudelaire about aesthetics, modernity, femininity, and politics, and his continuation of their exchange about picturing and writing,' in which

---

[5] Donaldson-Evans (2005, 21–34.). She is quoting an Italian proverb, translated by Montaigne as, 'Celui-là ne connaît pas Vénus en sa parfaite douceur qui n'a pas couché avec la boiteuse.'

[6] The same directorial subversive gesture applies to Luís Buñuel's *Tristana* (1971). Jørgen Bruhn discussed the limp in *Changing Borders: Contemporary Positions in Intermediality* (2008).

Disturbing Adaptations

'Manet contradicts customary idealizing prescriptions for portraiture and especially for the portrayal of femininity.' This subversive act draws attention to the medium instead of the object represented: 'The visibility of the presentation functions here to begin to draw our attention away from the model as portrait to the painting as entity' (Strauber 2006, 102, 117, 130). Throughout the film, we witness the *body becoming a picture*, through ekphrastic descriptions, *tableaux vivants* and the protagonist's puppet-like appearance – a mechanism recalling Manet's paintings. The uncanny visual effect relies on the striking discrepancy between the 'eternal feminine' and, in the words of Bessa-Luís's narrator, the woman turned into pure spectacle (*uma mulher-espectáculo*).

Books have a deep impact on the lives of Flaubert's Emma and Bessa-Luís's Ema: the novels they read are pre-texts, narratives that foreshadow their own destinies. A similar uncanny repetition appears in *Doomed Love*, the adaptation of Castelo Branco's homonymous novel about his uncle's tragic love story, in which Oliveira invokes both the writer and his uncle through a series of letter-reading and writing scenes.

8

Letters on the screen

The image of the written text in film has been often seen by theorists as a 'noisy intrusion' into the filmic imagery and the diegetic world. Often accompanied by a voice-over narration or a voice-off, it has been considered an uncanny presence, that entails, as Mary Ann Doane puts it, 'the risk of exposing the material heterogeneity of the medium' (1980, 35). The theoretical debate around on-screen writing surfaced in at least two contexts, recently connected by the conceptual and terminological framework of intermediality studies: the re-evaluation of the modernist tradition and the research of literary adaptations. As known, the coexistence of words and images on the screen became a mode of reflection on the ontology of the moving image in the cinematic modernism, a tendency most eloquently represented by Jean-Luc Godard's films.[1] Moreover, writing and reading on screen is seen as a consecrated metaphor of film, conceived as a writing and reading performance, a text, and not a closed (art) work. In the context of adaptation studies, the subgenres of so-called 'writers' movies' (about authors writing the story we are actually watching) and adaptations of epistolary novels has lately been given a phenomenological and cultural/anthropological significance, related to the absence or presence of the body, the ways of looking and spectatorship and the quality of the image (haptic or optic), as well as intermediality (still image vs movement, painterly or photographic vs cinematic).

This modernist mode of visual representation, bringing together texts and images, is not an invention of cinema and not even that of twentieth-century artistic vanguards. As Svetlana Alpers points out in her book, *The Art of Describing: Dutch Art in the Seventeenth Century* (1984), this tradition already existed in seventeenth-century Dutch painting:

---

[1] Agnes Pethő, in her book on cinematic intermediality, dedicates four chapters to Godard's New Wave films: the word-image plays, the types of emphasis and media archaeology (2011, 231–340).

132   *The Cinema of Manoel de Oliveira*

characterized by the inclusion of words with images that has the function of celebrating the new and unprecedented making that is a picture, while at the same time, and often in the same work, acknowledging the ineluctable absence of what can only be present in signs. It is an ironic and deconstructive pictorial mode.

Ibid., 172

Alpers also shows how Dutch painting before the seventeenth century simply served as a mnemonic device, recalling a significant – biblical or mythological – text and presenting its *substance* and not its *surface* to the eyes. This distinction between two ways of visual representation of texts seems to be working for adaptations of literary works on film, aiming either at a full diegetic effect by focusing on the story (the substance), or, by showing the text in question (or its writing and reading scene), is acting against cinematic transparency and reveals mediality or intermediality (the material 'surface' of the medium). Film adaptations of epistolary literary works represent a curious category in that they are often a hybrid, where the letter, its image, its writing and reading belong both to the story and to the visual (and figural) representation, halting the action and demanding a different kind of looking from the part of the spectator.

In adaptations of epistolary novels like *Doomed Love* the written text, the letter is often framed by pictorial compositions of the scene of letter writing/reading. Although considered a somewhat 'tired trope' by Belén Vidal, the letter remains one of the central figures of the so-called 'period films'[2] (besides the figures of 'the tableau' and 'the house') that lies at the core of an alternative tradition of experimentation with the 'literariness' of film (2012, 17). As she argues:

Due to its polysemic ambiguity between material object, text and sign, the letter encapsulates perhaps the most concrete manifestation of the figural in the period film: it literally demands of the spectator to 'read' the cinematic image and to 'see' (and hear) writing embedded in the aural and visual textures of film.

Ibid., 2012, 163

Defined by Garrett Stewart as 'reverse ekphrasis' – a 'full textual inversion by which pictured reading becomes the true mirror double of the read picture' (2006, 82) – the letter on screen is a complex figure of (inter)subjectivity, time, absence and desire, deployed inside the framework of narrative topics mostly

---

[2] Vidal prefers this term over 'historical film', 'classic adaptation', 'heritage film' or 'costume drama' because she finds it 'the least connoted' (2012, 9–10).

Letters on the Screen 133

typical of melodrama. In this genre, based on the 'rhetoric of the too late', the letter that arrives late is crucial in the creation of melodramatic tensions and has a drastic influence on actions and events. Relying on scholarly articles about *Doomed Love*[3] by Camilo Castelo Branco, I argue that in this novel, the trope of the late letter is a figure that has no effect over actions and events, and thus ceases to be a melodramatic ingredient. The same can be stated about the other, traditionally melodramatic tropes of the 'unsent letter' or the 'found letter'. The four adaptations of the novel examined in the subsequent chapters – Georges Pallu's silent movie from 1921, Lopes Ribeiro's film from 1943, Oliveira's version from 1978 and finally Mário Barroso's film from 2008 – differ in their interpretation of these tropes either as (melodramatic) narrative solutions or as manifestations of a modern subjectivity. In order to highlight the complexity of visual meaning making strategies in the version of Oliveira, I also propose an overview of visual and narrative representation of absence and presence, transparency and opacity, as well as the changing cultural, symbolic background of letter writing and reading as shown in the seventeenth-century Dutch painting and these four films.

The impulse of narrativization: The letter in the classic adaptations of the novel

There are two letters in *Doomed Love* that formally fit into the description of the 'late letter' as they start with the formula, 'by the time you read this letter, I will be dead', but they bear no melodramatic consequences. As Clara Rowland (2009, 75) argues, these two letters, in mirror position, have no connection with the action. The first, written by Simão before his crime, is never sent, the other, that of Teresa, arrives at the end of the novel, after the death of its author, just to summarize and conclude a love story that is melodramatic for the female protagonist (she falls victim of social circumstances, accepts it and dies), but escalates into a drama of the individual in the case of Simão. As Barros Baptista puts it, the hero's mistake – the choice to fall – is a modern one in the sense that it is not causing the action, but creates a destiny and a concept of destiny by interpreting a retroactively reconfigured action (2009, 112). In fact, Simão

---

[3] See, for example, the essays of Rowland (2009) and Barros Baptista (2009) on 'Simão's choice', reflected in his unsent letter.

chooses to symbolically die as a melodramatic character who assumes his failure, but at the same time, through the 'action gratuit' of killing Baltasar, he proclaims his freedom of choice, to be punished for a committed act instead of being reduced to passivity and helplessness by forces he cannot fight and circumstances he cannot control. This turn in the action from melodrama to modern drama can be sensed only in the film of Oliveira: in the scene of the killing, a completely indifferent Simão (who in the first part was so active in fighting against all odds) pays no attention to the bodily presence and fainting of Teresa. Although the lovers continue exchanging letters after Simão is being jailed, the remorse for causing Teresa's pain prevails in his letters over romantic love. Moreover, the version of Oliveira is the only one to represent the gap between what is written in the letters and what is done (a feature pointed out by Barros Baptista, 2009, 95) as a discrepancy between words and images.

In both the Ribeiro and Oliveira version, the last and late letter of Teresa is represented as a ghostly apparition of a body coming from the death: in Oliveira's film, stepping slowly to the fore from the dark background while reciting the text, in that of Ribeiro as a superimposition (Figures 8.1–8.2). According to Marc Vernet, superimposition has traditionally been a prominent figure of absence in European visual culture. It is adding the invocation to representation, making visible the invisible on the level of fiction, but on the level of discourse, it is also revealing a mechanism of film that remains invisible on the screen: it unites in the movement two different photograms. This is a case when the magic of film technology gives a new, poetic dimension to the story (1988, 104).

While Teresa's late letter appears as figuration of melodramatic temporality (it is the last letter closing the love story) and thus corresponds to the tradition of

Figures 8.1–8.2 The representation of the 'late letter' in Ribeiro's and Oliveira's version of *Doomed Love*.

sublimation of romantic love in Western culture (Vidal 2012, 167), the late, unsent letter of Simão is addressed to the reader and spectator, respectively, the only one to understand the turn from romantic love to a modern drama of subjectivity. The act of freedom of Simão ensuring his exodus from a suffocating social environment is somehow echoing what Lacan calls, 'the occult logic of courtly love': 'an altogether refined way of making up for the absence of sexual relation by pretending that it is we who put an obstacle to it' (1982, 141). In a psychoanalytical interpretation of the role of the letter in an unfulfilled love affair, taken forward by Slavoj Žižek, this becomes the 'third object' that 'finds itself at the place of the impossible Thing' (1994, 95). As Belén Vidal argues, expanding on this line of thought: 'The lovers' relationship is permanently structured through a third object, the letter: the letter appears as a sort of threshold: between present and past, the intimate and the social, but also between displacement of thought and the tangible presence of the body in space' (2012, 171,173). In the case of Castelo Branco's novel, this tangible presence is missing (the two meet only once, in a dark garden, for a few minutes), and, as Prado Coelho argues, the relationship as such is absent altogether from the novel (Coelho 1984, 97). In this respect, the letter adds nothing to the story, it only leaves a 'figural stain' on it, as Žižek puts it in his poetic question: 'is not the letter itself ultimately such a stain – not a signifier but rather an object resisting symbolization, a surplus, a material leftover circulating among the subjects and staining its momentary possessor?' (Žižek 2001, 8).

It is compelling how the adaptations from different periods of film history both in terms of technical and narratological competency use the letter either as a narrative device (the case of Ribeiro's version) or a redundant 'stain', simply an image absorbed to the visual figuration (the case of Oliveira's adaptation). Pallu's silent movie strikes us with its apparent redundancy: the image of the letter is often followed by inserts repeating its content. Moreover, this redundancy often works against narrative suspense and dramatic effect: for example, the inserts sometimes announce a series of future actions, like in the case of the murder of João da Cruz. This film documents a moment in the history of the medium of film practically acquainted with the whole arsenal of narrative techniques (parallel shots, shots illustrating the content of the letters, a big range of types of framing), but still finding it difficult to combine them smoothly in order to achieve an undisturbed narrative illusion. In fact, the whole film leaves us with the impression of fragmentation, due to a constant alternation between still and moving images, the images of the letters and inserts, as well as narration. This

136 *The Cinema of Manoel de Oliveira*

fragmentation and heterogeneity give the textual quality of Pallu's version and is responsible for its intermediality, defined by Ágnes Pethő as 'the experience of some kind of juxtapositions, jumps, loops or foldings between the media representations and what we perceive as cinematic reality' (2011, 5). We experience here a clear distinction between visual representation (that connected cinema to the history of visual arts) and narration (attracting cinema to the literary tradition), a duality that still existed in that moment of film history. Although the image of the letter served, together with the inserts, to fill the gaps of an imperfect film narration, it also acted against the realistic effect by showing the *surface* of the image that had to be read and thus required a different type of spectatorial gaze.

The practice of juxtaposition of silent images with texts in film has its roots in the painterly tradition of captioning in Dutch painting, carrying, according to Alpers, the text into the image. Many of these paintings present conversations: figures with heads bent, mouths open, hands flung out, expecting the viewer to supply the missing words (1984, 211).

In Ribeiro's film, the letter plays mostly an anecdotical part in adventurous scenes about the secret correspondence, creating suspense, or parallel scenes contrasting, for example, two different types of letter (one written by Teresa to Simão and the other by her father to Baltasar). Here, every detail is proof of an accomplished narrative competency of cinema and ability to enhance the illusion of reality with folkloric elements (physiognomy of characters, costumes, displayed traditions, even singing in a tavern, a spectacle typical of the sound cinema). The scene of letter writing and reading is yet another factor of narrative bravura aiming at entertainment, thus relying on unexpected turns in the story. It even introduces, in the scene with the beggar woman, a letter type that is not to be found in other adaptations of the novel: the intercepted letter, a trope typical not so much of the melodrama genre, but more of the thriller or historical drama, where the delay of information is crucial in view of the succession of narrated events. Ribeiro's version displays at the same time, just like that of Oliveira, the trope of the found letter that becomes in both cases a self-reflexive figure raising the issues of origin, authorship, fidelity to the literary work and authenticity.

At the beginning of both films, reference is made to the coincidence in biographies of Simão Botelho and his nephew, the writer Camilo Castelo Branco, who wrote the novel about his uncle's doomed love story in the same jail where the latter was incarcerated after committing the crime of murder. In Ribeiro's version, a voice-over narration accompanies the scene of writing, while in the

Letters on the Screen 137

film of Oliveira the link is made more visual with the recurrent, pervasive motif of the grids that surround the protagonist and the image of the manuscript, being also paired with a voice-over. Similarly, both films show in the last scene the love letters coming to the surface of the sea after the bodies of Simão and Mariana disappear. Again, and for the last time, the letter appears as a material substitute, a third object standing for the absent body and, being found, becomes a romantic figure of historical continuity, heritage and memory. Interestingly enough, while in Ribeiro's adaptation, the letters are floating on the water in the form of a book, in that of Oliveira, they are scattered on the surface of the water. This last image illustrates eloquently the different approaches of the two directors to the issue of the 'original text'. For Ribeiro, it is the Book, the Work of an Author that is unique and cannot be replaced or altered. For Oliveira, on the contrary, there is nothing else but a fragmented text that can be endlessly recreated, read and interpreted. In this respect, the letter itself is a figure of memory.[4]

In Oliveira's interpretation, the scene of letter writing and reading, as well as the image of the letter, appears as an excess to the narration, as a factor responsible for the gap between image and narration and as such belongs to the modernist stylization.

The gaze in focus: The letter in the version of Oliveira

Oliveira's representation of the letter scenes admittedly echoes one of the modes consecrated by the Nouvelle Vague, namely the reading aloud of texts. This performative approach to the letter can be identified in Godard's films,[5] and is systematically used in Truffaut's *Two English Girls* (1971), having the role to disturb narrative transparency. As Vidal points out:

> The reading aloud of the written text, alongside the actor's direct address to the camera is no less conventional than the voiceover that allows access to a character's thoughts and writing, yet it challenges the convention that would seal off the fictional space of the classical narrative.
>
> 2012, 174

---

[4] Oliveira repeatedly emphasized in interviews that he does not believe in authorship either, only in creators, or rather, re-creators. See, for example, his monologue in Wim Wenders' film, *Lisbon Story* (1994), stating that 'memory is the only reality'.

[5] As Pethő points out, 'in many of his films diegetic texts are not merely transposed onto the screen, but they are always subjected to some kind of action: they are read aloud, they are being translated, rewritten, misquoted, etc.' (2011, 8).

138   *The Cinema of Manoel de Oliveira*

In other words, 'the showing mode of realism gives in to the fragmentary literariness of the "telling"' (ibid., 175). In this cinematic approach, the letter becomes a figure conceived by Roland Barthes as a 'scene of language' in his *Fragments from a Lover's Discourse*. He writes about:

> Figures that take shape insofar as we can recognize, in passing discourse, something that has been read, heard, felt. The figure is outlined (like a sign) and memorable (like an image or a tale). A figure is established if at least someone can say: 'That's so true! I recognize that scene of language.'
>
> Barthes 1978, 4

Reciting the very subjective contents of the letter is comparable to the theatrical solution of the soliloquy, widely used by film adaptations of classic dramas. This mode of exposing innermost thoughts and intentions is presenting Castelo Branco's novel as participant in the discourse of individuality, characteristic of the modern European prose.[6] The adaptation of Oliveira elaborates on this aspect of the literary text: especially in the second part of the film, a rigorous framing of Simão's letter reading and writing body becomes a tool representing his complete isolation from the external world and a triumph of subjectivity. In these scenes, letters are surfaces onto which melancholy is projected, becoming what Agamben calls 'object images':

> objects that the melancholic sensibility has emptied of their habitual meaning and transformed into images of its own mourning ... [they] have no other significance than the space that they weave during the epiphany of the unattainable. Since the lesson of melancholy is that only what is ungraspable can truly be grasped, the melancholic alone is at his leisure among these ambiguous emblematic spoils.
>
> 1993, 26

At the same time, the character placed on one side of the frame with the other half empty or obscured (as if marking the absence of the addressee) makes these scenes mirror or match images of the letter-writing/reading images of Teresa (Figures 8.3–8.4). This visual symmetry, echoing the scene where the two lovers see each other for the very first time (in opposite windows, as if in mirrors), confirms Hamid Naficy's observation about the play of absences and presences underlying these scenes of epistolary film narratives: 'the very fact of addressing

---

[6]   About the trope of the letter and the modern novel, see more in Vidal (2012, 176).

Figures 8.3–8.4 The letter-writing and reading scenes in Oliveira's *Doomed Love*.

someone in an epistle ... transforms the addressee from an absent figure into a presence, which hovers in the text's interstices' (2001, 103).

This kind of framing of letter-writers and matching them with images of letter-readers actually follows a visual cultural tradition going back to the seventeenth-century Dutch painting depicting the letter-writing/reading scene. As Alpers points out about Gabriel Metsu's paintings with this subject, 'Separated by their frames, in their separate rooms, these lovers can forever attend to the representation of love rather than engage in love itself' (Alpers 1984, 197). Metsu invented the pendant, a man writing a letter to a woman, thus admitting the problem of absence by showing what or whom the letter stands for (Figures 8.5–8.6).

Besides a painterly framing of correspondents, Oliveira's images of them strike us with their lack of facial or bodily expression. Often seen as a Bressonian feature in his films, this also evokes Dutch paintings, depicting the same expressionless attitude. In Alpers' interpretation, this is related to a different kind of visuality and a subsequent demand for a new way of looking: 'What is suggested in the pictures – she points out – is not the content of the letters, the lovers' feelings, their plans to meet, or the practice and the experience of love, but rather the letter as an object of visual attention, a surface to be looked at' (1984, 196).

There are at least three ways of thematizing the gaze in Oliveira's version: 1. through the image of the letter emphasizing its materiality and calling for a different way of looking, reading, scanning or deciphering different kinds of signs; 2. with visual devices making the absent present or emphasizing the looking or peeping (mirrors, windows, curtains, paintings); and 3. with the representation of characters assisting at the letter-writing or reading scene as

Figures 8.5–8.6 Gabriel Metsu, *Man Writing a Letter* and *Woman Reading a Letter* (1662–5).

alter egos of the spectators. Indeed, the 16 mm stock quality, suitable for poetic purposes, but not very enduring, results in a more sensual-looking experience, the eye touching the surface of an almost dissolving texture. As Pethő points out, this 'sensual mode' 'invites the viewer to literally get in touch with a world portrayed not at a distance but at the proximity of entangled synesthetic sensations, and resulting in a cinema that can be perceived in the terms of music, painting, architectural forms or haptic textures' (2011, 5), so characteristic of the entire work of Oliveira. At the same time, the images of letters, folded and crumpled, urge the spectator to decipher or read them. The textu(r)al quality meaning both sensuality and a fragmented way of bringing together most heterogeneous signs, styles and discursive traditions from other arts (literature, theatre, painting, music) results in a very charged artwork. As Serge Daney claimed about this film of Oliveira, only few films in film history have pushed further the relationship between what is shown and what is seen.[7]

Mirrors, windows, paintings, curtains, just like letters, are figures of absence widely used in many Oliveira films. In the case of *Doomed Love*, these figures are often complemented by another one, described by Vernet in his *Figures de*

---

[7] Author's own translation from French: 'peu de films, dans l'histoire du cinéma, auront poussée plus loin l'examen des rapports entre ce qui est montré et ce qui est vu' (Daney 2001, 225).

l'absence (1988), namely the character looking directly into the camera, to the other side of the image, something out there, thus absent from the frame. The characters in full frontal shot reciting the letters that we cannot read represent a double figure of absence, while the content of the letters either recited or in voice-off are also discourses about absence. As Vernet points out, the gaze into the camera has the function of excluding any other partner outside the image who could attract a gaze not directed at the camera. In other words, here the character is his/her own partner and her/his gaze is equivalent to a soliloquy, emphasizing his absence, his isolation in a dreamworld (ibid., 46). The uniqueness of Oliveira's version consists of the representation of this absence and isolation of the characters despite their bodily presence on the screen, in the spirit of the second part of Castelo Branco's novel, where the characters are locked up in a jail and monastery, respectively, dying of illness and melancholy. As Vernet argues, the gaze into the camera, practised by the lovers while reading the letters aloud, also reveals the Elsewhere, the Death (ibid., 55).

The two letters in question, that of Simão and the last, closing one of Teresa, without any narrative function, also appear as pure figures of absence. The sentence, 'by the time you read this letter, I will be dead already', recalls one of the most paradigmatic works in film history, in which the letter comes to the fore against narrative transparency: Marcel Ophuls's, *A Letter from an Unknown Woman* (1948). Just like in that film, the letter of life and death is a ghostly presence that comes from another world and, through the voice-over, is opening up to the public and is invoking the spirit of its dead author.[8]

Finally, the presence of outsiders in the letter-reading scene has been traditionally considered, since the Dutch paintings I have already referred to, as thematization of spectatorship, voyeurism, but also as a representation of secrecy and intimacy. In these paintings, the letter is unreadable, its content is a secret to us: it appears as a hole, or, as Svetlana Alpers argues, as a 'vacuum at the centre': 'The letter stands in for or represents events and feelings that are not visible. Letters, as Otto van Veen put it neatly (quoting Seneca) in his *Amorum Emblemata*, are traces of love' (Alpers 1984, 196). In Oliveira's film, the spectatorial gaze is represented by the silent presence in the letter scene of Mariana and her father, who cannot read or write. Instead, they are trying to read on Simão's face the feelings provoked by the letter, which reiterates the distinction between reading a letter and reading an image. The illiterate Mariana

---

[8] On the letter scene of the film of Ophüls see Roger (2007, 35).

142 *The Cinema of Manoel de Oliveira*

and João da Cruz are the perfect messengers, just like the mute servant of Ophüls: they make letters move, while their authors are reduced to stillness. This contrast between the image of the letter being written or recited by the passive, melancholic lovers and the action carried forward by their helpers is most evident in Oliveira's version: this film is conceived like a Greek Tragedy, where Simão and Teresa are the choir, their immobile bodies echoing the texts of the letters, while the action is carried out by Mariana and João.

According to Alpers, the representation of letter writing and reading in Dutch paintings is related to the cultural fact of a high Dutch literacy in the seventeenth century, due to an increased necessity to communicate with the colonies that became a source of prosperity for the population. In Oliveira's film, just like in the two earlier versions, the trope of letter writing and reading is not given such a cultural dimension and the political and economic aspects of colonies are ignored as well. The Indies, where Simão is exiled, appear as a place out there, difficult to reach, even with letters or boats. Teresa's letters stop while the boat sails off and Simão dies at the very beginning of the road. Instead of being represented as a cultural artefact, a means of communication, the letter (its image, its writing and reading scenes) in Oliveira's film serves purely aesthetic purposes: besides its figural function, it stands for a revaluation of time and duration in the moving image, a Deleuzian paradigmatic change ostensibly present in Oliveira's work. In Deleuzian terms, the 'too-late' is not an accident that takes place in time either, but 'a dimension of time itself … opposed to the static dimension of the past' (Deleuze [1985] 1989, 96).

The oedipal gesture of Barroso: The absent letter

As we have seen, the main curiosity of the novel is that despite the epistolary genre, in it the melodramatic tropes of the unsent letter or late letter are mere empty forms, without narrative consequences, only responsible for communicating thoughts and feelings, or to emphasize separation, longing and duration of time. Accordingly, this late example of the epistolary genre, can be viewed as an intermediary form between a classic romantic novel and the modern psychological prose that consecrated the stream of consciousness and subjective monologue. The three adaptations discussed above present a wide use of the letter scene, either as a narrative factor or, in the case of Oliveira's film, an *image* concentrating aesthetic assumptions about the on-screen representation of time and absence. In contrast to this practice, Mario Barroso in his version perceives the letter as a pure cultural, and hence anachronistic, phenomenon, replacing it with mobile-phone conversations. This latter corresponds to the 'on-the-air sounds' category of Michel Chion, that 'usually situated in the scene's real time, enjoy the freedom of crossing boundaries of cinematic space' (1994, 52). The narrative device of the voice-off (termed as acousmatic voice by Chion), the ghostly voice coming from elsewhere, another world, becomes traceable, in this case, real, related to a body and is revealed as a pure technical issue. The voice reaching us through a mobile phone has the same role as the letter in Castelo Branco's previous adaptations: it is acting against cinematic transparency by revealing the technological foundations of the medium.

Some thirty years after the adaptation of Oliveira, with whom he worked together many times as director of photography, narrator or actor, Barroso realizes his own feature film that does not aspire to be The Adaptation of Camilo Castelo Branco's novel, but aims to be only one of these, as the title *A Doomed Love*, reflects. Moreover, he considers his film a free adaptation after the novel: it is not a period film, but set in today's Lisbon and marked by a teenage culture of the city, echoing, in this respect, Baz Luhrmann's *Romeo + Juliet* (1996). The novel itself is a repeatedly cited intertext in the film, characters read it, carry the book with them, talk about it and lend it to each other, as a sort of moral code or philosophy of life[9] of their generation (one of the characters even claims seeing the film, although she does not mention which adaptation of the novel; Figure 8.7).

In the film of Barroso, love is spreading as a contagion and the number of enamoured couples is multiplied, some of them are doomed (that of Simão and Teresa, Simão and Mariana, the incestuous relationship between his mother and brother), some of them have the promise of happiness (between Rita and Zé). But while Barroso makes visible the book, as pre-text of the film, he eliminates the letter as redundant, with an Oedipal gesture towards Oliveira's masterpiece, in which the letter scene is crucial in terms of visual stylization. This symbolic castration of both the classic adaptations and that of 'the master' (Barroso participated in a number of Oliveira's films as an actor), is paired with a new vision over the representation of absence. The letter scenes are replaced with original visual solutions for the unreachable, the ideal, thus unrepresentable woman. Teresa is hardly fully visible in the whole film: ingeniously recalling the window scene of the literary work, in which the two lovers see each other for the first time, her image is either a reflection

---

[9] This also has its tradition in the practice of literary adaptations: see, for example, Jim Jarmusch's *Ghost Dog: The Way of the Samurai* (1999), *The Jane Austen Book Club*, directed by Tom Swicord (2007) or the already analysed *Abraham's Valley* (1993).

Figure 8.7 The main character reading the book, *Doomed Love*, that becomes a moral code in the film of Mário Barroso.

on a windshield, on the screen of a computer (as another window), or appears in a dark room against huge closed windows. This post-modern refraction of the ideal body is in striking contrast with the overtly erotic, sensual scenes and the intense bodily presence of the main character, as well as that of Mariana, Rita, Simão's sister, or Zé, her friend. Indeed, while the previous three adaptations, just like the novel, only mention the Indies as a remote place, Barroso brings in the colonies by co-producing his film with a Brazilian company and casting numerous actors with colonial family backgrounds. This cultural-anthropological interest is closest to that of Ribeiro, but without his preference for the spectacular and historical authenticity. In terms of visual stylization and framing, Barroso's version is comparable to that of Oliveira, but instead of a purely aesthetical detachment, it offers a rather moral approach to the story (by opposing the ideal to the immoral) and is more preoccupied with (bodily) presence than absence.

The film of Barroso effaces the letter and replaces it with the acousmatic voice and the stylized image of the ideal woman. The earlier adaptations alternate the letter scene and story that results in a palimpsest-like effect: in them, writing and letters are being either absorbed by the image and narrative, or, in the case of Oliveira's film, emerge from moving images as carefully framed, still images. The last sequence of Oliveira's film, in which the written text merges with the image of the sea waves can be seen as a figure of the modernist discourse on *writing as image and image as writing*. After *Doomed Love*, the scene of letter writing and reading returns in many films of Oliveira, always concentrating his attitude about narrative, sound and conveying of emotions over the absence/loss of a beloved person.

9

Sounding letters

Emotional and musical dissonances in *Francisca*

An elaborated example of the letter as figure of absence appears in *Francisca*, an adaptation of Agustina Bessa-Luís's novel, *Fanny Owen*, based on a nineteenth-century tragic love story, documented by preserved letters of family members and the protagonists. In the film of Oliveira, the letter is represented as a proof of real events but, as Rita Benis argues, it does not change Oliveira's ambivalent relationship with truth, its quest being left open at the end of the film (Benis 2009, 37).

The opening letter-reading scene of *Francisca* appears, in addition to its slowness and stillness, as a tool of stretching the narrative frame inside-out through repetition. It is a pictorial scene, following abruptly the intertitle that situates the story in Portuguese history, written in red on a black background and accompanied by a loud and dramatic, late romantic-style musical score (signed by João Paes). This scene features a woman reading a letter that announces in a female voice-over the tragic death of a young couple, the protagonists of the film to follow, Francisca (Fanny) and José Augusto. Thus, in this case, the letter stands not only for the absent body of its writer, but also for that of the deceased couple.

While the non-diegetic musical score of the intertitle recedes a bit, we hear the content of the letter in a voice-over of its writer, who concludes that she cannot write more because she cannot see any more (presumably because of her tears). Then, the reading woman turns her eyes away from the letter and closes them in pain, the camera advances to the lace curtain, so close that we see its texture, and at the same time we hear, word by word, the content of the letter repeated, while the credits of the film appear on the same veil and the loud dramatic music fills the scene, aggressively intruding into the feminine privacy and intimacy of deep sorrow. It is a scene very charged emotionally, in which

146   *The Cinema of Manoel de Oliveira*

repetition happens in the same shot. The second occurrence of the voice-over (in another female voice) is echoing the same words, as if (re)sounding in the memory of the reader of the letter, who is also unable to read the letter, turning her eyes away, towards the lace curtain, a metaphor of the veil of tears. In parallel with this, the film image loses its transparency, becomes a haptic experience and opens onto itself through the texture of the curtain. The repetition of the same tragic message by two different female, mourning voices – one voice-over and the other what Serge Daney calls *through* voice, a voice whose source is *in* the image, both belonging to an imaginary space (Daney 2013, 20) – very similar in their timbre, expressing a kind of tired resignation, appears as a technique conveying cinematically the effect of a shocking message, as well as the coping strategy of the human psyche when faced with unbelievable, tragic news. This is in line with Daney's new approach to the voice-over, often identified with an absence in the image. He rather thinks the opposite is true: voices should be related to their effects (thus their presence) *in* or *on* the image. As he argues, 'my voice intrudes upon the image, affecting my interlocutor's face and body and triggering a furtive or perhaps overt reaction, a response. The viewer can measure the violence of my statement by the disturbance it causes in the person who receives it' (ibid., 19).

Shot in front of a large window, this letter-reading scene evokes, as Anne Hollander points out about similar scenes in cinema, an 'emotional atmosphere analogous to the spell of Vermeer's women, an uncanny evocation of female inwardness conveyed in a picture that seems to show a sequence of important moments without showing any action' (Hollander 1989, 445). Although the letter-writing and letter-reading scenes as cultural and social (visual) code are not central to the narrative, in *Francisca*, letters do play a cardinal role in the dramatic development of events and emotions: the flight of Fanny from home is planned in letters, the letters of Fanny to her parents are returned unopened, causing emotional distress and greatly contributing to her isolation and, finally, the letter of José Augusto's lover, intercepted by Fanny, is the last dramatic blow, leading to her physical and emotional destruction (Figures 9.1–9.2).

The displacement of emotions to the level of style (music, composition, decoration of dark interiors, lit only by candles) is characteristic of the melodrama genre, but also of Oliveira's somehow distant attitude towards the shadows of the soul, especially those of a female character. While Agustina Bessa-Luís, the writer of the original novel, *Fanny Owen*, is more concerned with the world of women and speaks about the need to reveal the essentially 'transvestite' aspect of

Figures 9.1-9.2 Letter-reading and intercepting scenes as key dramatic moments in *Francisca*.

the woman, and to present what has been hidden until now, in a melodramatic way (Saraiva 2009, 100), Oliveira is preoccupied with what he considers the historical truth, allegorically reflected in the personal drama. As Bessa-Luís remarked in one of her interviews, in *Francisca* observation and distanciation through aestheticization keep that seventh door of the castle of Barbe Blue (that is, the innermost emotions) closed (Mexia 1996, 3). This is an artistic attitude prevailing, as already argued in the previous chapters, in the films of Oliveira in general and his representations of women in particular.

The opening intertitle, accompanied by monumental orchestral music, introduces the story of Francisca and José Augusto as a product of the big political scene: with the conquest of Brazilian independence in 1822, an atmosphere of instability reigns in Portugal, marked by conflicts between conservatives and liberals, contributing to the appearance of the type of a young man who saw his traditionalist ideals unfulfilled, sceptic and inclined to sombre passions. From this historico-political overview, Oliveira abruptly establishes the link between the historical and the individual: 'this is the true story of a funest passion between Francisca and José Augusto'. By introducing the protagonists simply by their names, omitting their surnames and family relationships, Oliveira already outlines the drama of the individual (any individual) lost in chaotic historical events of monumental scale. It is exactly this generalization by omission that turns the romantic melodrama into an allegory of a deep social and political crisis. Just like the intertitles, the music of the film, both diegetic and non-diegetic, dissonant big orchestral and choral music using percussion and disturbing, breaking-glass effects, frames the story and symbolizes the unstable social and political background (inflexible moral codes leading to the isolation of Francisca), and a generalized atmosphere of disillusion

148   *The Cinema of Manoel de Oliveira*

leading to the emptiness of José Augusto. At the end of the film, in the restaurant scene bringing up the mysterious death circumstances of José Augusto, the idea of the opening intertitle is reiterated, and with this the narrative frame is realized. José Augusto is considered by the writer Camilo Castelo Branco (one of the characters of the film) an example of the chaotic condition of the society: talent without bon sense, barbarism mixed with culture, sensibility with egoism. A gunshot-like theatrical loud noise closes the scene and the same music from the ball episode of the very beginning starts off.

Oliveira's conscious decision not to use conventional scoring or any traditional (tonal, instrumental) type of music in scenes dealing with intense emotional content, or the use of traditional orchestral, classical music (in the carnival scene, for example) with a contrasting purpose (exaggerated cheerfulness in times of crisis) has to do with the same intention to signify the indifference of history to individual suffering. Michel Chion also distinguishes between empathetic and indifferent music in film, this latter exhibiting, as he puts it, a 'conspicuous indifference to the situation, by progressing in a steady, undaunted, and ineluctable manner'. The opening letter-reading scene is an example of this kind of musical score as backdrop of 'indifference' (Chion 1998, 8).

Despite the female name in the title, in both the novel and the film, great attention is given to the friendship between the two men, the writer Camilo Castelo Branco and José Augusto, both products of their historical times and in a desperate search for the limits of morality. It is rather through their conversations (in which Camilo mostly tries to dissuade José Augusto from ruining Fanny) that a very sketchy, two-dimensional portrait of Fanny is drawn. She appears as a symptom of psychologically disturbed men, trapped in a morbid fascination with death, characteristic of late Romantism. Although critics like to talk about a love triangle, the bonding between Camilo and José Augusto is much more developed in the narrative than the men's relationship with the catalyst of their (self-)destructive Byronism, an innocent young woman. The two men appear as the two sides of the same uncertain male principle balancing between light and shadow: Camilo's interpretive monologues about José Augusto reveal an urge for self-understanding. It is Camilo who discovers and names the psychological pattern in José Augusto's behaviour, coining Don Juan and Hamlet as its literary antecedents. Both references point at a problematic relationship with women, stemming from an early loss and sense of abandonment related to the mother. Loss and fear of a new abandonment are at the core of melancholia, defined by Freud and post-Freudians as mourning over an anticipated loss. It

Sounding Letters 149

generates a wishful thinking of death, denounced by the fictional character, Camilo, in both the novel and the film, claiming that: 'thinking of death at 20 years is not poetry but crime'. Contrasting this critique, the poetics of Oliveira seems to comply with Agustina Bessa-Luís's assumption that 'the real presence is in death' (1957, 386).

Melancholy coined as 'the dysentery of the soul' by the character Camilo, is permeating the images and sounds of the film: tableau-like compositions with motionless, puppet-like characters, lighting and colours that make living bodies look cadaveric and the disturbing dissonant music, all culminating in the long deathbed scene of Francisca. The overflowing pain emanating from her letters, full of 'indiscrecies' as José Augusto puts it, is sublimated as style in Oliveira's film, an excess marking both the visual and the auditive design. The contrast between image and sound, movement and stillness is the main source of a disturbing emotional effect: the loudness and rudeness of servants counters the silence of Francisca, the sombre choral, religious music (as if of a burial) overwrites the wedding images, and the image of a stormy sea is followed by its stilled, frozen version, framed by the window of the living room where Francisca welcomes her visitors. The poetic representation is characterized by a duality between the images of interiors as signifiers of unspoken emotions of the female character and the long dialogues and monologues uttered in expressionless voices by male protagonists seeking the meaning of events. The film of Oliveira takes to the extreme the poetic impact of the tension between image and sound, 'the aperture and the interstice between soundtrack and visual track', as Alfonso Crespo puts it (2013, 58). This is a natural feature of cinema also according to Michel Chion, who finds that there is no natural and pre-existing harmony between image and sound (1994, 17). As Chion claims and *Francisca* testifies, 'sound more than image has the ability to saturate and short-circuit our perception' (ibid., 33): loud and disturbing, both so-called pit music and screen music (non-diegetic and located directly or indirectly in the space and time of the action) anticipate the dramatic events, orchestrating their convergence and divergence by recurrence. As Chion argues, by repetition, the musical score can carry the perception of the image to another level, without formally contradicting or 'negating' the image (ibid., 38). This is the case of the repetition of the cheerful and fast-tempoed ball music at the close of the film, in line with the period-drama scene, but still adding a touch of irony by suggesting that time is rushing forward, leaving the clueless men sitting and thinking.

150   *The Cinema of Manoel de Oliveira*

The visual and textual equivalent of non-diegetic, orchestral, 'pit music' is the intertitle either positioning the scenes in time and place, or providing a narrative bridge between them. As a cinematic tool of the silent era, replaced later by the voice-over narrator, the intertitle traditionally prescribes the images to follow. But, in *Francisca*, images seem to contradict the content dictated by the written text: when this latter refers to historical events, images reply with middle-class interiors and when the text informs about action and adventure (in case of Francisca's flight from home), the obscure images reveal indistinct shadows moving slowly and silently. In accordance with Chion's remark, the mutual challenge here arises from the fact that: 'The text seems to create images as it wishes, but the image retorts, "you're incapable of telling me all"' (ibid., 174). The tension between the speakable (historical and family events conveyed in intertitles) and unspeakable (individual suffering figurated through stylistical elements) is not attenuated by the dialogues of characters, that is, theatrical speech with a dramatic, informative (and less psychological, affective) function. The characters' apparent indifference towards their own emotions and those of others is only comparable to that of the dissonant music towards the depicted events.

The musical scenes of *The Letter*

By contrast, in *The Letter*, the opening and closing musical scene, a live concert of Pedro Abrunhosa is perfectly congruent with the emotions it depicts: the enthusiasm of a crowd, affected by the loud pop music, with lyrics reminding of the confessional content of love letters. Intriguingly, in this adaptation of Madame de La Fayette's novel, *The Princesse de Clèves* (originally published in 1678), the letter as cultural communication code specific for the sixteenth century, when the story of the original novel is taking place, is almost entirely missing. As such, despite the title, it is a real figure of absence in the film, standing for the lack of communication between the two protagonists in love, who resist their own feelings in the name of an anachronistic sense of morality and fidelity: the Princess of Clèves (played by Chiara Mastroianni) and the Portuguese star, pop singer Pedro Abrunhosa. In the adaptation of Oliveira, transposing the story into a contemporary French and Portuguese context, the letter as the ultimate (and obsolete) sign of life appears at the end of the film, in a scene featuring the nun, the only confidante and friend of Madame de Clèves, reading aloud her

Sounding Letters 151

letter (an example of in-voice, to use Daney's category) informing her friend about her whereabouts and spiritual journey as a volunteer in a children-rescue mission in Africa. This scene is missing from the original novel, in which the princess is also withdrawing from public life and spends much time in a monastery and has no confidante or adviser. It is exactly the unbearable moral burden of keeping the promise to a dying mother and husband, that of not to marry the Duke of Nemours, that leads to her isolation. In Oliveira's film, the nun thus appears as an embodiment of an innermost, helping and self-defensive voice encouraging her to follow her emotions and allow the fulfilment of her love for Abrunhosa. The letter 'sounding' in the voice of the nun (she reads it aloud) also seems to support this hypothesis of the nun being a kind of alter ego to the princess. No other letter appears in the film, leaving the spectator with an unfulfilled expectation for the letter promised in the title. Instead of a narrative tool causing a dramatic turn in the love story, the film leaves us with a letter definitively closing down the communication between protagonists and the story.

By omitting the letter-writing and reading scenes, and the important episode of La Fayette's novel revolving around a misplaced letter from an unknown woman, causing a series of misunderstandings and adventures in the novel, Oliveira's film is, in fact, adapting in an exaggerated way the princess's strategy to forgo absolutely any contact, as stated in the final sentences of the novel: 'The princess had not only forbidden her (a messenger) to come back with any message from him, but even to report the conversation that should pass between them' (La Fayette 1678). While in the novel there is more contact between the two protagonists (they are actually forging a letter together to replace the lost misplaced letter, an incident that brings them even closer), the film is restricted to very short encounters and formal conversations between the princess and Abrunhosa. This is a perfect replica of *Doomed Love* illustrating the mystery of fatal attraction and romantic idealization.

Instead of the letter-writing scene typical of the seventeenth-century social and romantic interactions, as represented in the Dutch paintings of the same era, Oliveira refers to another type of the Dutch genre painting, those depicting music being made *in the painting*. In these paintings depicting a man and a woman making music together, the love story is perceived through the music: the musical scene becomes an allusion to the underlying romantic story (Hollander 1989, 448; Figure 9.3). In the same vein, in *The Letter*, we get to know the protagonists along musical scenes: live pop concerts of Abrunhosa alternate

Figures 9.3 Musical scenes as emotional/romantic scenes in seventeenth-century Dutch painting, Gerard ter Borch, *A Music Lesson* (1668).

with classical musical concerts that the princess attends regularly with her mother. Their encounter happens at a piano recital performed by pop star Abrunhosa: in contrast with his usual loud performance, this time he is singing with his own piano accompaniment. We may say that this is the only musical scene where the two completely different worlds of the protagonists meet and are attracted to each other.

The distance between the princess and the singer is depicted not only as a social, but also as a cultural and temporal one: the princess is a member of the French aristocracy, Abrunhosa is a Portuguese pop star conquering the world with his concerts. He lives in the present, addresses contemporary topics in his songs, wants to please his public and acts as any pop star, having superficial love relationships regularly aired by the media. The princess instead lives isolated and follows anachronistic moral principles. Even their looks express this incompatibility: Abrunhosa's self-created pop-star image, 'a man in black', with black hat and constant dark sunglasses (he never takes them off) and thick-soled sports shoes have a touch of the ridiculous next to the classy elegance of the princess.

Adaptation conceived as 'adoption' of an anachronistic literary 'object' here is thematized, after *Benilde*, *Abraham's Valley* or *Francisca*, as an irrational, fatal attraction between historical and contemporary social roles, signified by music styles and the characters' relationship to these. Abrunhosa actively makes and performs his own music, the princess is listening passively to classical music (the Schubert *Impromptu*s, among others, performed by Maria João Pires). The

Sounding Letters 153

singer plays a more active part in the love story, in line with his constantly performing life style: he is visiting, is sending messages, is trying to meet, while the princess, a passive audience of concerts, is constantly withdrawing and generally takes an avoidant behaviour. In Oliveira's film, the unbridgeable gap between the two is emphasized on a metanarrative level by different modes of representation which the characters belong to: Abrunhosa is playing himself, in live concerts and in other scenes, while the role of the princess is played by Chiara Mastroianni: he is a real, she is a fictional character, a difference somehow attenuated by Abrunhosa's stardom and idealized image.

The duality between reality and its representation is thematized from the very beginning of the film and opens off-stage, where we see Abrunhosa getting ready for the concert in his dressing room (while the cast list appears on the screen), then stepping on-scene with the words: 'May the music be with you!' Addressed both to his public and spectators, this opening sentence already emphasizes the role of music (classical and popular) as a signifying system in the film. In line with Chion's categories, the diegetic music in the film is empathetic, as it directly expresses its participation in the feeling of the scene (Chion 1994, 8). The *Impromptu* piece played a bit too hastily, almost hysterically by Maria João Pires at one of the classical music concerts, depicts the princess's state of mind, hidden behind socially prescribed manners. Her mask-like face, however, becomes transfigured by passion when listening to Abrunhosa's piano music and singing (a change immediately noticed by her mother). In contrast, the loud concert scenes, contrasting Abrunhosa's restrained, polite behaviour and general expressionlessness, appear as eruptions of unspoken emotions, also articulated in the confession-like lyrics of songs: 'I want you to be my voice,' 'I don't want to be the first to cry' and the last concert about love and death, meant to 'exorcize' the song inside him with the public.

The use of classical and pop music as signifiers of moral values and emotions is in line with Rick Altman's observation about film music: while classical music is bound to express universal feelings (like love, longing or loss), pop music is more related to personal, actual emotions (as the first person occurrences of Abrunhosa's lyrics attest; Altman 2001, 26).

Besides music, scenes of eavesdropping and peeping have the role to signify emotions that cannot be expressed or verbalized directly: as the princess formulates, she is afraid to be told what she already knows. There are two scenes that work as displaced love confessions reaching the person in question somehow 'illegally', involuntarily, making words useless: the princess sees Abrunhosa stealing a miniature photo of her and Abrunhosa overhears a discussion between the princess and her husband, in which she reveals being in love and that she knows that he took her photo. This scene of the indirect exchange of information evokes yet another visual tradition of seventeenth-century Dutch painting, that of paintings of characters eavesdropping on love scenes, visible only for the spectator, or, alternatively, characters peeping behind curtains. Moreover, Abrunhosa rents an apartment opposite the princess's house, to be close to her, constantly keeping an eye on her. His desiring gaze is represented rather by the compositions and scenes than the point-of-view shots, as his gaze is completely missing, being blocked by the dark sunglasses. The painterly, cultural reference confers, once again, a historical dimension to the cinematic representation, as if literary adaptation would trigger a regression of film language into its own past of visual codes contemporary with the novel. The anachronistic, old-fashioned topic of love restricted by morality attracts visual representations of carefully framed interiors as well-guarded private spaces. These visual codes, just like the other, regressive tool of intertitles filling the gaps in the visible story, become the adequate signifiers of the similarly obsolete story of a girl 'too perfect to be happy'. This is actually true for all female characters of Oliveira's films: as long as they are on a pedestal, they can be admired, but not loved. They can be possessed only as loss – the paradoxical mechanism of melancholia permeating this cinema.

References

Adorno, Theodor W. and Hanns Eisler. 2005. *Composing for the Films*. London and New York: Continuum.

Agamben, Georgio. 1993. *Stanzas: Word and Phantasm in Western Culture*. Trans. Ronald L. Martinez. Minneapolis, MN: University of Minnesota Press.

Alpers, Svetlana. 1984. *The Art of Describing: Dutch Art in the Seventeenth Century*. Chicago, IL: University of Chicago Press.

Altman, Rick. 2001. 'Cinema and Popular Song: The Lost Tradition'. In *Film and Soundtrack*, eds Pamela Robertson Wojcik and Arthur Knight, 19–30. Durham, NC: Duke University Press.

Barros Baptista, Abel. 2009. '*O erro de Simão*' ['The Mistake of Simão']. In *Amor de Perdição. Uma Revisão* [Doomed Love: A Revision], ed. Abel Barros Baptista, 81–112. Coimbra: Angelus.

Barthes, Roland. 1978. *A Lover's Discourse: Fragments*. Trans. Richard Howard. New York: Hill and Wang.

Benis, Rita de Brito. 2009. 'Agustina, Camilo e Oliveira. Uma aproximação de artes e temas a propósito das circunstâncias do caso Fanny Owen', Textos/Pretextos, 12: 32–43.

Bessa-Luís, Agustina. 1957. A Muralha. Lisboa: Guimarães Editores.

Bessa-Luís, Agustina. 2000. Vale Abraão. Lisboa: Planeta DeAgostini SA.

Bruhn, Jørgen. 2008. 'Tristan Transformed. Bodies and Media in the Historical Transformation of the Tristan and Isolde Myth'. In Changing Borders: Contemporary Positions in Intermediality, eds Jens Arvidson, Mikael Askander, Jurgen Bruhn and Heidrun Führer, 339–60. Lund: Lund Intermedia Press.

Chambers, Iain. 2017. 'Art as Anachronism'. Third Text. Critical Perspectives on Contemporary Art and Culture. Available at: http://thirdtext.org/carroll-chambers-review (accessed 30 October 2019).

Chion, Michel. 1994. Audio-Vision: Sound on Screen. New York: Columbia University Press.

Chion, Michel. 1998. Le Son. Ouïr, écouter, observer. Première édition. Paris: Armand Colin.

Crespo, Alfonso. 2013. 'Voices at the Altar of Mourning: Challenges, Affliction'. Cinema Comparat/ive Cinema, 1 (3): 57–65.

Dalle Vacche, Angela. 1996. Eric Rohmer's The Marquise of O: Painting Thoughts, Listening to Images. In Cinema and Painting: How Art is Used in Film, 81–106. Austin, TX: Texas University Press.

Daney, Serge. 2001. 'Notes sur les films de Manoel de Oliveira'. In La Maison Cinéma et le monde. 1: Le Temps des Cahiers, 225–7. Paris: P.O.L.

Daney, Serge. 2013. 'Back to Voice: On Voices Over, Back, Out, Through'. Cinema Comparat/ive Cinema, 1 (3): 18–20.

de La Fayette, Madame. 2009. The Princesse of Cleves. Oxford: Oxford University Press.

Deleuze, Gilles. [1982] 1986. Cinema 1: The Mouvement-Image. Trans. Hugh Tomlimson and Barbara Habberjam. Minneapolis, MN: University of Minnesota Press.

Deleuze, Gilles. [1985] 1989. Cinema 2: The Time-Image. Trans. Hugh Tomlinson and Robert Galeta. Minneapolis, MN: University of Minnesota Press.

Derrida, Jacques. 1978. 'Freud and the Scene of Writing'. In Writing and Difference, 196–232. Chicago, IL: University of Chicago Press.

Didi-Huberman, Georges. 2003. 'Before the Image, Before Time: The Sovereignty of the Anachronism'. In Compelling Visuality. The Work of Art in and out of History, eds Claire Farago and Robert Zwijnenberg, 31–44. Minneapolis, MN: University of Minneapolis Press.

Doane, Mary Ann. 1980. 'The Voice in Cinema: The Articulation of Body and Space'. Yale French Studies, 60: 33–50.

Donaldson-Evans, Mary. 2005. 'A Medium of Exchange: The Madame Bovary Film'. Society of Dix-Neuviémistes, 4: 21–34.

156   *The Cinema of Manoel de Oliveira*

Flaubert, Gustave. 1857. *Madame Bovary*. Paris: Michel Lévy Frères, Libraires-Éditeurs.

Gaudreault, André. 1988. *Du Littéraire au Filmique. Le Système du Récit*. Paris: Méridiens Klinksieck.

Gorfinkel, Elena. 2005. 'The Future of Anachronism. Todd Haynes and the Magnificent Andersons'. In *Cinephilia: Movies, Love, and Memory*, eds Marijke de Valck and Malte Hagener 153–67. Amsterdam: Amsterdam University Press.

Greene, Thomas. 1986. 'History and Anachronism'. In *The Vulnerable Text: Essays on Renaissance Literature*. New York: Columbia University Press.

Hollander, Anne. 1989. *Moving Images*. New York: Alfred A. Knopf.

Lacan, Jacques. 1982. 'God and the Jouissance of The Woman. A Love Letter (1972–73)'. In *Feminine Sexuality: Jacques Lacan and the école freudienne*, Juliet Mitchell and Jacqueline Rose, 137–61. New York: Norton.

Leitch, Thomas. 2007. *Film Adaptation and its Discontents: From* Gone with the Wind *to* The Passion of Christ. Baltimore, MD: Johns Hopkins University Press.

Mexia, Pedro. 1996. '*A Prudência esclarece-me mais do que a verdade. Diário de Notícias*'. Available at: http://www.guimarães-ed.pt/agustina/ablbib.htm (accessed 14 February 2020).

Naficy, Hamid. 2001. *An Accented Cinema: Exilic and Diasporic Filmmaking*. Princeton, NJ: Princeton University Press.

Pethő, Ágnes. 2011. *Cinema and Intermediality: The Passion for the In-Between*. Newcastle upon Tyne: Cambridge Scholars Publishing.

Pidduck, Julianne. 1998. 'Of Windows and Country Walks'. *Screen*, 39 (4): 381–400.

Prado Coelho, Eduardo. 1983. *20 Anos de Cinema Português* (1962–1982). Lisboa: Biblioteca Breve.

Roger, Philippe. 2007. '*Correspondances ophulsiennes*'. In *Lettres de Cinéma. De la missive au film-lettre*, eds Nicole Cloarec. Rennes: Presses Universitaires de Rennes.

Rowland, Clara. 2009. '*O Escolho do Romance*'. In *Amor de Perdição. Uma Revisão*, ed. 59–80. Abel Barros Baptista Coimbra: Angelus Novus.

Saraiva, Arnaldo. 2009. '*Conversa com Agustina Bessa-Luís*'. *Textos/Pretextos*, 12 (2009) (published with the permission of the Portuguese Radio and Television), 90–101.

Søndergaard, Sidsel Maria. 2006. 'Women in Impressionism: An Introduction'. In *Women in Impressionism: From Mythical Feminine to Modern Woman*, ed. Sidsel Maria Søndergaard, 11–28. Milano: Skira.

Stam, Robert. 2005. 'Introduction: The Theory and Practice of Adaptations'. In *Literature and Film: A Guide to the Theory and Practice of Film Adaptation*, eds Robert Stam and Alessandra Raengo, 2–52. London: Blackwell Publishing.

Steyerl, Hito. 2012. *The Wretched of the Screen*. London: Sternberg Press/E-Flux Journal.

Stewart, Garrett. 2006. *The Look of Reading: Book, Painting, Text*. Chicago, IL: University of Chicago Press.

Strauber, Susan. 2006. 'Manet's Portrait of Jeanne Duval: *Baudelaire's Mistress, Reclining*'. In *Women in Impressionism: From Mythical Feminine to Modern Woman*, ed. Sidsel Maria Søndergaard, 99–131. Milano: Skira.

Vernet, Marc. 1988. *Figures de l'absence* [*Figures of Absence*]. Paris: Éditions de l'étoile.

Vidal, Belén. 2012. *Figuring the Past: Period Film and the Mannerist Aesthetic*. Amsterdam: Amsterdam University Press.

Vidal Villasur, Belén. 2002. 'Classic Adaptations, Modern Reinventions: Reading the Image in the Contemporary Literary Film'. *Screen*, 43 (1): 5–18.

Žižek, Slavoj. 1994. *The Metastases of Enjoyment: Six Essays on Woman and Causality*. London: Verso.

Žižek, Slavoj. 2001. *Enjoy Your Symptom! Jacques Lacan in Hollywood and Out*. 2nd edn. London: Routledge.

Coda

A melancholic cinema?

In the light of the case studies of the previous chapters, Freud's definition of the uncanny (as the emergence of the unfamiliar in the familiar and the uncertainty whether something is what it seems to be) does not only apply to most of the topics of Oliveira's films, but is equally true of his vision of cinema, including his attraction to the magic of still and moving images, the stubborn repetition of certain topoi, the obsession with the image of the (dead and dying) woman, his relationship with a cinematic and wider cultural heritage, the link between recurring actors and their roles, as well as the effect all this has on the spectator. The applicability of the concept of *uncanny* to Oliveira's cinema as a whole, instead of generating contradictions, rather reveals a close interconnectedness between the different layers of his work, that constantly reflect each other. As I have been arguing in this book, the inherent intermediality of cinema, its organic connection with the myth of modernity (as a technology celebrating change but unable to break up with the historical tradition of visual arts, theatre and literature), overtly thematized, along with a series of anachronistic topics, also serve the uncanny effect which these films emanate. In this final chapter, I aim to reframe the features of repetition and return to the Oliveirian cinema from a new perspective: melancholia and nostalgia, and their unique, culturally specific mixture, *saudade*, as permeating its stories and images.

The obsessive repetitions revolving around dualities like the mysteries of life and death, divine and human, speakable and unspeakable, past and present, together with constant stylistic and figurative features like tableau compositions, chiaroscuro lighting effects, declamatory, monotonous monologues and dialogues, the image of women, to name but a few, all seem to point to what psychoanalysis would term as an 'unfinished business', that is, an experience or situation that keeps repeating in somebody's life until, as a lesson, it is learned or

160 *The Cinema of Manoel de Oliveira*

'processed'. What was, then, Oliveira's unfinished business? What is the loss that lurks behind so many of his films? Besides occasional preoccupations with various kinds of objects of loss in interviews and films (such as the death of his cousin Angelica and of his grandson David, the periodic loss of faith or a long political isolation), unexpectedly comes the open confession in a letter addressed to Julia Buisel in 1993, made public shortly before the death of Oliveira:

> My films, that is, in my films, I am only looking for the expression of a hurt. At times, they surely give me joy when through them I envision a Beauty that seduces me as something transcending me in many respects. But apart from these fleeting moments, the rest is only suffering, or better, 'the product of this suffering' is a mode of getting rid of them. It makes me happy, sad and even depressed.
>
> Buisel 2012, 98, author's own translation

In this very close description of artistic sublimation of melancholia, pain and sadness appear as a constant condition fuelling creativity. Julia Kristeva contends that aesthetic elaboration through a work of art, a configuration of which the prosodic economy, the dramaturgy of characters and the implicit symbolism are an extremely faithful semiological representation of the subject's battle with 'symbolic breakdown', can be considered as a cathartic 'therapeutic method' to attenuate this pain, without the necessity of understanding its cause (1987, 10). But the recurring topic of sadness over a real or anticipated loss in films by Oliveira points at the refusal of the melancholic to accomplish the work of mourning. As Slavoj Žižek points out, this 'takes the form of its very opposite, a faked spectacle of the excessive, superfluous mourning for an object even before this object is lost. This is what provides unique flavor to a melancholic' (2000, 661).

In fact, what makes of melancholia an unfinished business, is a confusion already signalled by Freud in *Mourning and Melancholia* (1917) and discussed more extensively from a cultural perspective by Žižek (relying on Giorgio Agamben), namely 'the confusion between loss and lack: insofar as the object-cause of desire is originally, in a constitutive way, lacking, melancholy interprets this lack as a loss, as if the lacking object was once possessed'. As Žižek elaborates:

> The explanation of this deceitful translation of lack into loss enables us to assert our possession of the object; what we never possessed can also never be lost, so the melancholic, in his unconditional fixation on the lost object, in a way possesses it in its very loss. In short, melancholia offers the paradox of an intention to mourn that precedes and anticipates the loss of the object.
>
> Ibid., 659–61

Fuelled by a real or anticipated, imagined loss – individual, familial losses and the vision of a declining Portuguese economic-political and cultural prestige, of which he feels responsible – in the films of Oliveira melancholia is eloquently represented both in the verbal performances of characters and in highly aestheticized visuals, painterly compositions and *tableaux vivants*. The monotonous, repetitive, narcissistic and masochistic monologues of characters, depicting the unbearable tension between desire and learned helplessness, present in all his films about failed romantic relationships (even beyond the so-called series of 'frustrated loves') are in line with Kristeva's description of verbal utterances of the melancholic: 'A repetitive rhythm, a monotonous melody emerges and dominates the broken logical sequences, changing them into recurring, obsessive litanies' (1989, 132). The painterly compositions of lying/dying women or seductive women isolate the still image from the narrative background and have the power to transform it into a concentration of repressed, unspeakable meanings that the melancholic character cannot verbalize. The male characters' fixation on emotionally unstable, manipulative, fanatic women, femmes fatales who bring destruction, can also be interpreted as the irresistible attraction to death of the melancholic.

The figural emerging as a painterly reference disrupting narration in the case of *Doomed Love* (1978), *Francisca* (1981), *The Satin Slipper* (1985) and *Abraham's Valley* (1996), for example, is meant to render visible death and the death drive as unspeakable contents inherent to melancholia, characterized by asymbolia or the impossibility of signification and figuration. As Kristeva puts it: 'If I am no longer capable of translating or metaphorizing, I become silent and I die' (1989, 42). This sublimatory approach to grief can be viewed as the repression of the individual and political in the aesthetic, that is, in the figurative modes of nostalgia and melancholia in films that showcase both real and anticipated losses.

Mourning and sublimation through beauty

According to Kristeva, sublimation alone withstands death. As she argues:

> The beautiful object that can bewitch us into its world seems to us more worthy of adoption than any loved or hated cause for wound or sorrow. Depression recognizes this and agrees to live within and for that object, but such adoption of the sublime is no longer libidinal. It is already detached, dissociated, it has

already integrated the traces of death, which is signified as lack of concern, absentmindedness, carelessness. Beauty is an artifice; it is imaginary.

1989, 99–100

In the cinema of Oliveira, the thematization of grief related to real loss, appears as a personal mourning process involving sublimation in at least two films: *The Divine Comedy* (*A Divina Comedia*, 1991) and *The Strange Case of Angelica* (*O Estranho Caso de Angélica*, 2010), the former dedicated to his grandson, the latter being the realization of an old project evoking the figure of a long-dead relative. As analysed in the second part of this book, in the chapter on 'Profanations', despite its title, *The Divine Comedy* does not establish a direct intertextual relationship with Dante's poem, rather being, as the title suggests, only one of the many versions of this latter by thematizing textual encounters across space and time, all revolving around deep individual crisis. The voices of the film represented by monologues and dialogues of Alyosha and Ivan Karamazov, the Philosopher, the Prophet and the Doctor confirm the observation on the religion-melancholy correlation of Kristeva, reinforced by examples from Dostoevsky:

> In different ways according to the religious climate, we might say that melancholy is affirmed in religious doubt. There is nothing sadder than a dead God, and Dostoevsky himself was to be troubled by the distressing image of the dead Christ in Holbein's painting, counterposed as it is to the 'truth of the resurrection'.
>
> 1987, 5–6

The Strange Case of Angelica, on the other hand, can be interpreted as a demonstration of an artistic sublimatory process of personal loss: the finality of death is countered by the beauty of the female body as aesthetic object (the woman as picture), and the stasis of the photograph is broken by the moving image (Figures C.1–C.2). But beyond that, the complexity of this film is due to

Figures C.1–C.2 The interchangeable photographic and cinematographic as figures of death and life in *Angelica*.

the thematization of an anticipated loss, the ultimate loss: the own death, the death of the artist played by his grandson, Ricardo Trêpa. The film can also be seen as an expression of the death drive, a desire to die *by* cinema, in order to be remembered *through* cinema.

According to Freud, there is no representation of death in the subconscious: the subconscious ignores death, and death cannot and should not be seen. As Kristeva points out, sublimation through beauty, the only way to resist death, stems from the refusal to accept loss: 'no, I didn't lose, I am able to remember, to signify, to call into existence through the artificiality of signs what is separated from me, and this ensures the entry of the subject into the universe of signs and creation' (1989, 35). Kristeva analyses in detail remarkable examples of artistic sublimation, that of Gérard de Nerval, Dostoevsky, Holbein and Marguerite Duras, showing how personal crisis reflects social (religious, political) crisis (Kristeva 1989). What I find intriguing in Oliveira's sublimatory solutions is that while the male artists discussed by Kristeva (just to take the example of Hans Holbein the Younger) are confronting death by representing the finality of the human (male) body, in Oliveira's work the representation of dying or dead male protagonists is very rare: if shown, it is from a distance, the body veiled or covered and it is not spectacular at all (the only exception seems to be *Past and Present / O Passado e o Presente*, where the body of the suicidal husband is shown surrounded by red flowers, as if staged by his wife). In contrast, the films of Oliveira abound with images of dead, dying or ailing female characters. Beyond purely poetical purposes, another explanation occurs, especially in the light of the above quoted letter, in which Oliveira asks Julia Buisel not to mention it to his wife, Dona Isabel, the person whom he loves most: 'This makes me suffer, also because I have a rebel and lonely soul of an animal. An excessively sensitive animal' (Buisel 2012, 98).

I contend that the stubborn return to the same type of romantic relationship and woman, although put in different cultural (philosophical, religious) contexts and iconographies in his films, points at Oliveira's own unfinished business with the eternal feminine, his own anima: accomplished in his male roles both in his private life (a patriarch of a big family, with many children and grandchildren) as well as professionally, this confession reveals a well-hidden fragility that cannot be said, but only shown and sublimated. While his socially culturally constructed image was, in turns, that of a dandy, a sportsman, a family man, a hermit, an acclaimed artist and lately, The Master, his extreme sensitivity, manifest in *Memories and Confessions*, passed unobserved, as a delicate detail.

164   *The Cinema of Manoel de Oliveira*

The archetype of anima finds expression as a feminine inner personality in the Jungian system, that, together with the animus, represents the inferior function of the shadow archetypes. According to Jung, the encounter with the shadow is crucial in the individual development. Jung also viewed the anima process as being one of the sources of creative ability, a medium between the ego and the unconscious. The need to reconnect with the anima and beauty is also detectable in the variety of types of female characters that correspond to the different levels of anima development: Eve, corresponding to the emergence of man's object of desire, Helen, the seductress, intelligent though not altogether virtuous, Mary, who seems to possess virtue by a perceiving man (even in an esoteric or dogmatic way) and finally Sophia, the level of complete integration and wisdom: the anima is now developed enough so that no single object can fully and permanently contain the images to which it is related (Jung 1968, 54–74). The favourite, fetish-actresses and female characters of Oliveira also correspond to these anima levels: Leonor Silveira and Leonor Baldaque represent at least three of them, the object of desire, the ambivalent seductress and even the worshipped woman in their roles (Eve, Helen and Mary), while Catherine Deneuve and Irene Papas mostly appear as the seductress and the older, wise woman (Helen and Sofia), respectively. In Jungian terms, these female characteristics are all projections of the anima:

> There are certain types of women who seem to be made by nature to attract anima projections; the so-called 'sphinxlike' character is an indispensable part of their equipment, also an equivocalness, an intriguing elusiveness – not an indefinite blur that offers nothing, but an indefiniteness that seems full of promises, like the speaking silence of a Mona Lisa. A woman of this kind is both old and young, mother and daughter, of more than doubtful chastity, childlike, and yet endowed with a naive cunning that is extremely disarming to men.
>
> Jung [1926] 1991, 5

Leonor Silveira embodies all these multiple female roles in the films of Oliveira, sometimes in the same film: Ema from *Abraham's Valley*, Judita from *Voyage to the Beginning of the World* or Alfreda from *Magic Mirror* have something from this mysterious, sphinx-like character, childlike, naive and seductive at the same time.

The dandy image assumed by Oliveira in his youth, also containing a feminine touch (detectable in a preoccupation with own image, a creation of himself as a

Coda 165

'work of art')[1] can also be integrated into this animus–anima dichotomy. Additionally, the female body as fetish (especially of legs and feet, in *Abraham's Valley* and *Party*, for example), as well as the pictorial images of women (of which *Angelica* is a remarkable example) as yet another form of fetishism (both of the director and the spectator) are also descriptive of this problematic relationship with the anima. Meant to replace the missing (desired, repressed) object, fetishism appears, according to Kristeva, as a solution of depression and its denial of the signifier: the fetishist replaces the psychological pain with a phantasm and passage to the act (1989, 54).

This urge to alleviate individual pain and loss through sublimation in some films intertwines with the sense of loss of a whole community: melancholia meets nostalgia in films analysed in the previous chapters: *Voyage to the Beginning of the World* (1997) or *Cristopher Columbus – The Enigma* (*Cristóforo Columbo – A Enigma*, 2007), revealing the ingredients of the Portuguese concept of *saudade*, 'breezy and erotic' but at the same time 'profound and hunting', as Svetlana Boym puts it (2001, 28).

Melancholia and nostalgia are the ingredients of *saudade* in Oliveira's films, ensuring the connection between an individual consciousness troubled by excessive sensibility or the Jungian anima, real or anticipated loss, and a collective, social memory, a longing for a lost unity and former greatness. As Kristeva and Boym argue, both melancholia and nostalgia, mourning and longing for a lost object are characteristic of periods of social crisis following revolutions, changes of regime and other economic changes and crises. Moreover, Ismail Xavier discovers a connection between societal crisis and artistic preference for a highly figurative, allegorical discourse ([1999] 2004). In this respect can the recurrent topic of aborted relationships be read as figuration of a declining patriarchal order, imminent after a long-lasting dictatorship. The all-pervasive moods of sadness, nostalgia, melancholia, deception, frustration, are a symptomatic imprint of this crisis that often manifest themselves as a 'rupture of energies' (Kristeva 1989, 8) in intense monologues, songs, disturbing music, unexpected gestures and desperate acts.

As Kristeva points out, 'At the boundaries of animality and "symbolicity" the moods – and sadness in particular – are the ultimate reactions to our traumas, our fundamental homeostatic recourse' (1989, 8). Moods are also 'diffuse tendencies towards emotional states; longer lasting than emotions, they prime

---

[1] Mathias Lavin writes about this image of the young Oliveira in his, *La Parole et le lieu* (2008, 11).

166   *The Cinema of Manoel de Oliveira*

us for having and repeating emotions, or clusters of emotional states, with a definite cognitive character' (ibid., 21).

Unfortunately, the role of mood in aesthetic composition and cinematic style has been little discussed in film theory, at least until very recently. Robert Sinnerbrink considers mood in cinema as a form of disclosure, an expressive way of revealing time and meaning (Sinnerbrink 2012, 156). In some cases – and I contend that this applies to most films of Oliveira – cinematic Stimmung can envelope and even transfigure narrative meaning, overriding conventional plot. Achieved by so-called mood-cues (music, visual framing, emotion scripts, prototypical scenarios and so on), mood becomes autonomous, taking on a primary rather than a supporting role in the composition of the fictional world (ibid., 161). This applies to the music in Oliveira's films (be it classical, intensely emotional as in *Francisca* or disturbing percussion music, like in *Non* or *Voyage to the Beginning of the World*), to the already mentioned painterly compositions of ailing / dying women and the prototypical scenario of doomed loves. The new perspective of Stimmung in cinema will be able to reveal the effect the 'paranarrative' or expressive dimension of cinematic aesthetics has on spectators. It would definitely nuance the psychoanalytical approach of melancholia conveyed in films, deeply affecting, in our case, a spectator irresistibly driven into, embodied and immersed in the compelling world of the cinema of Manoel de Oliveira.

References

Agamben, Giorgio. 1993. 'The Lost Object'. In *Stanzas.: Word and Phantasm in Western Culture*. Minneapolis, MN: University of Minnesota Press.

Boym, Svetlana. 2001. *The Future of Nostalgia*. New York: Basic Books.

Buisel, Júlia. 2012. *Antes que me esqueca*. Lisbon: Associação Cultural Il Sorpasso.

Costa, João Bénard da. 1981. 'Diálogo com Manoel de Oliveira'. In *Manoel de Oliveira*. Lisboa: Cinemateca Portuguesa.

Freud, Sigmund. 1917. *Mourning and Melancholia*. London: The Hogarth Press.

Freud, Sigmund. [1919] 2003. *The Uncanny*. London: Penguin Classics.

Jung, Carl Gustav. [1926] 1991. 'Marriage as a Psychological Relationship'. In *The Collected Works of C. G. Jung*, Vol. 17: *The Development of Personality*. London: Routledge and Paul.

Jung, Carl Gustav. 1968. *The Archetypes and the Collective Unconscious*. London and New York: Routledge.

Kristeva, Julia. 1987. 'On the Melancholic Imaginary'. *new formations*, 3 (Winter): 5–18.

Kristeva, Julia. 1989. *Black Sun: Depression and Melancholia*. New York: Columbia University Press.

Lavin, Mathias. 2008. *La Parole et le lieu: Le Cinéma selon Manoel de Oliveira*. Rennes: Presses Universitaires de Rennes.

Parsi, Jacques and Antoine de Baecque. 1996. *Conversations avec Manoel de Oliveira*. Paris: Cahiers du Cinéma.

Sinnerbrink, Robert. 2012. 'Stimmung: Exploring the Aesthetics of Mood'. *Screen*, 53 (2): 155–63.

Xavier, Ismail. [1999] 2004. 'Historical Allegory'. In *A Companion to Film Theory*, eds Robert Stam and Toby Miller, 333–62. Malden, MA, and Oxford: Blackwell Publishing.

Žižek, Slavoj. 2000. 'Melancholy and the Act', *Critical Inquiry*, 26 (Summer): 659–81.

Index

A Gentle Woman (*Une Femme douce*, Robert Bresson, 1969) 46
A Talking Picture (*Um Filme Falado*, 2003) 6, 10, 39–43, 60, 63, 66, 70, 76, 79–82
Abraham's Valley (*Vale Abraäo*, 1993) 6, 18, 19, 26, 32, 35–7, 89, 101, 115, 119, 121, 123, 125–9
Abrunhosa, Pedro 42, 101–4, 150–4
adaptation 1, 2, 3, 4, 8, 11, 20, 23, 25, 46, 63, 86, 92, 95, 98–104, 113–29, 131–54
Agamben, Giorgio 5, 6, 10, 39–40, 43–4, 46, 51, 63, 83–6, 92, 138, 160
Alcácer Quibir 62–3, 69
allegory 9, 10, 39, 40, 49, 63–70, 78, 82, 84, 126, 147
Almodóvar, Pedro 35
Alpers, Svetlana 131–2, 136, 139, 141–2
Altman, Rick 153
anachronism 5, 122–5
Aniki Bobó (1942) 1, 8, 41–3, 45
animism 3, 8, 43
Anxiety (*Inquietude*, 1998) 6, 8, 10, 63, 66, 105
Araújo, Nelson 1
archetype 164
Assmann, Jan 81
Augé, Marc 82
authorship 11, 136, 137

Baldaque, Leonor 90, 93, 164
Barros Baptista, Abel 22, 133–4
Barroso, Mário 61, 101, 133, 142–4
Barthes, Roland 8, 24, 27, 32, 138
Baudelaire, Charles 4, 7, 8, 17–20, 23–6, 39, 127–8
Baudelaire's Mistress, Reclining (Édouard Manet, 1862) 127
Belle Toujours (2006) 7, 11
Bellour, Raymond 8, 27–8, 49, 114
Benilde or the Virgin Mother (*Benilde ou a Virgem Mãe*, 1975) 1, 6, 8, 9, 11, 19, 47, 49–50, 90, 94, 114–18, 121–2, 152
Benjamin, Walter 6, 40, 67, 69, 84

Berger, John 24–5, 35
Bergman, Ingmar 77
Berlin: A Symphony of a Great City (Walter Ruttmann, 1927) 1
Bessa-Luís, Agustina 1, 23, 25, 36, 46, 59, 91–2, 100, 123–9, 145–7, 149
Bhabha, Homi 63, 95, 98, 108
Bloch, Ernst 6, 62, 86
Bonitzer, Pascal 8, 28, 32
Bordwell, David 1, 93
Boym, Svetlana 73–4, 165
Branco, Paulo 1, 10, 96
Bresson, Robert 1, 20, 22, 46, 104, 124, 126, 139
Buisel, Julia 160
Buñuel, Luís 1, 35, 70, 72, 128

Caravaggio, Michelangelo Merisi da 106–7
Cardinale, Claudia 96, 107
Carroll, Noël 27
Castelo Branco, Camilo 11, 20–1, 61–2, 113, 133, 136, 143, 148–9
Cavell, Stanley 18–19
Chambers, Iain 122–4
Chion, Michel 143, 148–50, 153
Cintra, Luís Miguel 61, 73, 93, 96, 99, 107
Claudel, Paul 98–9
Coelho, Prado Eduardo 135
Costa Andrade, Sérgio 1
Costa, João Bénard 1
costume drama 68, 101, 132
Crespo, Alfonso 149
Crime and Punishment (novel, Fyodor Dostoevsky) 87
Cristopher Columbus – The Enigma (*Cristovão Colombo – A Enigma*, 2007) 7, 60, 63, 66, 71–5, 95, 165
cultural mimicry 10, 63, 94–108
Cunha, Paulo 2

Dalle Vacche, Angela 8, 116–20
dandy, dandyism 18, 23–5, 163–4

Index

Daney, Serge 1, 52, 83, 84, 114, 143, 146, 151
Dante Alighieri 87, 162
death drive 8, 12, 18, 22, 26, 28, 30, 36, 105, 163
de Baecque, Antoine 1, 97
de Beauvoir, Simone 34
de Camões, Luíz Vaz 9, 60–1, 108
de la Tour, Georges 106–7, 117
Déjeuner sur l'herbe (Édouard Manet, 1863) 105
Deleuze, Gilles 22–3, 28, 34, 121, 142
Deneuve, Catherine 40, 71, 81, 96–7, 102, 164
Didi-Huberman, Georges 123
Doane, Mary Ann 131
doll, dollness 8, 23, 39–52, 82, 127
Dom Sebastian 64, 69–70
Donaldson-Evans, Mary 37, 128
Doomed Love (*Amor de Perdição*, Manoel de Oliveira, 1979) 1, 6, 8, 9, 11, 19–22, 24, 29–37, 45, 47, 61, 66, 89, 94, 113–15, 122–5, 129, 134, 139–43, 151, 161
Doomed Love (*Amor de Perdição*, Georges Pallu, 1921) 133, 135–6
Doomed Love (*Amor de Perdição*, Lopes Ribeiro, 1943) 134–6
Doomed Love (novel, Camilo Castelo Branco) 20–2, 113, 132–4, 136
Doomed Love, A (*Um Amor de Perdição*, Mário Barroso, 2008) 142–4
Don Quixote 9, 60–2, 72, 87, 89, 99, 100, 108
Dória, Diogo 61, 76
Dostoevsky, Fyodor 87, 95, 162, 163
Dutch painting 11, 106, 120, 122, 131–3, 136, 139, 141–2, 151–2, 154

Eccentricities of a Blonde-Haired Girl (*Singularidades de Uma Rapariga Loura*, 2009) 7, 9, 11, 43, 45–6, 61, 94, 115, 121
ekphrasis 126, 132
Elsaesser, Thomas 28, 33

Fanny Owen (novel, Agustina Bessa-Luís) 145–6
fashion 5, 7, 8, 17–19, 23–6, 35, 39, 46, 123
Felleman, Susan 8, 32–3
feminine, femininity 2, 18, 34, 89–90, 93–4, 121, 126–9, 145, 163–4

femme fatale 24, 91, 127
fetish, fetishism 8, 12, 18–19, 24, 25, 35–7, 39, 41, 44, 46, 51, 78, 89, 114, 125, 164–5
figure of absence 141, 145, 150
Flaubert, Gustave 23, 26, 98, 100–1, 125–9
Foucault, Michel 47, 80, 97
Francisca (1981) 1, 6, 8, 11, 19, 21, 30, 32, 34, 45, 47–8, 66, 89, 94, 114–16, 121–3, 145–50, 152, 161, 166
Freud, Sigmund 3, 4, 7, 43–4, 63, 70, 73, 83, 95, 148, 159, 160, 163

Gaudreault, André 1öl, 126
Gautier, Jean-Yves 75
Gebo and the Shadow (*O Gebo e a Sombra*, 2012) 7, 8, 11, 63, 107
glamour 18, 19, 24–6
Godard, Jean-Luc 28, 97, 131, 137
Gorfinkel, Elena 124–5
Greene, Thomas 124–5
Guimarães, Pedro Maciel 96–9, 101, 106

Hagener, Malte 28
Hitchcock, Alfred 46
Hoffmann, E.T.A. 7, 43
Hollander, Anne 122, 146, 151

Illness as Metaphor (Susan Sontag, 1978) 21
imitation 9, 28, 60, 63, 83, 87, 89
Impressionism 1, 105
intermediality 3, 11, 48, 97, 102, 128, 131, 132, 159

Jacobs, Steven 8, 32–3, 85
Jaffe, Ira 80–2
Johnson, Randal 2, 68, 70, 75, 80, 87, 88, 90, 91, 92, 99
Jung, Carl Gustav 164–5
Junqueira, Renata 2

Kovács, András Bálint 20
Kracauer, Siegfried 6
Kristeva, Julia 160–5
Kuhn, Annette 51–2

Labor on the Douro River (*Douro, Faina Fluvial, 1931*) 1, 29
Lacan, Jacques 95, 135

Index

Laderman, David 75, 77
Lavin, Mathias 2, 43, 44, 46, 50, 52, 80, 81, 165
Leitch, Thomas 125
Live Flesh (*Carne trémula*, Pedro Almodóvar, 1997) 35
Lopes, João 41
Lord Byron 23, 46, 148

Madame Bovary (Claude Chabrol, 1991) 100
Madame Bovary (Tim Fywell, 2000) 128
Madame Bovary (novel, Gustave Flaubert, 1857) 23, 26, 36, 98, 100, 125–8
Madame de La Fayette 42, 98, 101, 150
Magic Mirror (*Espelho Mágico*, 2005) 7, 10, 47, 63, 82, 89, 92–4, 114–16, 123, 164
Malkovich, John 39–40, 71, 81–2, 96–7
Manet, Édouard 8, 127–9
Marks, Laura 28
Marnie (Alfred Hitchcock, 1964) 46
Mastroianni, Chiara 102, 150, 153
Mastroianni, Marcello 75, 78–9, 96–7, 102
Medeiros, Maria de 89
melancholia 12, 69, 73, 116, 125, 148, 154, 159–66
melodrama 12, 20–6, 29–37, 45, 66, 73, 103, 125, 133–6, 142, 146–7
Metsu, Gabriel 139–40, 152
mimicry 94, 95, 98, 101, 103, 108
modernity 3, 7, 8, 17–20, 23–4, 45, 48, 113, 125, 159
Mon cas (1986) 70
Monteiro, César 61, 83, 96
mourning 11, 68, 73, 88, 138, 146, 148, 160–2, 165
Mulvey, Laura 8, 20, 22, 24, 26, 28, 30, 37, 51
music 3, 4, 11, 41, 67–70, 77, 79, 87–8, 101, 119, 122, 145–53, 165–6

Naficy, Hamid 138
neorealism 1, 41
Nietzsche, Friedrich 87
No, or the Vain Glory of Command (*Non, ou a Vã Glória de Mandar*, 1990) 6, 7, 60–2, 67–70

O dia do desespero (*The Day of Despair*) 18, 62

Orr, John 17, 19
Overhoff Ferreira, Carolin 2, 63, 69, 76, 80, 87–8, 104

Papas, Irene 40, 81, 164
parody 9, 10, 60, 63, 85–8
Parsi, Jacques 1, 97
Party (1996) 78
Pascoaes, Teixeira de 61
Past and Present (*O Passado e o Presente*, 1972) 1, 6, 8, 9, 11, 19, 66, 115, 118–19, 121–3
Pessoa, Fernando 71, 79
Pethő, Ágnes 52, 102, 131, 136, 137, 140
Piccoli, Michel 96, 97
Pires, Maria João 88, 152, 153
Porto of my Childhood (*Porto da Minha Infância*, 2001) 78
pose, posing 8, 23–6, 31–4, 91, 93, 104, 115–17, 119–23
profanation 9, 10, 63, 82–94, 162

Ramasse, Francis 21, 23, 34
re-enactment 10, 63, 83, 87–90, 95
Régio, José 70, 87
Remes, Justin 20, 27–8, 30
Renoir, Pierre-Auguste 48–9, 105
repoussoir 117–18, 120, 122
Rite of Spring (*Acto da Primavera*, 1963) 6, 10, 20, 63, 83–6
road movie 39–40, 75–7, 80
Rodowick, D. N. 42
Rohmer, Éric 1, 20, 28, 116–20
Rosenbaum, Jonathan 1, 24, 29, 11
Rowland, Clara 22, 133

Salazar dictatorship 1, 5, 59, 64, 66
Sales, Michelle 2
Sanchez, Vicente 124
Sandrelli, Stefania 40, 81
saudade 10, 12, 69, 73, 75, 79, 159, 165
Silveira, Leonor 19, 76, 78, 89–90, 93, 96, 107, 164
Sinnerbrink, Robert 166
slow, slowness 8, 22, 27–9, 41, 50, 80, 113–45
Soares, Ana Isabel 84, 86
Sobchack, Vivian Carol 20, 33, 37

172   *Index*

Søndergaard, Sidsel Maria 127–8
Sontag, Susan 21–2
Stam, Robert 125
Stewart, Garrett 30, 132
still life 118
Stimmung 166
Strauber, Susan 127–9
sublimation 74, 94, 135, 160, 162–3, 165

tableau vivant 3, 5, 8, 19, 23, 25, 28–34, 46, 85, 90, 97, 104, 115, 126–7, 161
The beautiful automaton 7–9, 44–7, 52
The Box (*A caixa*, 1994) 7
The Cannibals (*Os Canibais*, 1988) 6, 7, 44–5, 66
The Convent (*O Convento*, 1995) 71–2, 78, 95–7
The Divine Comedy (*A Divina Comédia*, 1991) 10, 63, 82, 87–9, 114, 162
The Fifth Empire (*A Quinta Império*, 2004) 10, 60, 64, 65–7, 70–1
The Hunt (1963) 7
The Karamazov Brothers (novel, Fyodor Dostoevsky) 87
The Letter (*A Carta*, 1999) 6, 9, 11, 42–3, 45, 63, 97, 99, 101–3, 150–4
The Lusiads (*Os Lusíadas*, Luís Vaz de Camões) 60–2
The Marquise of O (*La Marquise d'O*, 1976) 1, 20, 28, 118
The Old Man of Belém (*O Velho do Restelo*, 2014) 9, 60–1, 64
The Painter of Modern Life (Charles Baudelaire, 1863) 18, 24, 39
The Princesse de Clèves (La Princesse de Clèves, Madame de La Fayette, 1678) 42, 98, 101, 150–1
The Sandman (short story, E. T. A. Hoffmann, 1816) 7, 43
The Satin Slipper (*Le soulier de satin*, 1985) 10, 63, 98–9, 161
The Soul of the Rich (novel, *A Alma dos Ricos*, Agustina Bessa-Luís, 2005) 92

The Strange Case of Angelica (*O Estranho Caso de Angélica*, 2010) 7, 9, 17, 41, 43, 47–52, 162
The Tetralogy of Fustrated Loves 1, 27, 43, 123
The uncanny 3–11, 17, 30, 33, 41, 43–7, 50, 52, 60, 63–4, 68, 70, 82, 83, 86, 88, 92–4, 98, 122, 124, 127, 129, 131, 146, 159
The Uncertainty Principle (*O Princípio da Incerteza*, 2002) 6, 10, 63, 66, 78, 89–93, 104, 106, 116, 119, 121
The Uncertainty Principle: Family Jewel (novel, *O Princípio da Incerteza: Jóia de Família*, Agustina Bessa-Luís, 2002), 91
transitional object 12, 41, 47, 50–1
Trêpa, Ricardo 17, 48, 61, 64, 70–2, 107, 163
Tristana (Luís Buñuel, 1970) 35
trompe l'oeil 28, 33–4, 49, 92, 95
Truffaut, François 137

unfinished business 12, 93–4, 159–60, 163

Vermeer, Johannes 146
Vernet, Marc 134, 140–1
Vidal, Belén 50, 113, 115, 132, 135, 137–8
Visit. Memories and Confessions (*Visita. Memórias e Confissões*, 1982) 59
voice-over 35, 68, 84, 101, 126, 128, 131, 136–7, 141, 145–6
Voyage to the Beginning of the World (*Viagem ao princípio do mundo*, 1997) 6, 7, 10, 11, 63, 75–9, 97, 106, 108, 164–5
voyeur, voyeurism 7, 9, 26, 34, 44, 86, 141

Wild Strawberries (*Smultronstället*, 1957) 77
Winnicott, Donald 51
Word and Utopia (*Palavra e utopia*, 2000) 60, 67

Xavier, Ismail 9, 63–70, 80–1, 83, 165

Žižek, Slavoj 135, 160

CPSIA information can be obtained
at www.ICGtesting.com
Printed in the USA
LVHW052001100223
739200LV00007B/722